ANATOMY OF SUCCESS

The Ultimate System for Achieving Your Personal and Professional Goals

Ronald A. Kaufman

D1042465

POWELL/MANN PUBLISHING

Dedicated to all my students and clients
who I learned so much from, and to my
family and friends for their continual support
during the seven plus years it took to
complete this project. And a special expression
of gratitude to my father for
being there for me when I needed him.

Contents

• • •

Foreword

• • •

Doing the foreword for this book is very rewarding for me, because I have seen the positive results people can achieve using its techniques. Ron Kaufman has delivered training for my career development programs for over five years. The hundreds of people who have attended his workshops, constantly praise his work for how much it helps them in both their business and personal lives. Examples of participants' comments are:

"I gained how to use my most valuable tool, my brain. I feel I have tremendous potentional now."

"I believe in myself today more than I ever have. I am motivated, educated, inspired to be the best that I can be, and to do the best I can."

"Information I believe you need to be successful in your career as well as your personal life."

"Most important of all, I found out who I am and what I want."

Whether the participants are seasoned professionals with advanced degrees, or young people just starting out, he has effectively guided and coached them to fulfill their potential. Those who are parents uniformly say they wish their children could receive the same life enhancing tools and strategies that they've learned in Ron's classes.

Anatomy of Success captures in great detail and depth, the outstanding system that Ron teaches in his workshops. In specific "how to" terms, Ron guides the reader through various exercises, examples, and formulas, which develop clarity, focus, and understanding, enabling someone to achieve their goals. It's like a manual for the mind—a reference book to be used on a daily basis to maximize generating worthwhile results.

Time and time again, I have witnessed Ron's work build people's self-esteem, self-confidence, motivation, and a sense of hope for a bright future. This results in a greater level of achievement and personal satisfaction. Now, using the proven tools, techniques, and methods in this book, you can gain some of the same benefits as those who have attended the workshops. It's a great gift, for the use of these principles will enrich both the giver and the receiver.

> Richard Katz, President
> Human Resources Marketing Services, Inc.

Additional Client Testimonials

• • •

"Extraordinary! A precise practical program for decision making, motivation, and action to achieve the success, satisfaction, and fulfillment we desire. A must!" —*Marty Gronewald*

"It was very empowering. I absolutely loved it and can't wait to use all the knowledge that I received today, and especially see all the results." —*Lara Slaughter*

"A very comprehensive and dynamic program for success. It should be taught in all schools." —*Doe Gentry*

"Excellent! Ron provided a step-by-step, practical method for achieving our goals and dreams. I particularly liked the way he made it seem so simple. Bravo!" —*Gerry Foster*

"I'm especially impressed with the spiritual, positive aspect of your presentation and encouraging integrity. Also your emphasis on giving and helping others." —*Ruby Miyasato*

"Makes the brain stimulated to the point of restructuring old beliefs and ideas." —*Linda LaTique*

"A polished collection of ideas organized into a process. I got more than ideas, I got in touch with a way out of my dilemma." —*Al Gerlach*

"Well presented, well organized outline and guide to achieve the elusive goals in life, and overcoming the obstacles that inhibit our progress." —*Fred Arm*

"I believe there is great need for this type of program; would increase morale and productivity." —*Charmaine Clark*

"A valuable addition to my life and my ability to feel good and succeed in my endeavors." —*Patricia Jackson*

"Great program, and the best techniques. It works!" —*Rick Rodriguez*

"Excellent, Ron is a fabulous teacher—very motivating—caring—respectful." —*Reva Solomon*

"Highly recommend for everyone's personal/professional growth." —*Liza Mocorro*

Preface

Success and top achievement begin with clear, specific, positive goals. Goals focus your energy and give you direction. To reach your full potential, you need detailed objectives with a practical plan to fulfill them. What kind of house can be built without a thorough blueprint?

Welcome to *Anatomy of Success*. As you read this book, think about its contents, and use the ideas and techniques in it, you have made a choice that can dramatically enhance your life, now and forever. You will be able to enrich yourself, as well as other people throughout your lifetime. And just one idea can cause a positive transformation in a person's life!

Setting and achieving goals, and having certain results in your life, is what this book is about. Its comprised of techniques, methods, and ideas of things to do, and in some cases, things not to do, to manage your life.

Survival can be determined by what we do with our mind as well as our body. A large percentage of people die within a few years of retiring from their jobs. They struggle and strain to reach what they think is their ultimate dream, retirement. Then because their whole life and sense of self was tied into their job, without the job, they have little to identify with, no plans or sense of purpose, and they die. Having goals not only enriches your life, it can literally extend it!

Goals can be defined as results that we desire to have, and toward which we expend and use energy. This energy can be mental, physical, or both. We are goal oriented beings. Deciding to get out of bed in the morning, bathe, eat breakfast, go to work, see a movie, listen to music, visit with friends, read the newspaper, or feel something, are goals. The better we are at setting and achieving our goals, the better the quality of our lives.

Some people say that they don't want to have goals, and that they love to be spontaneous and go with the flow. Think about it, having no goals and being totally spontaneous, is a goal. Their goal is to have no structure, no plans, no commitments, no obligations, no responsibilities, and just live moment to moment. They are expending energy to have a specific desired result.

Accomplishment and goal setting are closely intertwined. Any activity we engage in, will be more productive when we first set a definite purpose for it. Whether it's doing a project at work, exercising, or meeting a friend for lunch, establishing a definite outcome for whatever we do, will yield better results. Before you do something, ask yourself what is the purpose or reason for doing it. We can't consciously pay attention to everything that's going on around us at all times. Therefore, being selective through setting goals, yields the highest dividends.

Setting clear precise objectives, alerts us as to what to selectively pay attention to. We will notice certain things, and filter out others. This can apply to even going to a party. You can go a party to connect with old friends, to make new acquaintances, get information about something, network for business, socialize, and/or let your hair down to burn off stress. Give yourself focus by first getting exact about what you want. Otherwise you can end up in a fog and limit yourself. Often people never reach their full potential due to ineffective goal setting. Lack of clarity prohibits them from using their innate talents and abilities. How can you hit a target if you don't know what it is?

People don't set goals for many reasons: fear of failure, fear of success, limiting beliefs, poor preparation, lack of motivation, conflicting values, indecision, or perhaps because they just don't know how to do it. Some of the effects are confusion, procrastination, and frustration. *Anatomy of Success* addresses these issues, giving you a step-by-step formula for you to follow to realize the results you want. This program gives you what to do, and HOW to do it.

Without goals we are like the proverbial ship without a rudder. We go drifting around aimlessly wherever the winds and currents take us. When you use *Anatomy of Success*, you have a method so that you can direct where you go. You are able to develop a detailed map and plan to get you to your desired destination.

What changes do you want in your life in areas such as health, love, career, wealth, self-confidence, knowledge, sports, etc.? Maybe you would like to have a new job, to be married, to earn a certain amount of money, to end world hunger, to have a specific golf score, to learn a new language, to travel throughout Europe, or to find out what your goals really are. As you apply this system, you are using a proven method to produce greater achievement in your life.

Knowledge is power, and the awareness this system gives you is crucial to success. Just being aware of something in itself causes a shift, by altering what you focus on and pay attention to. You also receive a greater sense of control. This increases self-esteem and optimism, and the confidence to take action. And taking action is essential to securing your desired outcomes.

Defining success can be very subjective and personal. To one person it's having a lot of money. To another it's having power and influence. For some, it's being good at what they do. In one survey of men, over 84% said it's being a good father. And success for certain people, is giving your best and helping others to be their best! This last definition is more of an attitude than a measurable level of achievement. It's a way of approaching things that anyone can use, and therefore anyone can feel like a success and live a fulfilling life. Someone can successfully obtain results in an area of their life, but if it's at the expense of others, then by this definition they are not a success. Have you ever known someone who "had everything," and yet was still unhappy?

Success for most people, ultimately comes down to a feeling. Whether it's feeling happy, content, satisfied, powerful, secure, worthwhile, free, or successful, we achieve to feel. More on this topic in the values section of the *Building a Foundation* chapter, and in *The Benefits* chapter. Regardless of how you currently interpret success, this book will assist you in obtaining it.

The roots of this system began when I was a teenager, "trying" to grow up in Chicago. I've always had a tremendous curiosity about everything, especially people. I would wonder, why were some people so happy and full of life, and others so sad and miserable? What was the reason? It wasn't looks, money, health, or power. Many people had all of these and yet they had no joy in them. And some people had none of these, and yet projected great happiness.

Anatomy of Success started to become formalized when I fulfilled a lifelong dream, by producing a motion picture titled *Everyday.* I was a stockbroker for many years but I always loved movies. So I wrote a script, raised the capital, and began production.

Producing a film was not as easy as I had thought. It was constantly dealing with little details, changing priorities, and overactive egos. Chaos was everywhere. Since I was the largest investor in the film, all the problems were costing me money. Out of the need to be organized and efficient, I began structuring and developing this system.

After doing production work for several years, I became an executive with what's known as a product placement company. I did promotions with major motion pictures and film studios. I represented companies, such as Cadillac, Panasonic, and Ivory, and arranged for the placement of their products in films. With over ninety clients to handle, and working on over two hundred films per year, it was necessary for me to further refine a procedure for setting, organizing, and achieving goals. Now you can profit from my years of experience, as have so many others in my seminars and private consultations. This book is based on my workshops that have proven to be so effective for my students.

Over the years I have been very fortunate to be able to observe, interview, and study successful people. Two things these successful people have in common, a dream and passion about its attainment. They have a burning desire, a willingness to *WIN*, to do *Whatever Is Necessary* to reach their objectives. They constantly learn from whatever results they receive. Continually asking "What can I learn from this?" makes a world of difference in terms of constant growth and improvement. In some way, they or someone who works with them, is completing every step and part of this program.

It's recommended when using these techniques, to do each step and each section in the order as presented. Complete each part as much as you can, before moving to the next one. This is an active process where as you get feedback, you go back and refine various sections until you accomplish what you want.

The examples throughout the book, might be from one person or from many people. As you look at them, please keep in mind that they are only examples and may or may not apply to you. The idea is to provide you with possible answers to help to stimulate your thought processes, and open up the potential for new viewpoints and insights.

Do all the questions apply to every type of goal? Yes. However with smaller goals, such as where to go on vacation or which desk to buy, you probably won't need to ask all of them. Many of the answers are already built in. Working on a major goal, such as family, career, or health, use all of the parts with as much detail as possible, for maximum results. Merely asking the questions causes connections to take place, improving your ability to produce results.

Anatomy of Success also works in group situations. It gets people involved and committed, building teamwork. It helps everyone understand what the objective is, its importance, and what their responsibility is for its completion. This sense of ownership reduces stress and improves morale. Effectiveness increases, adding to the bottom line.

What about changing a goal? Your original intention might be to sail around the world, or to lose twenty pounds, or to become the president of a company. However, you may go part of the way and find out that it's far enough. You may stop off in Tahiti and discover that you've found your paradise. You lose ten pounds and realize you're now at a comfortable weight. After becoming vice-president on your way to the top, you see that the view is just fine from where you are, and that you don't have to climb any higher.

Writing everything down is very significant. *Plan On Paper, POP.* Writing everything down helps to establish awareness, ownership, commitment, and understanding. It also saves time and energy. Trying to remember things can require tremendous effort. Have you ever said, "Oh I'll remember that, no need to write it down," and later you forgot? So *POP* and let the paper do the work for you. In addition, writing involves several of the senses, making your ideas more concrete and real, providing a greater feeling of control.

Another benefit of using *Anatomy of Success* is that it actually enriches the brain. Many of the questions you will answer cause thinking at deep levels. This in turn produces an increase in connections between brain cells, enabling you to use more of your mental capacity. The more we use the mind, the stronger it becomes. Like any muscle, use it or lose it.

Motivation and procrastination frequently come up when goal setting is addressed. So often people get pumped up about a goal, but within a short time, they become discouraged and give up. This can happen, because being motivated is not just one thing. Having desire, money, and skill is not always enough to bring a dream into reality.

Persistence and MAXIMUM MOTIVATION is actually made up of seven major components. To be consistently fired up, you need:

1. A clear specific *measurable vision* of what it is that you want.
2. To *know yourself*: your *values, beliefs,* and *self-concept,* and be in alignment with them; and to know your *skills* and *abilities.*
3. To install within yourself the right *beliefs to empower* you.
4. To be aware of, and *neutralize,* any *limiting beliefs.*
5. To have enough worthwhile *benefits* to getting your goal.
6. To have enough *negative consequences* if you don't achieve your goal.
7. To have a practical *plan of action* to make it all happen.

These are a few of the many concepts and techniques that are explained in *Anatomy of Success.* If one part of the process is missing, a whole project could fall apart.

Stress management is another area that these topics deal with. Stress is often caused by a lack of clear goals and purpose, not knowing oneself, living in conflict with who one really is, and having negative limiting beliefs. Using the tools in this book will assist you in dealing with the things that could cause the unproductive levels of stress.

Important goals can require a lot of time to map out. But it's a small investment compared to the results and lifetime of benefits you'll receive. How much time, money, and energy are wasted because of incomplete planning? By using *Anatomy of Success*, you have a clear logical practical way of thinking, bringing you expanded possibilities.

This book is divided into several parts. The first sections give you ideas on effective communication, self-awareness, and constructing a foundation to build upon. The next sections are the actual goal setting system. And the final sections are checklists and information on career and relationships. Many of the concepts and techniques you'll be able to use immediately, and others may take some time to fully put into effect.

It's suggested to always have a copy of this book available to you. Whenever you have a few idle moments, such as waiting in line, read a section to nurture yourself. The mind is always occupied with something. Use *Anatomy of Success* to make sure that it's filled with thoughts that you choose, and that benefit you. Just glancing through the pages can have a positive effect on you at the unconscious level.

Future results are largely determined by the choices we make today. Choose to use what is contained in this book, and put yourself in charge of controlling what your future becomes. Not only your tomorrows, but the tomorrows of those you care about. Many parents in my seminars have reported how sharing these ideas with their children has yielded excellent results. Right now, we don't know which of the ideas, tools, and techniques in this book will be the most useful to you for each goal, so use them all and find out for yourself.

The first chapter deals with the importance of words and language patterns, and enhancing your internal and external communications, now!

Chapter 1

POSITIVE LANGUAGE PATTERNS

● ● ●

EMPOWERING VOCABULARY

"Sticks and stones can break my bones, but names can never hurt me," is an old childhood rhyme. Is that really true? Not hardly. Being called a name or having a negative label put on us, can hurt, and can do damage way beyond their casual expression. This chapter is about the impact of words and how we can produce positive changes for ourselves and others, by choosing to change our vocabulary. The goal here is to expand your options so that you can determine the direction of your thoughts, and to lay down a solid base that other concepts and techniques can be built upon. Effective wording improves thinking, decision making, and your state of being.

"The most important conversation,
is the one we have within ourselves!"

Words can be looked at as symbols for people, places, things, feelings, experiences, etc. They basically represent the meaning of something to us. They are elements that assist us in communicating within ourselves, as well as with other people. The words we use can determine how we see and feel about the world, and therefore create our reality. They can either strengthen or weaken us. Too often out of habit, the words we use happen automatically, and we are unaware of the one's that can be harmful to us.

Deciding consciously to change your language patterns, changes your thinking, which changes the actions you take, and therefore changes your experiences. This change in communication will enable you to achieve different results in your life. What we focus on reinforces it. You can choose to focus on success and learning, or failure and frustration.

Making deliberate shifts in the words you use, can create huge differences in the quality of your life, and the possibilities that become available to you. As in a recipe or formula, change the amount, quality, or sequence of combining the ingredients, and the whole outcome will change.

Many words are very powerful in how they link us up to every other time we had a similar experience where the same word was used to represent that experience. For example, when we say we *hate* something, it links us up to everything else we have ever *hated*. The word *hate* is a symbol for a wide assortment of unpleasant things from our past. Every time we use it, our brain makes connections with hateful memories, thus producing a similar emotional state. Even using the word *hate* in jest, can bring about a negative reaction in our mind and body.

Studies over the years have shown that negative emotions can decrease our immune system and make us more susceptible to illness. The energy in our body follows our thoughts. Every thought or idea causes a physical reaction. Ever notice how some people are frequently talking how *sick and tired* they are of something, and how they tend to be *sick and tired*? We have all experienced various physical responses such as increased heart rate, difficult breathing, and sweating, when we have thought about a future fearful event. The event hasn't happened and yet by communicating with ourselves in a certain way, we literally change our body chemistry.

Heart attacks, percentage wise, happen most often on Monday mornings. The stress of the new workweek, can produce tension, worry, frustration, and sadness. Negative emotions can trigger a drop in the heart's blood supply, which can trigger a heart attack. Downhearted feelings can actually double this risk.

How much do you lose in various aspects of your life, because of creating the wrong effect? We are always creating some kind of impression, is it the impression you want? If not, you can achieve a different response by adjusting the words you use, and the manner in which you present the words. Constantly work towards the goal of achieving the finest results that you can. This will also help to minimize a sense of isolation, and maximize a sense of feeling connected. Since very little can be accomplished in this world without the input of others, it's essential to use and have effective communication.

"What we concentrate on, we tend to create."

Talking about something reinforces it, therefore only say what you want to be true! When we make ourselves the object of a seemingly innocent joke, if it's done with enough frequency, it can become self-fulfilling. For instance, people will talk about how *bad* their memory is, almost bragging about it. Repeated over and over again, the subconscious begins to accept that you have a *bad* memory as true, and sure enough you have a *bad* memory. Others may also at the subconscious level, start to believe your imaginary shortcomings are true. They then start to treat you in a manner consistent with the image you have created, and thus their response can cause you to think less of yourself. Simple kidding around, can have very negative consequences.

Language has power, and by knowing this, you can select words that allow others to hear and understand you. Certain words provide a way of maintaining the focus of what you want. They can assist you to be in the frame of mind that you desire. Looking for *Positive Language Patterns*, gives your brain the opportunity to find alternative ways of expressing your experiences to yourself and others. These tools get you off automatic pilot and in control. Having choice means you can regulate how an experience will affect you. You can choose to use your old patterns of expression which produces certain results, or use empowering language to give you different results. Now it can be you who decides.

"Labels" limit is another concept that we're dealing with here. When we label something or someone, we put a meaning on it that can limit our awareness, experience, and understanding. Labels are a form of beliefs, and like all beliefs, they filter our perceptions. Our beliefs only allow us to be conscious of things that are in agreement with them, and we unconsciously filter out everything else. We essentially only see, hear, and know things that are consistent with our beliefs. It can take tremendous evidence to the opposite to penetrate the belief filters. In the case of positive empowering labels, labels can work to our benefit. But with negative labels, the effects can be very destructive. Because of their importance, beliefs are discussed in depth in several chapters throughout this book.

Perhaps the next time you start to put a negative label on someone by calling them something such as stupid or a jerk, experiment with a different approach. Step back, look to understand the facts, and search for why they behaved the way they did. Label the behavior with the actual things they do or don't do, not the person. Then ask yourself why you feel the behavior is unacceptable. Put yourself in charge of your responses.

What if someone's behavior is so distasteful, that at the moment, you can only view them as a jerk, a fool, or a slob? Suggestion, if you must put a negative label on someone, at least leave out the bigotry and prejudice. Prejudice goes beyond race, religion, and nationality. Other forms might include weight, height, gender, appearance (four-eyed, pizza face, elephant nose, buck toothed, bald, etc.), age, education, financial condition, social status, family, intelligence, and physical ability. And remember, prejudice usually comes from some kind of weakness such as fear and insecurity. Otherwise there would be no need for it.

Just call them a jerk, instead of calling them a fat jerk, or a short jerk, or an ugly jerk. Be part of the solution, and not the problem. Of course, getting rid of *jerk*, or any negative label, would also be a good idea. You could just deal with the actual factual behavior. You could objectively discuss the situation with them, and help them to understand how their behavior is affecting others. They truly might not know until someone tells them.

This chapter provides you with a list of commonly used words and phrases that can be limiting in various situations. Along with them, are other ways of expressing ideas or experiences. When I established just a few of these *Positive Language Patterns* with my staff when I was doing film promotion work, the reduction in stress was dramatic. Using the old ways of speaking you could cut the sense of tension with a knife. Using these new forms of expression reduced the intensity to a manageable level, and greatly increased our productivity.

The goal here is to give you options, take you off of automatic response, and to put you at choice. I'm not suggesting to never use negative phrasing, but to deliberately choose your words and therefore your thoughts, and for you to be in control of your experiences. And if you think about it, the only thing we can control with certainty, is our thoughts. Figure 1-2, at the end of this chapter, lists the following examples, with space for you to write in the positive alternatives.

Empowering Communication

O   try   ⟶ GOAL, OBJECTIVE, OUTCOME, TARGET, AIM,
PURPOSE, AMBITION, INTENTION, MISSION,
COMMITMENT, PLAN, VISION, QUEST,
DREAM, WISH; RESULT; WORKING ON,
USING, IN THE PROCESS; EXPERIMENTING
WITH

The word *try* by definition, refers to an unsuccessful attempt to achieve a result. Frequently we hear people say they *tried* to get a raise, a client, a loan; that they *try* to be optimistic, to be considerate, to get ahead, to stop smoking, to be on time, etc. These unsuccessful attempts create negative associations, making use of the word *try* produce negative impressions in ourselves as well as in others.

When someone *tries* to do something, the assumption is that it won't happen, that they're only giving it a halfhearted effort. Someone tells you that they'll *try* to get back to you or that they'll *try* to make the delivery on Friday, odds are it won't take place. People are constantly saying how they're *trying* to lose weight, *trying* to get a new job, and *trying* to save money. *Trying* implies they're not fully committed to make things happen. By changing one's language and replacing *try*, it will change the focus, and therefore change the results achieved.

Remember the brain takes things literally. If you keep saying you are *trying* to get a job, no one including yourself, is likely to take you too seriously. A lot of people when they come to my workshops are *trying* to find a job. They're not even *trying* to get a job, only to find one. It becomes clear to them very quickly, how their choice of wording affects their thinking, and has limited what they have been able to accomplish. By shifting to, "My *goal* (*objective*, *outcome*, *target*, etc.) is to get (or have) a job as a . . .," there is a whole shift in their perspective and the approach they take.

Job applicants when answering interviewing questions, will often say, "I always *try* to do the best that I can." This creates a very weak impression in the listener. By saying, "My *goal* is to always do the best that I can," a very different meaning is created. This communicates that you are committed to learning and improving, and that you will produce far better results than someone who *tries* to do their best.

Listen to other people speak, and notice how unconvincing it is when they say they're *trying* to do something. How do you feel when you hear public figures say they're *trying* to end hunger or poverty or unemployment? Then notice how much stronger it is when someone says their *goal* is to end hunger, or their *objective* is to eliminate poverty, or the *target* they're aiming for is full employment. This change in presentation, gives a sense that the speaker is actually serious about taking concrete action to accomplish something. The principle is to direct the focus to a specific *RESULT* that is desired. This shift in attention will help to motivate you as well as others.

Other alternatives to *try* could be, "I'm *working on* being at my preferred weight by eating healthy foods and exercising daily." Or you could say, "I'm *using* exercise and healthy eating to have my desired weight." This works a lot better than saying "I'm *trying* to lose weight." How often do we like to lose something anyway? "I'm *in the process* of getting a college degree, by taking classes at night," versus "I'm *trying* to get a college degree." Construct your statements in a positive way so that they are declarations of your commitment to take action, and to have a particular outcome.

Leave the use of *try* to past learning, and to one other area where its use is appropriate. When you are *experimenting* with different options to find out which one is best, *trying* works. *Trying* various routes to get to work on time, *trying* different types of exercise to find one you like, *trying* assorted software to see which one is most effective, are examples where *trying* is useful. Otherwise catch yourself when you use the word, and immediately restate your thoughts in a positive productive way.

○   rejected   ⟶ DIFFERENT

Feeling *rejected* can be a very powerful emotion to experience. It can invade one's entire being. When we say someone *rejected* us, it can link us up to every other time we have felt this way. A single event can be totally blown out of proportion.

Let's look at this concept from another viewpoint. To be *rejected* is to be turned down, denied, or refused. You want something from someone and they say no. To effectively manage this, let's use the truth. When you get a no, what it really means, is that what you are offering and/or the way in which you are offering it, is *different* from what the other person perceives or believes they want or need. From their outlook, based on their current experience and understanding, you or your product, is *different* or incompatible with what they feel they require. And that's the TRUTH! If a perceived value was there for them, if their needs were being met by their impression of what you are offering, then they would buy or accept your proposition.

Rejection does occur at times because of insufficient information, because something is not explained fully or properly. Regardless of the reason, positioning not getting what we want because it is *different* from what the other person believes they want, is more useful than thinking of it as *rejection*. You can then look at why it's *different*, and work at using another approach to find a common ground that works for both of you.

Not every proposal is appropriate for every person. Is what you're offering really right for the other person? If it is, regroup and use a different strategy. If not, stop wasting your time and theirs, and go on to another prospect.

When working on personal relationships with clients, the word *rejection* repeatedly comes up. They meet someone or go out with someone, and if it doesn't work out, they feel *rejected*. Exploring this logically and realistically, if someone doesn't want to have a relationship, it doesn't have to indicate that there's anything *wrong* with either one of you. All it means is that what they believe they want, is *different* from what they perceive you want or have to offer. That's all it means. If you don't get what you want by being who you are, then it's time to look elsewhere, or perhaps in some cases, to re-evaluate who you are.

What if you learn what the *differences* are and you change to minimize them? You change your appearance, manners, attitude, language, values, religion, friends, job, hobbies, etc., to win this person over, but then what have you got? At some point in time, you will want to be yourself and the relationship starts to fall apart. How many times do we see this happen? Often when someone finally feels secure in a relationship, they go back to their true self and wonder why things go downhill from there.

Study after study has shown that in most long-term successful relationships, each spouse considers the other their best friend. Friends accept each other as is. Friends are compatible in values, lifestyle, and viewpoints. Friends feel free to be themselves with each other. Rather than feeling *rejected* and that there is something *wrong* with you, realize that there are *differences*, and choose to move on.

Are there times when you are perfect for someone and they still say no? Yes! Often the reality is, that they said no to you because you were just right for them. Many people have very negative beliefs about life and themselves, and literally don't believe they deserve to have happiness. Your perfect for someone, but they don't have beliefs to support having the great kind of relationship that you would provide. You're "*too good to be true.*"

Fear of not being worthy can be so powerful, that the other person pushes you away. Is this ringing any bells? And sometimes, the other person's self-esteem is so low, that they at some level feel that there must be something wrong with someone who would want to be with them. To paraphrase something Groucho Marx once said, "I'd never want to join an organization that would have someone like me as a member."

Unfortunately due to faulty personal beliefs, many people feel this way, and they don't know it.

Work situations can present a similar story. You apply for a job or a promotion that you are totally suited for, and you don't get it. The boss believes that work is a struggle, filled with chaos, confusion, and challenges. You're perfect for the job, you'll bring calm, clarity, and competence to the position. Therefore you are inconsistent with their model of the world. You're a threat to what they accept as true, to what they understand and are familiar with.

If you want to feel lousy, talk about how you were *rejected*. If you want to make the best of things, step back accept the truth, and that there are *differences*. Understand, learn, and grow. Know and accept yourself, and allow your self-esteem to blossom.

O   general   ⟶ SPECIFIC

Miscommunicating information is a huge problem. The costs in terms of lost time and money is immeasurable. How many times do we hear "I thought you meant," and experience not being understood, or not understanding someone else. Often people either are too general and vague, or they only give the details without putting them into a category first.

Very little can be accomplished in our increasingly complex world without a clear, concise, and correct exchange of information. A lack of it is a major reason for errors. If someone tells you they want *several, a lot*, or *quite a few*, of something, how many is that? Getting definite and specific will benefit everyone, contributing to accuracy and awareness.

To have effective communication, before you can transfer data to someone else, you first need to have clarity in your own thoughts. Why are you having this communication, what is your reason? Always aim for the *UER*, the *ULTIMATE END RESULT* that you want. Because of having this interaction, what do you want to have happen? A major reason many people never reach their full potential, is because they use limited thinking, and never figure out what their *ULTIMATE END RESULT* is. In the *Wording Your Goals* chapter, we'll deal in detail with how to construct and form your goals for peak productivity, and how to know you've achieved what you want.

People sometimes have difficulty in coming up with the *UER*. A simple question that helps, is to keep asking "So that," until enough information is gathered. In my job interviewing class I ask, "What's your goal for taking this workshop?" Someone will reply, "To be able to be more comfortable in an interview." I then ask, "So that?" They might say, "So that I'm confident during the interview." Again, "So that?" They respond with, "So that I give a good interview."

Coaching with more "so that's," they finally arrive at the *UER*, "So that I get a job as a _____, at a salary of _____, doing _____ type of work, for a _____ type of company, etc." In one of the last chapters, *Career Checklist*, there is a checklist to aid someone in answering these kind of questions.

Once you've gotten clarity, begin your message with the general topic that you're talking about. This provides a frame on which all the details can be tied to. Then give enough *specific* details so that your listener gets an accurate picture. This picture needs to be *specific* enough so that the vision you have created in your listener's mind, is the same vision that you have in your mind. Can they see what you see? Remember, the brain thinks in pictures.

The amount of information required to accomplish this, will depend on what your listener knows of the topic, as well as their state of being. Are they in an open and receptive frame of mind where they can fully process and comprehend what you are communicating? A person can only understand what they have had an experience of. Is the message complete enough, for this person, at this time, to create an experience in them that achieves the desired understanding? If not, it's up to us to explain things in a way that the listener has the necessary experience. Yes this may take work, however, the gain far outweighs the possible effort.

After you believe you have been clear and *specific* enough, ask your listener to feed back to you their understanding of the information. Say, "I want to be sure I've been clear, so I'd appreciate it if you would give me your understanding of what we've discussed." With this approach, you're taking responsibility for the accuracy and completeness of the communication, and showing respect for the other person. If we're not getting what we want, it's up to us to do something about it. If someone doesn't understand what we're saying, it's usually our responsibility, and we need to change our approach.

More/Less/Better Syndrome

Another concept that ties into being *specific*, is what I call the *More/ Less/Better Syndrome*. This pattern can cause weak, blurry, and obscure goals, which can equal poor performance. You must be able to clearly see what you want before you can productively direct your energy towards it.

Therefore, 80% to 90% of the time, replace *More/Less/Better* with ideas such as in this section, and reap the benefits. "We rarely get more than we ask for!"

Let's deal with *more* first. Whenever you find yourself saying something preceded with *more*, say it again without the *more* and see if it enhances your objective. You will probably find that most of the time it does. For instance, when you have an important meeting to attend, do you want to be *more* confident, or do you want to be confident! There is a world of difference between these two states.

Scaling it out from one to ten, moving your confidence level from a three to a five is much *more* confident, but it's still a weak unclear target to strive for, and limits you. A potent outcome would be for you to be totally confident, to be at a level of ten, and to do what you can to come as close to a level of ten as possible. This is a critical distinction. This shift in thinking is essential for you to free yourself from restrictive patterns. I've had people in my workshops embrace and use this one concept of dropping the *more*, and transform the results they produced in all areas of their lives.

Look at the following lists, cover the *more* sides, and notice the difference. "I want to be . . .":

more — confident	more — accurate
more — successful	more — motivating
more — peaceful	more — comfortable
more — compatible	more — decisive
more — loved	more — creative
more — healthy	more — disciplined
more — youthful	more — ambitious
more — fulfilled	more — persuasive
more — energetic	more — organized
more — practical	more — assertive
more — relaxed	more — optimistic
more — balanced	more — forgiving
more — thorough	more — independent
more — attractive	more — patient
more — powerful	more — perceptive
more — efficient	more — persistent
more — effective	more — poised
more — understanding	more — productive
more — competent	more — punctual

more — knowledgeable	more — cheerful
more — trustworthy	more — worthwhile
more — coordinated	more — focused
more — respectful	more — careful
more — positive	more — sincere

Remove the *more*, get *specific*, and give yourself definite destinations to move toward. Powerful goals act as magnets drawing us to them.

More can be useful as a starting point, to begin the process of getting clear and specific. But the key is to always work for total clarity, by determining what the *UER* you want to have is. The *more* powerful the goal, the *better* the outcome, are functional ways of using *more* and *better*, because we're talking about being in process when the *UER* is still incomplete and difficult to measure.

The following are other variations people habitually say, and *more* effective ways of representing the goals. Shift from *safer* to *safe, healthier* to *healthy, kinder* to *kind, easier* to *easy, faster* to *fast, happier* to *happy, wealthier* to *wealthy, stronger* to *strong*, and *calmer* to *calm*. And then you need to be as *specific* as you can, so that you know what *safe, healthy, kind*, etc., mean to you.

Work out enough detail so that you can explain what you want to someone else. If I say I want to be wealthier, there's no clear picture. Someone giving me one dollar fulfills that goal. If I say I want to be wealthy, and to me being wealthy consists of having over $50,000,000, now I have a *specific* target to aim at, and something that other people can understand.

Less is the next concept in this group. It's common to hear someone say that they want to have *less* stress in their life. If they average 100 stressful experiences per day, if they move it down to 90, they got what they asked for, but it's still a lot of stress. What would an effective objective be? What is the total opposite of stress? Instead of aiming for *less* stress, work for peace, calm, serenity, joy, tranquility, harmony, happiness, and bliss. Always go for the complete positive result of what you want to have.

People say they want to be *less* nervous, have *less* competition, *less* sickness, etc. Poor targets equal poor results. Always turn negative statements around, and look for the most positive ways of expressing your ideas. *Less* nervous could be completely calm and confident, *less* competition could be mutual understanding and cooperation, and *less* sickness could be total health.

Better is a concept that can be along similar lines to *more*. If you express that you want things to be *better*, what does that imply? What instructions are you giving to your brain? If you say you want a *better* relationship, to feel *better*, or a *better* job, it's unclear and very weak. To establish the best outcomes for yourself, talk specifically, in total detail, about what you want.

Arguing with your mate 50 times a week, and then declaring that you want a *better* relationship, might advance you to quarrelling 45 times per week. That's an improvement, however not at a very satisfactory level. Continuing to ask for a *better* relationship, the arguing can drop to 40, 35, 30, 25, or even 20 times per week. It's *better*, but it's still a lot of conflict. Weak goals equal weak results.

Instead of *better*, how about setting a goal of, "I always want to have an outstanding, mutually loving, caring, supportive, satisfying, nurturing, compatible, respectful relationship with my mate." That creates a whole different outcome and target to aim for. Then you'll need to define what loving, caring, supportive, etc., represent. What will and won't happen that tells you these conditions are being met? By answering these types of questions, you'll have a picture to move toward developing. You'll have something to guide your behavior in the right direction. In a later chapter, there is a large checklist to aid you in establishing your relationship boundaries.

If you feel lousy, do you just want to feel *better*, or do you want to feel *great*!? Telling someone else that you hope they feel *better*, is weak compared to saying that you hope they feel *wonderful*, *great*, or *totally fantastic*. The effect your words could have, could actually support the healing process.

What is a *better* job? Would it be one that's challenging, creative, rewarding, secure, exciting, interesting, etc., and what would you specifically be doing that would give you the feelings that you desire? Many people in my workshops come in stuck, because they never understood how to get clarity in their careers. Once they do, they are able to get unstuck, and to push forward. Again, one of the last chapters has a career checklist to assist in this process.

Instead of stopping with wanting things to be *better*, set a goal for yourself to make things the most satisfying that they can be. And then ask yourself what you need to do to make this a reality. As you look at the following illustrations, notice how *better* is limiting, and how you can benefit by getting focused, and going to the *UER*. Do you want to:

- have *better* health -or- be completely healthy
- have a *better* home -or- have an ideal home
- have a *better* job -or- have a fabulous job
- be a *better* mate -or- be an outstanding mate
- be a *better* parent -or- be an excellent parent
- be a *better* driver -or- be an absolutely safe driver
- be a *better* manager -or- be an entirely effective manager
- be a *better* golfer -or- be a terrific golfer
- be a *better* friend -or- be a great friend

Again, once you have established your optimal goal concept, you need to get specific as to what will exist so that you have things the way that you want them. What is being completely healthy, an excellent parent, a totally effective manager, etc.? What is the proof and evidence that your wishes are accomplished?

Business success depends on constantly improving everyone's performance. A major complaint and frustration for many workers, is that they do not clearly know what's expected of them. They do not fully understand how their performance is being measured. Besides quantity, quality, and timeliness, what else goes into how they are being evaluated? What does telling someone they need to do *better* work mean? How can they give management what they want, when they don't exactly know what it is? Too often instructions are delegated with:

- increase/decrease
- bigger/smaller
- lighter/heavier
- thinner/thicker
- taller/shorter
- more/less

These statements are okay as places to begin, but without clarification, errors too often will follow. Telling someone to *increase* capacity doesn't generate a picture. Conveying to *increase* capacity by at least 10%, no later than October 1, leads to the desired results.

Always clearly establish the *UER* that you want! Make it measurable so that people can understand your wishes, and know what to do, how to do it, and when to do it. And when possible, tell them why you want something done in a certain way and at a certain time. When people understand what's expected of them, and the reasons why its expected, they are assisted in performing to their potential. Again, how to get specific is covered in the *Wording Your Goals* chapter.

Are there times when it can be practical to be vague and unspecific? Yes. Negotiation, sales, and some forms of therapy, are situations where letting the other party fill in the blanks might be useful. But in most communications, especially within ourselves, confusion and vagueness can produce very disappointing conclusions.

Remember, a key to effective communication is being flexible. *More*, *less*, and *better* are fine as starting points, and are the best choices in some situations. They work when you are in process, for awareness, and when you are sorting things out where precise measurement is difficult. The technique is to work towards the most constructive wording possible. Give yourself specific strong powerful outcomes to motivate yourself, and to maximize what you achieve. The *better* the goals, the *better* the results.

○   hate   ⟶ LOVE, PREFER, WANT

As we said in the beginning of this chapter, *hate* is a very powerful symbol of what we don't want, or of something very negative. When you find yourself saying you *hate* being late, *hate* waiting in line, *hate* getting lost, or *hate* wasting time, immediately stop and tell yourself what you do want. Shift things around to the positive opposite. Some alternatives could be:

- ○   "I *hate* being late" -to- "I *love* being on time"
- ○   "I *hate* being sick" -to- "I *love* being totally healthy"
- ○   "I *hate* arguing" -to- "I *love* cooperation and agreement"
- ○   "I *hate* wasting time" -to- "I *love* being efficient"
- ○   "I *hate* waiting" -to- "I *love* being served immediately"
- ○   "I *hate* being ignored" -to- "I *love* being appreciated"
- ○   "I *hate* rudeness" -to- "I *love* politeness"
- ○   "I *hate* being lost" -to- "I *love* knowing where I am"
- ○   "I *hate* confusion" -to- "I *love* clarity and understanding"
- ○   "I *hate* being bored" -to- "I *love* being interested"
- ○   "I *hate* stupidity" -to- "I *love* smart behavior"
- ○   "I *hate* sloppiness" -to- "I *love* neatness and order"
- ○   "I *hate* being angry" -to- "I *love* being peaceful"
- ○   "I *hate* repetition" -to- "I *love* variety"
- ○   "I *hate* being insecure" -to- "I *love* being confident"

So the next time you start to say how you *hate* when your neighbors are noisy, refocus and think about how you *love* when your neighbors are quiet and considerate of others. Look to put *love* in your life wherever you can, with all its enriching qualities. *Love* increases our immune system, *hate* decreases it.

Prefer and *want* are other choices when your feelings about something are less intense. "I *prefer* having a situation with a lot of variety," versus "I'm uncomfortable doing repetitive tasks." "I *want* to be confident and poised," versus "I dislike being nervous."

Are there situations when *hate* with all its energy might serve you? It's an individual matter. But at least save it for major situations, and put *love* in your life whenever possible, in day-to-day dealings.

○   don't ——► DO

Changing your focus from what you *don't* want, to what you *do* want, is a crucial point. When you restructure your thoughts, you are able to restructure your life. Whatever we pay attention to becomes our reality. What we focus on shapes our experience. When you watch television, you switch channels until you find something you like. We can do the same in life.

Keep switching what goes through your mind, until it's what you *do* want. To effectively move away from something, it helps to have something worthwhile to move towards. Let the word *don't* be a powerful trigger for you. Whenever you find yourself saying what you *don't* want, immediately turn it around and ask yourself what you *do* want. Make the last impression in your brain be a positive one. Doing this adjustment will transform the results you create.

The mind is very literal. If you *don't* want to be sick, poor, alone, etc., stop focusing on these things and giving them energy. Immediately focus on the positive opposites, of what you *do* want, such as health, wealth, and companionship. Stating what you *don't* want, is fine as a starting point for being aware of and acknowledging what is, but make sure you always end on the positive of what you *do* want. You must constantly direct what your brain is filled with, or someone else will probably do it for you.

Mowing the lawn was one of my responsibilities when I was a teenager. This was not something that I enjoyed doing. I kept talking about how I *hated* doing it and wishing that I *didn't* have to do it. Well one day I got my wish. The subconscious mind often gives us what we want when we ask long enough and loud enough. Being very literal, it provides solutions when we put enough emotion into our requests.

Our power lawn mower had large steel blades that could cut through almost anything. Whatever got in its way, was quickly pulverized. While mowing, and complaining, one day, with the grass tall from my neglect and wet from the rain, the right rear wheel fell off the mower. After unsuccessfully *trying* to put the wheel back on, I proceeded to finish mowing the tall wet grass. I was now complaining even more about how I *don't* want to cut the lawn.

A short distance later, because of the tall wet grass and having only three wheels, the lawn mower became stuck. Cleverly, I pushed the back of the mower with my right foot, while wearing gym shoes. My gym shoes were wet from the grass and as I pushed the mower, my foot slipped under the mower and into the spinning blades.

Power was spelled with a capital "P" for our mower, and the blades went through my shoe and big toe like the proverbial "hot knife through butter." Needless to say I was stunned, so much so that I basically felt nothing, at first. I was whisked away to an emergency clinic where my toe was fully reunited with my foot. The healing was slow and uncomfortable, however, I never ever had to mow the lawn again. Was this a good trade-off? No!!! But I got what I asked for. No more boring mowing the lawn for me. I also learned about the power of the mind and how we need to be clear and specific in our thinking, about what we *do* want, and HOW we want it.

Always look to end communications on the positive *do*. "I *don't* want any errors or mistakes," vs. "Please make sure everything is perfect and correct." "I *don't* want to get fired," vs. "I want to keep my job." "I *don't* want to be abused," vs. "I want to be treated with respect and kindness." You could say to a loved one, "I *don't* want to cause you pain, stress, and grief," or "I only want to bring you pleasure, happiness, and joy." In a job interview, you could say, "I *don't* want you to think I'll quit," or "I'm only interested in a long-term situation." The last impression in the mind, is the one that tends to get acted upon.

Here are some additional samples of routinely used *don'ts*, with possible opposite *do's*:

"Don't be late"	"Please be there at . . ."
"Don't forget to"	"Please remember to . . ."
"Don't leave"	"I want you to stay"
"Don't yell"	"Please speak softly"

"Don't slam the door"	"Please close the door quietly"
"Don't feel awkward"	"I want you to feel comfortable"
"Don't be tired"	"Please have a lot of energy"
"Don't be rude"	"Please be polite"
"Don't run"	"Please walk slowly"
"Don't stop"	"Please continue to . . ."
"Don't drive so fast"	"Please drive the speed limit"
"Don't slouch"	"Please stand upright"
"Don't drop the ball"	"Please hold onto the ball"
"Don't be so rough"	"Please be gentle"
"Don't be dirty"	"Please be clean"
"Don't criticize me"	"Please be supportive of me"
"Don't be unreliable"	"Please be responsible"
"Don't tell me no"	"Please tell me yes"
"Don't be stupid"	"Please think logically"
"I don't want to hurt you"	"I want you to feel good"
"I don't want to be old"	"I want to be youthful"
"I don't want to be sick"	"I want to be healthy"
"I don't want to be poor"	"I want to be wealthy"
"I don't want to be alone"	"I want a loving mate"
"I don't want to be fat"	"I want to be my ideal weight"
"I don't want to be stressed"	"I want to be relaxed"
"I don't want to lose"	"I want to win"
"I don't want to be critical"	"I want to be accepting"
"I don't want to feel inept"	"I want to feel competent"
"I don't want to argue"	"I want to have cooperation"
"I don't want noisy neighbors"	"I want quiet neighbors"
"I don't want to be depressed"	"I want to be cheerful"

There are times we may try to be of assistance to others, however through the use of *don't* we can produce the opposite result. Have you ever heard someone say *don't worry*, or *don't feel sad*, or *don't be angry*? What are the emotions that these phrases communicate? *Worrying, feeling sad*, and being *angry*. These types of comments just serve to inflame the situation.

First they are telling the person that what they are feeling is *wrong* and that they *should* feel something else. And by repeating the undesirable state, it's like throwing fuel on the fire. A better strategy is to acknowledge and respect what someone is experiencing, and then to find out if they would prefer something else. Get their permission to be of assistance, otherwise you can end up putting your values on them. If you learn from them that they would prefer feeling another way, then help them to achieve it. Unless someone is in danger, be considerate by following, "do unto others as they want done unto them."

What's the opposite of *don't worry*? Ideas such as *calm, hopeful,* and *peaceful* could be substituted. Approaching something that is of concern by analyzing the facts and looking for possible courses of action, would be a more functional way of dealing with a future uncertain outcome. Looking for solutions would yield better results than reinforcing a state of worry which limits a person's abilities.

What's the opposite of *don't feel sad*? Words such as *cheerful, good, happy,* and *comfortable,* could have the desired effect. Someone feels *sad* because something did or didn't happen, or they feel something will or won't happen in the future. Quite often their ego and sense of self is on the line. Assisting them to see things objectively, what they could learn from an experience, and how they could use an experience to assist them in the future, can help to get them going again.

Don't be angry, deserves special attention. *Anger* is so widespread, that for some people it's an almost constant companion. People are *angry* about the weather, traffic, waiting, taxes, work, the government, other people, etc. It's like the old story when a tense young man was asked what he was *angry* about, and his reply was, "What have you got?" Some people are so unhappy within themselves that they try to blame everyone and everything else for their condition, instead of taking responsibility for doing something about it. Many people are shortchanged growing up, but as adults it's up to each one of us to learn from yesterday, and push forward toward the future of what we want.

Anger and the threat of violence, is constantly used to resolve issues in everything from films and television shows, to cartoons and music videos. Even some commercials have an indirect message of violence. We need to be aware of how repeatedly we are bombarded with hostile themes in the media. Then we can protect ourselves from the negative influences, by choosing not to expose ourselves and our loved ones, to it.

When someone is *angry,* or experiencing any emotion, realize that there is a totally valid reason for it, regardless of how irrational it might seem to us. Based on someone's values, beliefs, physical condition, life situation, etc., it's perfectly logical from their point of view for them to respond the way they do. It might not be proper or desirable, but it is logical to them, otherwise they wouldn't do it. The fact that they are *angry,* means that there is a reason for the anger. From this perspective, find out the cause of their reaction, and assist them in moving to resourceful states such as *understanding* and *control*.

Physicality or physical pattern plays an important role in dealing with *anger*. In many of the acting classes I've taken over the years, you learn to first get in the physical pattern of the emotion you want to communicate to your audience, and the emotion will follow. To fully have anger requires muscular tension. Where is this tension usually felt? In the fists, arms, chest, stomach, and especially in the jaw. After acknowledging someone's *anger*, get them to sit down and talk about what they are responding to that is causing the *anger*. Sitting will help to relax their body, and talking will help them to relax their stomach, chest, and jaw. It's almost impossible to totally experience *anger* with the mouth open, and a relaxed jaw. Relaxing the facial muscles with a small smile also helps. In this less intense state, you can support them in working through whatever is really bothering them.

What's the real issue underlying *anger*? Commonly it's that a person believes something should or shouldn't happen. Frequently *anger* is an expression of a build-up of many small incidents that weren't handled when they first occurred. To assist someone, keep them focused on what they *do* want, and what they can do to get it. Getting them in a resourceful state from a position of awareness and truth, will help this process. Look for respectful ways to support others in dealing with their emotions.

Listen to yourself, as well as to others, and start catching the *don'ts*. When they happen, use them as starting points, to guide you to specifically identify what you *do* want, and what others want.

○   depressed   ⟶ BLAH, HAZY THOUGHTS, NO ENERGY

Depressed is a word that is frequently overused and can be very self-perpetuating. It's used so commonly and lightly that we stop being aware that it's being said. I'm not talking about clinical "depression" or "depression" from physical causes. I'm talking about the little ups and downs we experience in life that we label as *depression*, and how the use of this word, can make us feel even worse.

By breaking down into specifics, what we are actually experiencing during the state we call *depression*, we can get a better handle on it. What if you said that you felt a little *blah* today, that your thinking was *hazy* and *unclear*, and that you were listless and had *no energy*? A detailed description of your state of being is more manageable and it gives you more choice as to how you feel. Just stick with the facts, and leave out the emotion.

Shifting physicality is also very powerful here. To fully enter the state we call *depression*, we need to be in a certain physical pattern. In my workshops, when I ask what's the posture of *depression*, participants know immediately what it is. The head is down, the shoulders are slumped forward, the breathing is low and slow, the face has a frown on it, and the body is lifeless. Also the tone of voice is usually whiny, with the words and thoughts very negative. By shifting your physicality, to the opposite of the above, and by changing your language, you can put yourself in a resourceful state so that you can deal effectively with the thing that you are responding to in a negative way.

By pulling your shoulders back, putting your head up high, breathing high in your chest, putting a smile on your face, talking in a warm loving confident tone about what you *do* want, and visualizing yourself having what you want, you will not be able to fully experience the feeling called *depression*. This is one of the reasons a good brisk walk can lift the spirits. Remember that every mental and emotional state has physical aspects built into the body with a muscle memory. Get into a distinct physical pattern and a particular emotion will follow. This is what many actors do when they are performing a scene. The desired emotion follows the physical form.

Changing physicality is a technique that was very helpful in dealing with one of the people on my staff. She had a tendency toward *drama*, and would get herself so down that she couldn't work. When this happened, I asked her to walk up and down the hall several times at a fast pace, with her head up high, and her arms swinging fully. I also asked her to think about something she loved to do, which was dancing. As she did this, she would start to smile, and her focus would begin to shift. After just a minute or two, her mood changed and she was able to get back to work. So to perk someone up, get them moving and concentrating on a bright future of what they *do* want.

Beliefs play a major role in the emotion of depression. As with *anger*, we usually believe something should or shouldn't have happened, or believe something will or won't happen. Because of this, we therefore feel we should be *depressed*. But consider this, does everyone respond to the same thing in the same way? Do we always respond to the same thing in the same way? So much of our reactions occur due to our emotional state at the time of an event. And our emotional states are essentially caused by our beliefs.

○   fear/nervous   ⟶ APPREHENSIVE, UNCOMFORT-
ABLE, ENERGY; EXCITED

We can gain greater choice and control over *fear* by using words such as *apprehensive*, *uncomfortable*, and *energy*. I'm not recommending denial of a negative feeling. What I'm suggesting is positioning the feeling for what it is, *energy* that is generated due to thinking about a future event in a certain way. The type of thinking that we engage in comes from our beliefs, which may or may not be true.

Thinking certain thoughts, usually predicting an undesirable result of what we *don't* want, is necessary to achieve the mental and physical conditions that we label as *fear* and *nervousness*. By using less emotional terms to describe our ideas, we put ourselves in a more resourceful state, which enables us to handle things more productively. We can then shift focus from what we *don't* want to what we *do* want, and plan what needs to be done to get it.

In some cases we can change the perspective completely, by calling the *energy excitement. Fear* and *excitement* are often at a similar level of intensity. Instead of telling yourself you are *nervous* about meeting a client or going on an interview, use that *energy* to be *excited* about all the benefits you'll gain from the meeting or interview. Or you could simply acknowledge the *energy* surging through you, and imagine how you will use this *energy* advantageously to be dynamic, enthusiastic, and effective. The principle is to make the greatest use of whatever happens, and to constantly learn.

Skydiving is a sport I used to engage in, so I've had experience with intense *fear*. It's been said that the only *fear* that we are born with is the *fear* of heights and of falling. Even this instinctive *fear* can be put in a different perspective, and handled in any way that we wish.

When I began skydiving, with each jump I was in a complete state of terror. Several times I was so afraid, that I was not going to jump and just go back down in the airplane. My negative self-talk created a heartbeat that felt it would burst out of my chest, limbs that were numb, and total delirium in my brain. Nothing had actually happened, but my fatalistic internal dialogue put me into a state of hysteria.

Yet one day, after listening to experienced skydivers, I was communicating with myself differently. It was so different, that I had no *fear*. I thought about how terrific it was for me to be doing something so *exciting*. I thought about how proud I was handling something that I was so afraid of. I thought about how fortunate I was to be feeling life at such an intense level. I chose different thoughts, and I produced a different result.

Overcoming this *fear* and turning its energy into *excitement*, has served me through many rough times over the years. What are some *fears* you have faced and pushed through, no matter how small they might be? It could be asking someone for a date, participating in an athletic event, or making a speech. Celebrate and congratulate yourself on your wins, and make a list of them to use as a resource for dealing with other challenges that come your way.

○ dysfunctional   ➝ THE FACTS, THE TRUTH

Many people go around saying that they, and everyone else, come from a *dysfunctional* family. Therefore, we're all *dysfunctional*. Remember that labels limit, and that what we identify with, becomes our reality. Thinking of oneself as *dysfunctional* becomes self-fulfilling, and will probably cause limiting, ineffective, and *dysfunctional* behavior.

What if instead, you looked back on those aspects of your childhood that you had no control over, in purely *factual* terms? There may have been fighting, arguing, yelling, criticism, physical attacks, hunger, dirt, sickness, lying, aloneness, crying, etc. What are the *facts* without any emotional labels? Simply describe what actually happened. By viewing the past based only on the objective details, it can take a lot of the harmful negative charge out of it. Otherwise, you might continue to relive the pain forever.

What would you have *loved* to have from people when you were growing up? Would you have *loved* it if the people in your life were kind, loving, caring, giving, honest, nurturing, supportive, understanding, calm, patient, clean, accepting, capable, sane, available, healthy, happy, fun, etc.?

> *"We can't change the past, however we can change how we view, understand, and position it."*

Feeling like a victim and feeling sorry for ourselves, causes us to continue to suffer, and it can totally weaken and disable us.

What if you look at the *truth*? Because the *fact* is, that each person does the best they can with what they have. Everyone has a script, and only functions in ways that are consistent with this script. Until the script is edited, until the programming a person has is reconfigured, replaced, or enlarged, they are limited by it. This means that people have the ability to be more than they are, but too frequently, they don't have the mindset to be able to access and use what they have. As with being *angry* at someone, I'm not suggesting to like what someone did, but to understand it so that you can let go of it, for your own benefit.

Addictions is an issue that can be in a similar vein. As long as someone keeps telling themselves they are *addicted* to something, it will be true. Since human beings function from chemical processes occurring throughout the mind and body, changing the activities that cause the chemical reactions, could change the addictions. So changing the food, the water, the environment, and the physical activity would change the chemistry. And thinking certain thoughts also has a powerful effect on the body chemistry. We think certain thoughts and we change our heart rate, our blood pressure, our breathing, our temperature, our hormones, etc.

What if someone instead of saying they are *addicted*, they told themselves that currently, they have an urge to have or to do something? But they know that acting on this urge is harmful to them, and possibly to other people that they care about. What if instead of saying, "I'm an alcoholic," someone said, "Alcohol is toxic and poisonous to me. It destroys my health and my life, and therefore I'm a total nondrinker (or non drug user, or nonsmoker)?" Many people in my workshops with addictions used this line of thinking successfully.

What if they constantly examined the beliefs they've had that contributed to an urge? What if they made a list of all the times when an urge was not present? What we study, we strengthen. What if they constructed a self-image, a set of beliefs, and a set of goals of what they wish their life to be? What if they compiled a list of other people who had the same urge, and who no longer have it? And what if they established relationships with people that are supportive of the desired behavior, such as being a nondrinker?

Making things different can be difficult and can take a lot of time. However, many people have successfully made changes, and since time is an illusion, often they have done it as quickly as it took them to decide to do it. Each of us is capable of so much more than we may realize. Many things are necessary to have change last, which will be covered in subsequent chapters.

In other sections of this book, we will explore ways to edit and rewrite one's script. For now, instead of the label *dysfunctional*, search to understand other people's scripts, and why they behaved the way they did. You may have received less than you wanted or deserved when you were growing up but it's over with, and why continue to have pain and be held back due to other people's limitations?

○   angry,   ⟶ FASCINATING, CURIOUS, INTERESTING,
    frustrated   WHY

Under *don't* we discussed dealing with someone else's *anger*. Now we'll talk about dealing with your *anger*, and utilize some of the same reasoning. Have you ever become very *angry*, and later you found out you didn't have all the facts and that your *anger* was unfounded? Have you ever become *angry* with someone for doing something that you've done in the past, like cutting in line, or driving too fast or slow? The idea here is to consider that if someone is doing something you feel is inappropriate, get *fascinated*, *curious*, and *interested* as to *why* they're doing it. You might say to yourself, "Isn't it *curious* that this waiter is rude considering that he works for tips." "Isn't it *fascinating* how fast some people drive, risking their license as well as their life." "Isn't it *interesting* how the bank teller took a break when I got to the head of the line." Search for understanding, instead of responding.

Wondering *why* people do things or *why* things happen, keeps you in control. As stated before, the fact that someone does something, indicates that there is a reason *why* they did it. If there were no reason, they wouldn't have done it. Regardless of how silly, horrible, or stupid someone's behavior is to us, the fact that it happened tells us that according to their reality it made sense. I'm not suggesting to like or even accept someone's negative conduct, including our own, but to seek to understand it. The thinking here, is to get *curious* instead of getting *furious*, *interested* instead of *irritated*, *fascinated* instead of *frustrated*.

We once had 20 television sets shipped to a film location, and they didn't arrive on time. Normally this would have created a great deal of *anger* and *frustration*. Now, using these principles when something went wrong, my assistant would in a singsong way, say, "Oh Ron, we have another *fascinating* situation!" My staff thought this was silly. But, did getting emotional and all stressed out help us to be productive? No! We can't change what has happened, however, we can change how we choose to respond to it. In the past, we wasted too much time on the drama and worry of what we didn't want, and made things more difficult for ourselves. Now we shifted to focusing on what we did want, on solutions, and what we needed to do to achieve our objectives.

Also stepping back and asking yourself *why* you're getting upset, is very useful. Getting at the truth of your reactions allows you to decide what to feel. I'm not talking about denial, I'm talking about what's real for you. Is the *anger* a smoke screen for some other unsettled *issues*? Things will happen, and by staying objective you can make the most out of whatever comes your way.

Anger, as discussed under *don't*, is tied into someone's beliefs. Something should or shouldn't happen, based on one's model of the world. Things tend to only have the meaning that we give them. Otherwise everyone would respond to the same things in the same way, and obviously we don't.

If someone inappropriately yells at you, do you think less of yourself, or do you think less of them? One belief could produce *anger*, and the other belief could produce understanding and empathy. If someone is rude to you, do you respond the same if you had just received a promotion or if you were just laid off? If you had just won a large sum of money or just lost a large sum of money? If you had just received a compliment or just received a character assassination? What belief or beliefs control how you react? What beliefs are behind the interpretation and evaluation of a situation that causes a negative reaction? Change a belief, and you change your response! Belief management techniques are explained in several later chapters.

Am I suggesting to never get *angry* or *frustrated*? No. There are times when an emotional display could be the best alternative. Sometimes, under certain circumstances, it's the only way to get some people to be aware of and to understand how important something is. Sometimes it's the only way to get justice and what you deserve. But in regular day-to-day activities, being *fascinated, curious, interested,* and wondering *why,* will probably serve you and everyone else a lot better.

Health will also benefit from a calm manner. *Anger* puts a tremendous strain on our body, and can lead to serious health problems. It stimulates the release of the hormones adrenaline and cortisol, which prepares us for fight or flight. The heart rate and blood pressure rise, which can damage blood vessels, contribute to plaque build up, and a heart attack. Blood cells become sticky, also encouraging plaque formation. Fat cells are stimulated into the bloodstream for energy, and if not used up, convert to cholesterol and more plaque. And the immune system is reduced, making illness more likely. Managing emotions and maintaining a peaceful viewpoint, can be a matter of life and death.

It's like the analogy of putting your hand in a fire. If you take it out quickly enough, no damage. If you leave it in the fire for a short time, you will get burned. And if you leave your hand in the fire long enough, your skin will literally melt off. When anger first starts to surface, immediately shift your physical pattern: open your mouth, release facial tension with a smile, breathe deeply, change your posture, make sure your hands are open, and relax all your muscles. Then ask, "Why is this happening?," and "What belief is causing me to react this way?" Short-circuit the flow of electrical connections through your body, before they have a chance to do any damage.

Understanding your *anger* and repositioning your thoughts and physical pattern, in some cases may not be sufficient. For many people some basic changes are needed. Poor health, an improper diet, insufficient sleep, a stressful home situation, a noisy hassled work environment, etc., all can contribute to a less than favorable state of being. Many changes might be necessary for you to have *anger* be a choice, instead of an automatic response. Start with the goal to be in charge of your feelings, then know your beliefs, commit to understand the beliefs of others, and make positive changes as needed.

What if you lose it and blow your top, what then? Get physical! You need to quickly burn off the adrenaline in the most constructive way possible. Take a very brisk walk, move furniture, clean out a closet, run up and down stairs; burn off the energy. Once you've regained your composure, then deal with the issue that initiated the negative response. Have you ever said or done something when you were *angry*, and regretted it later?

Another point to consider, is how we affect others when we're *angry* or *frustrated* about something. For instance, you have an argument with someone at work. You tell the story to a friend, and you tell it with all the emotion, drama, and intensity of when it actually happened. You relive it and experience all the negativity all over again.

What's happening to your listener? They now go through and experience the whole lousy mess themselves. They might feel all the negative feelings, the tension, the stomach churning as if it happened to them. A friend of mine used to regularly have conflicts with co-workers. When we would go out to dinner I would hear the latest battle, told with a great deal of emotion and realism. My friend would step-by-step, word-for-word act out the entire scene for me, to where I became a participant in this drama, and experienced all the negative feelings.

By the time our food arrived my guts were churning, and indigestion followed. This became so chronic, that I stopped having dinner with this friend. Recommendation, be good to your friends. Never ask them to have a bad experience, only help them to have good experiences. What emotion or state do your words ask or cause another person to have?

If you tell a less than joyful story, tell it in an objective matter-of-fact way. Give the details, express how you feel about it, but do it in an unemotional manner. Since we so often laugh about the negative things that happen, later, why not tell them as soon as possible in a light humorous way? What if you were going to talk about the incident on an upbeat television talk show, how would you relate the story? Is there any possible benefit to anyone if you and your listener both feel horrible after you tell your tale? Who likes to be around people who are *angry* and upset? As someone once said, "You can't bond with someone who is angry."

The message here is for you to be at choice and in control. For you to decide what you feel anytime anywhere, instead of allowing someone or something else to decide for you. After all, what is life other than a series of experiences. And as long as we're alive, life happens!

O   failure   ⟶ FEEDBACK, LEARN; DIDN'T GET THE RESULT

Positioning our less than totally successful results as *failures*, we link up to other *failures* and can put ourselves in a negative frame of mind. This then limits our willingness to engage in other ventures where we might *fail* again. The focus shifts from possibility to improbability, from *let's go for it*, to *why bother*. Someone then feels like a *failure* which is a self-concept that is self-fulfilling.

Successful people see nonperforming actions from another viewpoint. When they *fail*, they frame it as just another experience. They look at it as *feedback*, as something they can *learn* from. We can *learn* from anything in life, if we have the right attitude. We do this asking questions such as, "What can I *learn* from this?" and "How can I use this experience to assist me in the future?" Also, "I *didn't* get the result I wanted. What do I need to do differently in the future to achieve what I want?" This is basically the optimistic way of looking at things.

Optimists are always *learning*, they have positive expectations, therefore they are persistent, and consequently they produce more results. Pessimists commonly have low expectations, give up easily, wallow in self-pity, and produce less. Pessimists ask, "Can I achieve . . .?" which presupposes maybe yes, maybe no. They focus so much on the possibility of *failing*, that they do things in a halfhearted fashion, and cause *failure*. Optimists ask, "HOW can I achieve . . .?" which assumes something can be achieved, and they do things with the best of their ability. Pessimists become envious of others' successes, and become unmotivated. Optimists gain inspiration and hope from others' successes, and become motivated, "If it can happen for them, it can happen for me."

Are there situations where being pessimistic is a useful outlook? Most definitely. It takes an optimistic posture to start things, and at times it takes a pessimistic attitude to keep things in line and to avoid trouble. Some fields such as accounting, law, medicine, and engineering, looking for what can go wrong and therefore being prepared for it, is a functional policy. When engineers build bridges, it's probably optimum for them to be as pessimistic as possible. When I did film production work, I always had to look for what could go wrong, and have several backup plans ready to go. You never could predict when a camera would break, an actor would get sick, or what the weather would be. Not preparing for all the possibilities, was a prescription for inefficiency.

Which attitude will serve you better? If you are in a job interview, being optimistic is most advantageous. If you are investing your money, being pessimistic could be the wisest choice. And if you are starting a new business venture, some of both will most likely yield the greatest results. Again flexibility is the key. Being too pessimistic can drain the life blood out of a project and destroy it. Being too optimistic can cause a lack of sufficient planning, and can also cause a washout. In any situation, there is a certain amount of information that needs to be gathered to be able to make the best decisions. But putting a time frame on the accumulation of the data is necessary to avoid the paralysis of analysis.

○ deadline ⟶ TIME FRAME, TARGET DATE,
TIMETABLE, SCHEDULE, COMPLETION
DATE

Calling a specific point in time a *deadline* can create needless stress and pressure. It can make something become more serious than is necessary. Naturally there are times when it is crucial that a project be finished within a certain period of time, and using the word *deadline* would be fitting and productive.

In some situations other words for *deadline* can be more useful. We can ask, "What is the *time frame*, (the *target date*, the *timetable*, or the *schedule*) for the completion of the project?" By using these types of words, we take the emotion out of the communication. When we tell people the *deadline* we can cause resistance and tension to occur. It can remind them of other *deadlines* in their history that represent less than pleasant memories. When it makes sense, objectively refer to completion times and work towards keeping things in a positive perspective.

Time is another area where getting *specific* is very important. How frequently do we hear, "I need this as soon as possible," or "This has to be done in the near future," or "Do this when you can." What do these statements mean? When is *as soon as possible, the near future,* or *when you can*? Is it any wonder there are so many foul-ups in scheduling.

Regardless of who creates the time frame, make sure that a *specific* schedule is determined and agreed upon. Set a time that is the latest that something can be completed by. "I need this project done no later than 3:00 P.M. on Wednesday," versus "I want this project done by the middle of the week." To be able to effectively manage our own time or the time of others, *specific* periods need to be established. There is a separate chapter on time management later in the book.

○ unbelievable, ⟶ TERRIFIC, GREAT, EXCELLENT,
     amazing,   MAGNIFICENT, SENSATIONAL,
     incredible   SUPERB, OUTSTANDING

Saying something is *unbelievable, amazing,* or *incredible,* is best when used under extraordinary circumstances. It could be a feat of athletic prowess, the weather, how someone or something behaved; a special singular event that may never be repeated. It might be of a positive or negative nature. If on the other hand, it's relating to something good that happens to you, a different tack is probably more favorable.

Positive experiences can be enjoyed or diminished through language. If you say it's *unbelievable* that you got a promotion (a raise, a date, a loan, etc.), you're basically saying that deep down you don't believe you deserve it. In essence, you're putting yourself down. The message to your subconscious is that you got lucky, and that it will probably not happen again. Some people will even spoil the good things that come their way, due to being *amazed* at having them. Look at how many celebrities have destroyed their lives, often at the height of their success.

Glory in the pleasant things that occur in your life. Talk about how *terrific* your health is, how *great* your job is, how *magnificent* your relationship with your mate is, how *superb* your vacation was, and how *excellent* your golf game is. Fill your thoughts with positive realities that will contribute to more of the same, versus feeling it's *incredible* that your wishes have come true.

○   problem   ➤ SITUATION, ISSUE, CIRCUMSTANCE

Problem is a word that tends to be overused and can form mountains out of molehills. It's sensible when something is of major proportions and where you need to make people aware of its importance. But in most interactions, it's usually more practical to take the emotion out of events by using neutral words like *situation*, *issue*, and *circumstance*. When we label something a *problem*, it links us up to every real and imaginary *problem* we've ever had. When we call an event a *situation*, it takes the intensity out of it and aids us in dealing with things in a logical objective manner.

In life, things that need to be dealt with, occur on a regular basis. As challenges surface, a lot of drama can go into them due to paying attention to what's wrong and what isn't working. Time and energy can be wasted looking at what we *don't* want. By calling them *situations*, by asking what the *issue* is, or by explaining what the *circumstances* are, we can leave most, if not all, of the emotion out. Now we can rationally focus on what we *do* want, focus on solutions, and on what we need to do to have what we want. This one shift in language, dramatically reduced the tension in my office. It changed how we were impacted by what happened on a day-to-day basis.

○   sorry   ➤ THANK YOU, I APPRECIATE

Sorry is another word that is at times overused. When we're *sorry* we're apologizing for doing or not doing something. This is fitting in many situations. In some cases though, a compliment may be more worthwhile. For instance, when you put someone on hold on the telephone, it's more effective to *thank* them for waiting, instead of saying you are *sorry*. Or when someone has to wait for you in person, *thanking* them for their patience and understanding could be more beneficial for both of you.

Apologizing in some cases, can inflame a situation making it worse. A sincere appreciative compliment keeps both parties on a positive footing. Sincerity is a vital element here. Many companies have their operators say "thank you for waiting," but the tone of their voice doesn't match the intention of the words. For optimal results, remember that someone's time is very valuable, and that if they patiently wait for you, they deserve a genuine expression of your appreciation.

○ I'm weak   ⟶ NOT COMFORTABLE, NOT CONFIDENT, NOT COMPETENT; IMPROVE, STRENGTHEN

Talking about one's *weaknesses* can be very self-fulfilling. Just speaking about them can make you feel *weak*. No one excels at everything. So what? Many things we are not talented in, are because we haven't had the time, desire, or need to be, not because we can't. Instead of saying you are *weak* in public speaking, which can make you feel *weak* as a human being, separate the behavior from you as a total person.

Saying you're *not comfortable*, *not confident*, or *not competent*, yet doing public speaking, is much more effective. In this way you are saying that it is a skill you do not currently have at a level you feel is a suitable one. These statements are not indictments of you as a person. Presenting things in this manner, serves to keep you open to utilizing the skills that you already have to acquire additional skills. And it helps you to feel good about yourself

The next step, would be to specifically state what you want, how you'll know you have it, and figure out what you need to be and do to get it. These are some of the topics that will be discussed in depth when we get into the actual goal setting system.

Another approach, is to talk about *weaknesses* in terms of what you want to *improve* in, or *strengthen* yourself in. Rather than saying that you are *weak* in using computers, express that computers are something that you want to *improve* your skills in, or that you want to *strengthen* your computer skills. Communicating this way, sends a positive message that you can do something, and that you just haven't fully learned how to, yet!

Always keep in mind, that the subconscious takes things very literally. Stay focused on what you want, create a clear vision of it, and maintain a sense of possibility that will free you to tap into and expand the resources that you have.

○ compromise   ⟶ ADJUST, ADAPT

The word *compromise* can have some negative connections. It's commonly used when people are talking about careers and relationships. I hear things such as, "I *hate* making *compromises* and giving in." There can be associations to being weak and not standing up for one's rights. There can be a feeling of resentment, and self-pity about not getting what one wants. And there might be a sense that the other person is being selfish and uncaring. Whatever the meaning, the result is negative.

Rather than feel like you are *compromising* or being *compromised*, perhaps a different attitude will serve you better. Why do we do anything? It's because we get something out of it. As is discussed in *The Benefits* chapter, we do everything in life to achieve and have a feeling. When we do something for someone else, we do it so that we can have a specific emotion. Even when we devote our lives to others to the point of self-sacrifice, we do it to have a feeling that is in alignment with our values and beliefs. What I'm talking about here, is that if you do something, it's a choice that you are making, and to make the best of it. Otherwise don't do it. The option of saying no is always available, however not always practical, as in a work setting.

There are things in life that we would rather not do. But due to consequences, we go ahead and do them. We do them because it's useful, realistic, and beneficial. Instead of *compromising*, look at what you do as your chosen decision to *adjust* or *adapt* yourself to the current situation you find yourself in. You can *adjust* at your job to an additional work load. You can *adapt* to new working conditions. Make it your conscious choice to have things affect you in a way that is rewarding for you. Eliminate resentment or it could continue to take from you.

O   can't   ⟶ DIFFICULT RIGHT NOW

Telling ourselves we *can't* do something can be a very limiting and self-fulfilling belief. When we believe we *can't* do something, the actions we do engage in are usually executed in a halfhearted manner. Why bother with our best effort when it's unlikely that we'll see the fruits of our labor. Naturally this attitude all but guarantees minimal results. With this belief, if we begin to get close to achieving a goal, we will at times sabotage our own efforts to be consistent with what we accept as true.

When we believe we *can't*, there's no hope or expectation of success, and the possibilities are vague and unclear. Of course, there are mental and physical boundaries each human being has, but they are probably much larger than we may ever know.

Replacing it's *difficult right now*, for *can't*, paints a different picture. It leaves the door open for future potential. It recognizes the present, and acknowledges that things can change. Think about times in the past when you felt you couldn't do something, such as riding a bike, learning the alphabet, swimming, or using a computer, that you finally succeeded at. After repeatedly *working* at it, you were able to do it. Of course you were always able to do it, you just needed to learn how and to have experience at it.

The next time you say you *can't* do something, stop and say, "It's *difficult right now* for me to do this." Accept that you need to get more information, learn more, and do more, if you want a certain outcome. *Difficult right now* sets you up to keep going and to keep working on a project. It moves you from "Can I do this?," to "HOW can I do this?" It supports you in more fully utilizing your abilities and resources. Edison reportedly did over 10,000 experiments before developing the electric light bulb. Over 10,000 times it was *difficult right now*. In a minute, an hour, a week, a month, etc., it could be a very different story.

○   diet   ➞ HEALTHY LIVING

We constantly hear about this *diet* and that *diet*, and yet being overweight is still a major issue for so many people. When someone goes on a *diet*, it basically has sacrifice and pain built into it. How long is someone willing to feel deprived?

One needs a different program, a healthy lifestyle. Choosing *healthy living*, to take care of oneself, to be good to oneself, is the mindset that could help someone to make decisions that are life enhancing. What are the benefits we can have through *healthy living*? We can feel good, have energy, be clear thinking, be productive, and essentially maximize our experience of life.

Beliefs again are so crucial with this issue. Being overweight might be consistent with a person's beliefs and self-concept, and therefore a constant struggle occurs. If someone believes that being overweight keeps them from being hurt, or that it's a sign of success, or they feel like a failure, or it gives them an identity, etc., they will make choices that fulfill their script. I'm not talking about clinical obesity, or where there is a chemical imbalance in the body. I'm talking about the different choices someone can make that determines their physical condition.

"What we concentrate on, we tend to create." Get totally clear about how you want to look and feel, and all the things you need to think and to do, to have this outcome. Then get a safe and fun exercise program, and only have in your home foods that are healthy, and prepare them in a

healthy manner. Remember as stated under the *More/Less/Better Syn-drome*, the objective is to eat and to be *healthy*, not *healthier*, or *more healthy*. Lightly fried foods are *healthier* than deep fried, but not *healthy*. Optimal goals move us toward optimal living. In the *Wording Your Goals* chapter, there's a fleshed out example for being *healthy* that you can use as a model.

○   stupid,   ➝ LEARN, WHY
    dumb

Do you ever hear someone say, "I can't believe what a *stupid* thing I did," or "that was really *dumb* of me"? This type of self-talk can be very debilitating and self-perpetuating. Remember the subconscious mind accepts, records, and stores everything. Even when said in jest, repeated negative self-talk can be internalized as the truth. And if other people hear you speak about yourself in this manner often enough, they might also begin to accept your *stupidity* as true.

Internal dialogue about being *stupid*, combined with the responses of others to witnessing your *stupidity*, can alter your reality to the extent that you are *stupid*. We can through repetition, create a negative expectation in ourselves as well as in others about our abilities, even though it's untrue.

Instead of labeling yourself, due to certain actions, as *stupid, dumb, an idiot, a fool, a jerk, brainless, witless, a dope, worthless, a loser*, or *a moron*, step back and ask yourself, "What can I *learn* from this? *Why* did this happen? *Why* did I choose to do, or not do, something?" Give yourself the respect to be able to *learn* when things don't go your way. There's always a reason for what we do, or we wouldn't do it. I'm talking about the real truths about what we do and don't do. Again, I'm suggesting to explore the beliefs that caused you to make the choices that you've made.

If you forgot to pay a bill and the phone is cut off, you may need a better system for handling bills, and to be more organized, or you may want some excitement in your life and something to get angry about. You may feel down on yourself, so you create a hassle to reinforce how worth-less you are. Maybe there are people you don't want to be able to reach you. Or perhaps you are just so preoccupied with other things that paying bills is ignored. Whatever the reason, as with *failure*, use results as *feed-back*, *learn* from them, and make the necessary adjustments for the future.

○   obstacles, barriers,   ➝ GOALS, OBJECTIVES, STEPS
    stumbling blocks

Many times when I'm speaking with someone about their goals, they'll talk all the *obstacles*, *barriers*, and *stumbling blocks* that prevent them from being successful. Whether it's money, age, education, experience, height, weight, gender, nationality, etc., they perceive things as insurmountable hurdles. Often framing certain factors as impossible to deal with and overcome, gives a person excuses to not take action and therefore enables them to maintain their narrow self-concept. Procrastination takes hold, and forward progress is halted. This scene expresses the person's beliefs, and it becomes self-fulfilling.

Employing a different way of looking at what one may encounter on life's path, will be more rewarding. Rather than defining things that come up that need to be handled as *obstacles*, look at them as additional *goals*, *objectives*, or *steps*, that simply get put on your list of things to do. They are just more actions that you will need to take in order to reach your destination. If you position things as *obstacles*, *barriers*, and *stumbling blocks*, then that is what they are. They become bigger than they are, and then can be very difficult to cope with.

While I was producing my film, schedules had to be repeatedly changed, which caused actors, investors, and crew to drop out. One part of the puzzle was replaced, and another part would fall out. To stay in the game, I kept focused on my *UER*, and filed any setbacks as just additional *steps* that I needed to take. Without this attitude, I would have given up.

Whatever went wrong in the making of the film, simply became more actions that had to be undertaken. It's another example of shifting from what you *don't* want, to what you *do* want. Keep in mind, that labels limit, and labeling things that need to be handled as *obstacles*, can create massive limits.

Are there times that the amount of *steps* that need to be taken are just too many? It depends on how valuable a goal is, and how its pursuit will affect other aspects of your life. Getting more education is a case in point. Many times people will not get additional education due to the time, cost, and isolation of classwork and studying. "It'll take too long," "I'll need to get a part-time job," "I won't be able to see my friends." Then the time required to complete the schooling has gone by, and what do they say? "I should have taken those courses, I would have finished them by now."

○ pain ⟶ UNCOMFORTABLE, STRONG SENSATION

Pain can be a vital signal from our body, or our mind, that something is out of balance. It is an important warning that something needs to be checked out and attended to. However, there are minor everyday *pains* such as muscle soreness from overdoing exercise and healing from an injury, that can be blown out of proportion. When you know the origin of a *pain* through medical professionals, and you would like to reduce its intensity, using different wording can help.

Sensing *pain* requires a level of tension. When muscles are totally relaxed the transmission of sensations is decreased. That's part of why someone can be hypnotized and undergo surgery without any discomfort. The way that we represent the sensations that we call *pain*, can reduce the severity of the feelings. Instead of verbalizing, "I have a horrible *pain* in my shoulder that's killing me," which creates more tension and increases the *pain*, another way may work better. The idea is to fully analyze what specifically you feel in your shoulder, describe in detail what's being felt, and to relax your body as much as possible. In this detached mode, by eliminating emotional labels such as *horrible* and *killing me*, you can reduce the discomfort.

You might say, "I have an *uncomfortable* feeling in my shoulder, so I want to take it easy for a few days." Or, "I have a *strong sensation* in my shoulder, and movement is *uncomfortable*." Using more neutral language and imagery, can serve to relax the body, lessen the sensations, and assist the healing process. Acknowledge what you are experiencing, and keep things in a proper perspective. Focus on what is actually happening, and what your desired result is. Notice when you use negative imagery, such as "my stomach (back, neck, foot, hand, knee, etc.) is killing me," and eliminate it from your communications. Toward the end of this chapter, see Figure 1-1 for more of these type of examples.

In addition to physical sensations, there can be mental situations where the concept of *pain* is used. Examples such as "it *pains* me to give in," and "so and so is a *pain* in the neck," cause tension and stress, and can be self-fulfilling. Be kind to yourself, stop putting *pain* in your life wherever you can, and look for ways to put things in the most beneficial terms possible.

    ○   wrong   ⟶ FROM MY EXPERIENCE, WHY DO YOU
                               FEEL THAT WAY?

When we tell someone they're *wrong*, what happens? They can get defensive or angry or hurt, and a confrontation can occur. Nobody wins. And have you ever told someone they were *wrong* and found out later they were right, and you had to apologize? I don't know about you, but I love to not need to apologize.

How can you disagree agreeably? First keep in mind that whatever we know is limited to our experience, just as the other person's opinions are limited to their experience. Begin by recognizing the other person's ideas, and then present your views with, *"From my experience* it seems that . . ."
Then follow-up with finding out where their information came from by asking, *"Why do you feel that way?"* Be sure to use an appropriate tone. Ask in a genuinely curious, wanting to know and understand, fashion.

Uncover the source that generated their conclusions, and help them to understand your position. You may find that they have logical reasons for their viewpoint, even though they are incorrect. Appreciate their thoughts based on their experience, and then move towards a mutual understanding of what is realistic in a situation. Create a safe environment where people can admit they were incorrect and still keep their dignity. Work towards a win/win of mutual support and discovery where everyone can learn and benefit.

What if both parties are stuck in their positions and refuse to budge? In that case you still acknowledge the *differences* and the understanding that based on the circumstances, each of you feels correct. Also acknowledge that you respect each other's views, and that in the future with additional information and experience, the views may change. In some cases, such as a work situation, a choice may need to be made without an agreement. But at least with understanding and respect, the decision will be more comfortable for everyone.

○   but, however   ⟶ AND

But, and the gentler *however,* basically erase what was said just before them. Sometimes this is useful, sometimes not. If you say to someone, "That was a great job you did, *but* . . .," you've eliminated the compliment. If you want the compliment to stick, use the word *and* instead. "That was a great job you did, *and* in the future, I would like these changes." In this manner, the positive part of the message remains and is built upon.

There might be times when you deliberately want to erase something. For instance, in a job interview they tell you they want someone with ten years experience and you only have five. You could respond with, "I realize you're looking for someone with ten years experience, *however* I feel that with the solid experience I have, with my skills, and with my hardworking attitude, I believe that I'll give you the results you want." Show that you recognize their feelings, present why you're qualified for the position, and end on a benefit to the employer.

○ overwhelmed   ⟶ SMALLEST STEP

Clients regularly come to me saying how *overwhelmed* they are. With this kind of self-talk, they put themselves on overload, and they shut down. Then because they do nothing, they compound the sense of *overwhelm* as the amount of undone tasks increases. The solution here is to use the techniques on time management in a later chapter, and to reorganize your approach.

When things start to feel like they're too much to handle, stop, step back, and regroup. Ask yourself, "What can I do right now to move me toward my objectives?" Depending on the circumstances, the first thing to do is to make a list of the results you want, and what steps it's going to take to get them. Then take each step and keep breaking it down into the *smallest possible steps* you can, regardless of how obvious some of them may seem. Shift from *overwhelmed* to one *smallest step* at a time. By planning on paper, or *POP*, you gain an overall view of what needs to be done, and a sense of control over the situation.

Writing things down and *POP*, seems to be resisted by many people. Because of this, they often forget to do things, and they have much more stress in their life than is necessary. Recommendation, always write things down, and keep the information organized in specific places. To *try* to keep things in memory takes a lot of energy, and too often is ineffective. Write things down, and let the paper do the memorizing for you.

○ sick   ⟶ TEMPORARY IMBALANCE

Much the same way the word *depressed* can be self-induced, the word *sick* can become very influential. We dissected the various aspects that make up the state we call *depression*, and we can do the same thing with feeling *sick*. What goes into sensing that we are *sick*? We might have aches and pains, feel chilled or boiling hot, feel tired, have trouble breathing, feel dizzy, etc. By describing the individual aspects of your experience, you have better mastery over what's happening.

You can lightheartedly say, "I have a *temporary imbalance*. I'm congested and I have a fever, so I'm going to relax and give my body time to heal." Or you could say in a disgusting tone, "I have this horrible cold that's making me miserable." Research has shown that when we are tense, stressed out, and upset, that our natural immune system is decreased. An emotional response to an *imbalance* in the body actually can make the *imbalance* worse. Being relaxed, thinking about being healthy, thinking about things that are pleasing to you, increases the immune system and supports your body in becoming balanced again.

Of course it's critical to get professional medical help and a correct diagnosis when you feel out of sorts. When you know what the cause of your situation is, then use positive communications to assist you in healing. The *Effective Visualization* chapter will give you additional ideas on this issue.

○   nagging   ⟶ I APPRECIATE THAT YOU CARE

When someone *nags* at you to do or not do something, it's because they care, right? If they do it for some other reason, than they're out of place doing it. Conversations often get into debating sessions with one person feeling attacked and becoming defensive. A heated discussion occurs with nothing being accomplished, except perhaps anger and resentment. This type of interaction is very common among family members and friends.

The next time some well-intentioned person tells you that you should exercise, should stop smoking, should quit your job, should go out more, etc., tell them, "Thank you, *I appreciate that you care*, and that you respect and understand my situation." Remember that your tone must be sincere, this must come from the heart, or the other person will feel that you are being sarcastic. When someone would *nag* me about when this book would be finished, I would say, "Thank you for asking. I appreciate your interest, and I'm looking forward to when it's done." It takes two people to have an argument. Choose to extinguish a possible disagreement before it erupts.

It may take many repetitions of "*I appreciate that you care*," before the nagging stops. But it's a minimal amount of effort compared to the benefits. Of course you could get defensive, or attack them back, neither of which has a pleasant outcome. It takes two to play this game.

How does this apply in a work situation? If your boss tells you how terrible your work is, *appreciate* the feedback, and find out what specifically they would like changed. You can get defensive, argue, or try to explain what happened, but these strategies may not work. Your boss is your customer, and your job is to satisfy their reasonable needs. If their needs are too out of line, then it might be time to get a new customer.

Nagging can sometimes be brought upon ourselves by us complaining about things. If we complain about something such as our health, love life, or career, we're opening the door for comments and recommendations. A complaint says there's pain, and the listener might *try* to alleviate it for us by providing a solution. If we're getting an undesirable behavior from someone, at times we could be responsible for it. Again it goes back to our beliefs, which cause us to unconsciously do something that brings about a certain reaction from others. More about this in the sections on beliefs.

O   should,   ⟶ CHOOSE, WANT TO; IT MIGHT, IT SEEMS,
    need to   IT APPEARS

"I *should* do something," or "I *need to* be or do something," can be overdone. These words can create too much pressure in certain situations. "I *should* exercise everyday," may make exercise seem like a burden, and therefore you may not consistently do it. Instead, talk about choices you can consciously make, and why it benefits you to make them. "I *choose* to exercise everyday so that I can feel good and be healthy." Instead of talking about sacrificing and how you *need to* give up all your favorite junk foods, say "I *want to* eat nutritious natural foods so that I'll be healthy, and have the energy that I want." Feeling that you are at *choice* and in charge, is usually preferable to feeling that you must do something. A sense of control is directly related to our sense of happiness.

There are times in this book that I use *should* and *need to*. In the framework of the topics discussed, I feel that these words are appropriate. There are some people who spend a tremendous amount of time and energy in *trying* to eliminate the *should's* from their vocabulary, as well as from everybody else's. It becomes ironic that they are basically promoting that you *shouldn't* use *should*. I've often heard people say to someone, "You shouldn't say should!" They are therefore doing what they are telling another person not to do. My goal is to give you options where you can decide what works best for you at a specific time and under specific circumstances. To secure certain results on a consistent basis, there are things we *should* and *shouldn't* do. Whether it's health, career, or relationships, there are behaviors that work and those that don't. When your actions only involve yourself, make choices. When your actions involve other people, then some *should's* in your behavior, make sense.

If you want to have a successful job interview, some of the things you *should* do are:

- know exactly what you're looking for in terms of duties, responsibilities, and compensation
- research the prospective employer and know their business
- thoroughly know yourself, the experience, skills and traits that you have that would make you valuable to this employer
- practice, out loud, answering interviewing questions
- have a written list of questions to ask them
- prepare for possible objections and be ready to handle them
- have extra, unfolded copies of your resume
- be dressed appropriately
- have all the information required to fill out an application form
- have a list of your references
- be on time for the meeting
- be polite and friendly
- find out what they believe their needs are, and show them how you are the solution to their perceived problems
- thank them for the interview

Again, the best way to communicate something is determined by the goal and the conditions. What will provide you with your desired result?

When communicating with others about their behavior, you can soften your comments by using *it might, it seems,* and *it appears,* with a benefit and a reason why. For example, you could tell someone, "You *should* drive slower," or "*It might* make sense to drive slower, be safe, and avoid getting a ticket." You could say, "You *need to* go to sleep now," or "*It seems* like it's a good idea to go to sleep now, so that you'll be effective tomorrow." You could comment, "You *should* stop eating fatty foods," or "*It appears* that eliminating fatty foods would help you to feel good and be energetic."

Someone complains about being lonely, you can say, "You *should* get a pet," or "How would you feel about getting a pet?" If they complain about their weight, you can say, "You *should* start exercising," or "Have you considered going on an exercise program?" If they complain about having a lousy job, you can say, "You *should* get more training," or "Have you thought about getting additional training?" Other possibilities are:

- "How do you think it would be if . . ."
- "What would it be like if . . ."

- "Would it make sense for you to . . ."
- "Would it work for you if . . ."
- "I have some ideas about . . ., if you're interested."

Instead of giving someone an order or a command, you can speak to them in a supportive caring fashion, with suggestions. Rather than put someone on the defensive, you can show them respect. Notice when you tell people they *should* or *shouldn't* do something. Ask yourself if what you are saying to them is more for your benefit or theirs. Are you accepting them and their uniqueness, or *trying* to control and change them? Unless you see their behavior as potentially harmful, appreciate and enjoy them for who they are.

⚪ negotiate ⟶ DISCUSS, TALK ABOUT, CONSIDER, ARRANGE, GET AGREEMENT, WORK OUT, MODIFY, ADJUST

Negotiating is often very uncomfortable for people. The word can bring up fears about not getting a fair deal and being taken advantage of. It can be associated with conflict, with two opponents being locked into competitive positions. The result may be both sides unsatisfied with the final outcome.

Suggestion, begin the deal making with the *UER* for each participant. First establish what everyone wants, and that the goal is to have a mutually satisfying agreement. (Note: clearly know your boundaries and your criteria of what a good deal is for you, before you sit down). Then as things progress and disagreements appear, use neutral words such as *discuss, talk about, consider,* and *arrange* when working out the details.

In a job interview, if the compensation package is unacceptable to you, respond with statements such as: "Can we *discuss* the salary?" "Is there any way that we can *talk about* (*modify* or *adjust*) the salary?" or "Is it possible to *consider* a different compensation plan?" The last example is depersonalized without a reference to *we*. In some cases this works well, because it's about the two of you working out a fair deal for everyone in an objective fashion. The concept here is to take the competition out of the equation, and to create long-term mutually beneficial relationships.

⚪ with my luck ⟶ I'M LOOKING FORWARD TO

In jest people talk about their *bad luck* and how what can go wrong will go wrong. The subconscious mind has a hard time knowing what's true and what's not. This is especially the case when a way of speaking is repeated so often, that it becomes a habit. And after awhile, not only do you believe in your *bad luck*, everyone else who hears you, starts to believe it too. Successful people view their successes as expected and they take full responsibility for them, reinforcing the belief in future successes. When they don't succeed, they learn from the experience and use the learning to be successful in future situations.

Unsuccessful people tend to see their successes as accidents that only happen rarely for them, they finally got lucky. They position their *failures* as expected. They then tend to remember other *failures* and go through a session of self-criticism. Unfortunately this reinforces their self-concept of being disadvantaged and unlucky, and the cycle keeps repeating itself.

Stop talking about the negative, "*With my luck* I'll probably never get . . .," and only talk about what you *do* want. "*I'm looking forward to* getting the . . .," keeps you focused in the direction that you want to go. Our choice of words forms our thoughts, and links us up to what we expect and believe is possible. Which thoughts are most desirable for you?

Additional Ideas

There are some commonly used expressions that may mean nothing, but they can generate a negative message. Many times we hear people say things such as:

"To be honest with you . . ."
"Between you and me, . . ."
"I'm going to level with you, . . ."
"Frankly, I . . ."
"Truthfully, I'm . . ."

Usually these things are said simply as filler while people think of what they want to say. However, what are some of the possible meanings these sayings can communicate? That the person is lying, insincere, or can't be trusted. Eliminate these phrases, and you will greatly increase the credibility of what you say.

Candid is a word that can at times be used to substitute for the above. It can work, when you are being open, and revealing private information about yourself. It doesn't have the same negative connections that *honestly, frankly,* and *truthfully* have. But there is a potential downside to it, and if you do use it, do so sparingly.

Sometimes it's difficult to understand what some people are saying. They seem to be rambling on and on, with disconnected thoughts. We can tell them that they're unclear and confusing, or assume we know what they're saying, and move on. Either of these approaches can be ineffective. To remedy the situation, use questions and statements such as:

- "Is what you are saying . . .?"
- "If I understand you, you're . . ."
- "Could you give me an example of . . .?"
- "What's another way you could state that?"
- "Help me to understand how . . ."
- "It seems as though. . . . Is that correct?"
- "It appears that. . . . Is that accurate?"
- "Is what you mean, that you . . .?"
- "Would it be realistic to say . . .?"

By using this type of communication you can check out your assumptions or remove any uncertainty, in a respectful manner. The other person won't feel attacked or belittled, and productive dialogue can take place.

Another idea to consider, is that of labelling things in terms of absolutes. We'll do something, or see something, or have some type of experience, and conclude that it was the *best* or *worst*, the *greatest* or the *most horrible*. I'm not saying that this is always a *bad* thing to do, but that there may be some other alternatives that are more useful at certain times. This concept of removing absolutes is appropriate for many experiences, but not for making decisions, especially when a purchase is involved. When deciding between alternatives, such as which car to buy, which job to take, or where to go on vacation, then the *best*, *greatest*, or *most* advantageous choice is what you are looking for.

When you say it was the *best* party that you ever went to, it can diminish how fondly you remember other parties, because this one was the *best*. Then the next time you go to a party, there could be a tendency to compare it to the *best* one, and therefore not enjoy the current party to the fullest extent. This could happen with anything, a vacation, a sunset, or piece of apple pie. The *best*, the *greatest*, and the *most* delicious, can have a person living in the past and limiting what they can have in the present. And when the *most* incredible party in the history of the world is over, there could be a sense of loss because it's past tense.

Instead of absolutes, the suggestion is to use descriptive wording that will link up the positive aspects of one thing, to many others. In other words, it was a *great, wonderful, terrific, outstanding, excellent, magnificent, superb,* or *fabulous* party, instead of the *best* party. This way it brings to mind other enjoyable party experiences, instead of diminishing them, while maintaining the present experience as pleasurable. It was a *beautiful* sunset, or a *magnificent* sunset, in place of the *most* beautiful sunset ever seen. This pie is *delicious* or this pie is *outstanding,* rather than this pie is the *most* delicious I've ever eaten.

Removing absolutes can also be very helpful when dealing with negative situations. Remember only talk about what you *do* want. When you say it was the *worst* party that you have ever attended, what kind of impression and memory is created in your mind? First, it links you up to every other unpleasant party you've ever been to, which can make this party seem even more unpleasant. Then the next time you're at a party and something similar is present, it could bring up all the unpleasant memories. In addition, because this is the *most horrible* party in the history of the human race, a barrier is created that could prevent you from enjoying whatever useful opportunities that are there.

Have you ever been to a party or event where at first you thought it was *terrible,* and later it turned out to be *okay?* The idea is to leave yourself open to all the positive possibilities that are available to you. Remove the emotion by simply commenting that you didn't enjoy the party, or that it wasn't your type of party.

One-upmanship is something that is often observed. This is where one person tries to outdo another in both positive and negative circumstances. In other words, someone might complain about something, and the listener rather than being understanding, will compete. They might say, "You think you're cooped up, I haven't been outside in over two months." "You think your boss is critical, my boss . . ." "You think you've got problems, let me tell you how bad I have it right now!"

Rivalry also can happen with positive events. "You think you had a terrific vacation, let me tell you about when I . . ." "You think that was a wild party, let me tell you about the time I . . ." "You think that was a great (concert, meal, sale, bargain, etc.), let me tell you about . . ."

Instead of having a contest of *best* or *worst,* nurture and support. Be a good listener. Help others to explore how they feel. Perhaps show how you understand them due to having a similar, not better or worse, experience. "A critical boss can make for a long workday." "That sunset must have been quite a sight to behold. I love a great sunset." Be a resource to others for coping with life's challenges, and for enriching the good times.

Compliments can sometimes be minimized by responding to them in a certain way. When receiving praise, approval, or recognition, someone could say, "Oh it was nothing." This diminishes the positive comment, and may also diminish the positive feeling the speaker had which prompted the remark in the first place. Over a period of time this can shut someone down, and cause them to stop giving compliments. Suggestion, when you get sincere praise, respond with gratitude such as, "Thank you, I appreciate you saying that." Contribute to their joy, versus decreasing it. There is giving, in graciously receiving.

Asking for assistance or *help* can be phrased in several different ways. In some situations, asking for *help* is the best choice. Many times when dealing with customer service people, asking for their *help* will get you what you deserve. In some situations though, asking for someone's *help* can make them feel put upon and obligated. For instance, when seeking a new job, asking certain people for their *help* could cause them to shy away from you. By asking them for their *advice*, *ideas*, *suggestions*, *recommendations*, *thoughts*, *view*, *perspective*, or *opinion* on something, can come across as a compliment. These words communicate that you respect them to the extent that you value what they have to say. You can get what you want, and make someone feel good in the process.

METAPHORS, SIMILES, and ANALOGIES are colorful ways of expressing and explaining ideas, often by comparing and contrasting things. Negative ones may seem harmless, but they can be very powerful in causing tension and stress. See Figure 1-1. Notice when you use them, and choose to replace the negative ones with the facts, ending on what you *do* want. Remember the brain accepts things literally, and repeating, "Lately I have the memory of a gnat," or "My life is as exciting as watching paint dry," can become self-fulfilling.

It's important to keep in mind that as you begin to use these language patterns, to not impose them on others. Be a resource for people. Only suggest positive language patterns to others when they've given you permission to help, and it's fitting for them. When someone is in a highly charged emotional state, it isn't the right time for suggestions about their vocabulary. Use constructive words yourself and be a positive model and an example, that over time, others may choose to follow. When someone says, "I'm *trying* to lose weight," you can respond with, "Do you have a *target* that you're aiming for?" If they say, "I *hate* being alone," you can say, "What kind of relationship do you *want* to be in?" If you hear, "They rejected me," you can ask, "What do you think the *differences* are?"

Consider the options, and use language that works most successfully for you. Stop using words that restrict you, and which reinforce limitations. Only say what you want to be true. Use ways of expressing yourself that empower and strengthen you, and those around you. By using these ideas, you can make a dramatic improvement in the quality of your life. Right now, write down a list of words that you want to change your usage of, and the words that you will replace them with. Use Figure 1-2 as a starting point, using the ideas from this chapter. Make this a goal for yourself.

"What we concentrate on, we tend to create."

Choosing effective wording to express yourself, is crucial for effective goal setting and for motivation. It helps you to have clarity. Clarity is needed to know what to do, how to do it, and when to do it. Clarity is necessary to be able to enlist the effective assistance of others. And clarity is one of the major building blocks of motivation, supporting the persistence required to fulfill your desires.

Remember, for the best results, use positive specific communications of what you *do* want. Always look to establish the *UER*, the *ULTIMATE END RESULT*, in all areas of your life. As it's been said, "We rarely get more than we ask for." The better you do the asking, the better the results. Again, we'll cover how to effectively construct your goals in the *Wording Your Goals* chapter.

So the next time someone says, "You have got to try the cheesecake, it's to die for," ask them, "Do you mean that it's so good, that it's to live for?"

The next chapter is about self-awareness and prepares you for the goal setting system.

FIGURE 1-1:
Mischievous Metaphors, Sorrowful Similes,
and Adverse Analogies
• • •

"I'm sick and tired of this (job, relationship, diet, etc.)."
"I'm bored to death of this (job, relationship, diet, etc.)."
"I hate going to that snakepit of a job."
"Going to work is a nightmare."
"It kills me that they never say thank you."
"My heart breaks when they don't call back."
"My heart aches when . . ."
"My heart bleeds for him."
"I was shattered by what they said."
"My life is a disaster waiting to happen."
"I'm a rusting old battleship ready for the junkyard."
"I feel all tied up in knots."
"I'm at the end of my rope."
"I look like death warmed over."
"He's such a pain in the (neck, back, gut, etc.)"
"I feel like I'm boxed in."
"My schedule is a nightmare."
"I'll just die if . . ."
"It eats me up alive that they're so critical."
"It burns me up when . . ."
"I'm a stubborn old mule that can't change."
"It's as if I'm constantly digging myself out of a hole."
"My brain is fried from all this pressure."
"I'm at war with myself."
"I feel like I'm being buried alive."
"I'm drowning in a sea of confusion."
"I'm in a rut."
"I can't stomach the way . . ."
"No matter what I do, I'm just spinning my wheels."
"The rug's been pulled out from under me."
"The world is caving in around me."
"I feel as if I'm falling apart."
"I can't breathe in this relationship, I feel like I'm suffocating."
"I have the weight of the world on my back."
"I feel like a ton of bricks just fell on me."
"The criticism is a knife through my heart."

FIGURE 1-1:
Mischievous Metaphors, Sorrowful Similes,
and Adverse Analogies (continued)

• • •

"Listening to him pains my brain."
"I seem to have a dark cloud hanging over me."
"I have a monkey on my back that's driving me crazy."
"I'm torn between two different choices."
"I'm an emotional basket case."

FIGURE 1-2:
Creating Positive Language Patterns

• • •

TRY = _____

REJECTED = _____

GENERAL = _____

HATE = _____

DON'T = _____

DEPRESSED = _____

FEAR/NERVOUS = _____

DYSFUNCTIONAL = _____

ANGRY/FRUSTRATED = _____

FAILURE = _____

DEADLINE = _____

UNBELIEVABLE = _____

PROBLEM = _____

SORRY = _____

FIGURE 1-2:
Creating Positive Language Patterns (continued)

• • •

I'M WEAK = _____

COMPROMISE = _____

CAN'T = _____

DIET = _____

STUPID/DUMB = _____

OBSTACLES = _____

PAIN = _____

WRONG = _____

BUT/HOWEVER = _____

OVERWHELMED = _____

SICK = _____

NAGGING = _____

SHOULD = _____

NEGOTIATE = _____

WITH MY LUCK = _____

Chapter 2

BUILDING
A FOUNDATION

● ● ●

GETTING TO KNOW "YOU"

Self-awareness, understanding, and direction is what this chapter is about. The purpose is to construct a base that will function as a solid foundation for all your goals. This foundation will be built upon in the subsequent chapters that make up the actual goal setting system. The information gathered in this chapter will help you to start clearing away any obstacles and barriers that might be restricting you. We will also be dealing with some of the elements of motivation that were mentioned in the preface.

In this chapter we will discuss values, beliefs, self-concept, limiting beliefs, empowering beliefs, modeling success, success self-concept, skills/abilities inventory, success inventory, and your wish list. Therefore, it's very important to complete this chapter before moving on to the next one. So have a lot of blank lined paper available to do all of the exercises. There's a lot to be done in this chapter, but once it's completed, it will serve you for the rest of your life. An investment of time now, will give you lifelong returns.

Many people never sit down and take the time to do this kind of work. They are then limited due to the confusion, conflict, and misunderstanding that results. We want to be sure that the attainment of one goal is in alignment with other goals, and that harmony is achieved. Remember, self-knowledge and self-awareness are very powerful and freeing, and are a major part of motivation.

When I present *Anatomy of Success* as a seminar, people pair up and take turns guiding each other through various parts. One person asks the questions and jots down their partner's responses in a given section. Then they switch roles and repeat that section before moving on to the next one.

53

This is an excellent way to learn the system. When you are answering the questions, it's easier to allow your mind to think freely. Then, when you are asking the questions, you can objectively see how the process works.

Whether you pair up with someone or do the steps yourself, the key is to complete each section as best as you can, before going on to the next one. Since achieving objectives is a process, some parts of the system are ongoing and may never be totally completed. But like exercising, a certain level of activity is necessary to have satisfactory results. If you have difficulty finding some answers, just asking the questions creates connections to occur in your brain. These connections will give you access to information at a later date, and give you greater focus and direction.

There are many sections in this chapter that have an exercise. For optimal results, read each section completely before doing the exercise in it. Be sure to study the examples provided, so that they can help to guide you through your own exploration.

Values

Procrastination and a lack of motivation can have many causes. In the last chapter we talked about how a lack of clarity is one of them. Another is to have goals that are incompatible with who you are. Part of who we are, are our values. Simply stated, a value is something that we spend time, energy, and resources to have. It is something that we feel is very important and worthwhile to us.

If your values are in conflict with the fulfillment of a particular goal, a great deal of stress can occur. You may find that after achieving a lifelong dream, your life is worse off because of it. Therefore, a certain amount of analysis and comparison is essential for satisfaction.

Let's say that "family" is your number one value, but you spend so much of your time pursuing your career, that you don't have the time and energy to have quality relationships with your loved ones. And you finally get that promotion you've always wanted, which means you're out of town 50% of the time. Satisfying one outcome, can limit the possibility of reaching another one. It's vital to view each goal in terms of its impact on others, and to have a balance.

Have you ever worked for a company where your personal values were in conflict with the values of the organization? Or been in a relationship with someone where you had different values? How much pressure and difficulty did you experience because of this? Consequently, it is very important to know what your values are and live your life in agreement with them.

It's productive to constantly monitor your values to be sure that they're in alignment with your goals. Do values change? Yes. Think back to when you were younger. Do you ever talk about how funny it is, that back then something was so important that is now meaningless? As we grow, as we experience life and learn, our values can change. So it's very advantageous to do a values assessment on a regular six-to twelve-month basis.

How do you learn what your values are in a given area? Simply ask yourself questions such as, "What's most important to me about . . .?" "What's truly important to me about . . .?" or "What's really worthwhile to me about . . .?" In this chapter we're working with your life values, so the question could be, "What's most important to me about life?" As you answer this question, just let your mind freely associate and respond. Other helpful questions are, "What do I constantly think about?" "What do I focus on?" and "What do I long for?" There are no right or wrong answers, it's just what's true for you now.

Confusion can sometimes occur about what a value is. Values are not things. A key is to translate any totally material or "thing" answers into the underlying value, which is connected with behaviors and ultimately feelings. For instance, someone might say a value is money, whereas the actual value might be security, belonging, control, independence, contributing, excellence, etc. Money in itself is not really a value, it's what the money provides for emotionally, that has the true importance. Money enables someone to have experiences, such as taking a trip around the world, but it's the feelings that the experiences provide that have the real meaning. It's the adventure, fun, growth, freedom, etc., that travel might mean to someone, that is the actual benefit.

Things may help us to have the experiences and feelings that we consider to be of value. Accordingly, a big beautiful house may provide prestige, safety, and comfort, and a red sports car might provide excitement, power, and romance. In a way, career and family could also fit into this concept. Having a career may represent the realizing of values such as a sense of purpose, power, prestige, variety, self-esteem, creativity, etc. And family might translate into love, belonging, companionship, respect, sensuality, etc. Again, there are no right or wrong answers. I'm not saying to not use money, career, and family as values, but to think things all the way through. This is about knowing yourself and the benefits of this knowledge.

Determine your current values by asking yourself, "What's most important to me about life?" On the bottom of Figure 2-1, circle or underline 8-12 values that are really important to you now. Then head up a piece of paper with the title "Life Values," as shown in Figure 2-1. What if you have difficulty getting responses? Ask yourself, "What if I did know the answer, what would it be?," and "What do I pay attention to, where do I put my time and energy?" Remember questions are powerful keys to the mind. Keep asking questions until you have the information that you seek.

The example in Figure 2-1, and the possible values under it, are from several people, and is for illustration purposes only. If you have other values, please add them to your list. Once you have your life values written out, the next step is to prioritize them in terms of importance. Begin with the value at the top of your list and compare it to every other value until you come up with the most important one, and write the number one in front of it. In the example, you would ask, "What's more important, friendship or health?" The answer here came up health. Then you would compare health to all the other values, and so on, until all of them are sequenced in order of significance.

Sometimes two values might seem to be equally worthwhile, and it's difficult to put them in order. Here's the tie breaker question, "If you were about to get on an airplane going to your most favorite place on earth, and you had two suitcases, but you could only take one of them, which one would it be?" One will always be more valuable than another.

After you've prioritized your values, rewrite them in the order that you've determined. Check the list again to be sure that you feel the hierarchy is correct for now. This list is a resource for you to refer to often. It will help you to be sure that the achievement of a goal is in sync with what is of fundamental importance to you, and so that you maintain a satisfactory equilibrium in your life. And ask yourself, are your present values giving you the quality of life that you desire, or is it perhaps time to redo your values?

Another thing to look at, is to what extent your values are being realized. How do you know a value is being fulfilled at a level that you want? How do you know you have it? What would you need to have or experience that tells you a value is or isn't happening the way that you want it? For instance, if health is one of your highest values, what specifically would you have because of it in terms of energy, strength, endurance, things you would feel mentally and physically, etc.?

FIGURE 2-1:
Life Values

• • •

LIST AND PRIORITIZE		PRIORITIZED		CURRENT LEVEL
(8)	respect	(1)	health	8
(1)	health	(2)	companionship	7
(6)	growth	(3)	love	9
(5)	honesty	(4)	security	5
(7)	freedom	(5)	honesty	9
(10)	loyalty	(6)	growth	9
(2)	companionship	(7)	freedom	7
(9)	fun	(8)	respect	3
(4)	security	(9)	fun	3
(3)	love	(10)	loyalty	3

Possible Life Values:

abundance	cooperation	integrity	respect
acceptance	courage	intimacy	responsibility
accomplishment	creativity	justice	romance
adventure	decency	kindness	safety
affection	efficiency	knowing	sameness
aggressiveness	empathy	logic	sanity
ambition	excellence	love	satisfaction
beauty	excitement	loyalty	security
belonging	fairness	modesty	self-esteem
career	fame	naturalness	sensitivity
carefulness	family	neatness	sensuality
caring	fitness	nurturing	sharing
challenge	freedom	openness	simplicity
change	friendship	optimism	sophistication
cheerfulness	fun	passion	spirituality
cleanliness	gentleness	patience	spontaneity
closeness	giving	persistence	stability
closure	gratitude	pleasure	success
comfort	growth	poise	togetherness
commitment	happiness	politeness	tolerance
communication	harmony	power	tranquility
companionship	health	praise	trust

FIGURE 2-1:
Life Values (continued)

● ● ●

compassion	honesty	prestige	understanding
competence	honor	privacy	variety
considerateness	humility	purpose	wealth
contributing	humor	quiet	winning
control	independence	recognition	wisdom

On a scale of 1-10, 10 being the highest, rate each of your values in terms of how close to your ideal level they are now occurring in your life. For example, if health is your number one value and you're sick all the time, then its current level would be rated a one. If you have excellent health, then it would be rated a nine or ten. This rating can be very useful in uncovering possible sources of tension and in putting things in perspective. Love might be a person's highest value, but if they're deep in debt and just lost their job, love might only get a two on a realization scale. Achieving security may temporarily put other values in the background, and create an imbalance.

Behavior is basically the bottom line. However, during turbulent times, things can get out of whack. When dealing with survival, values can become distorted. If health is your highest value, and you are going through a rough period at the office, not exercising or eating healthy foods temporarily, would not invalidate the value. But, if you constantly eat junk food, smoke, drink excessively, and never exercise, then saying health is a major value would be incompatible with reality, and cause stress. The question to ask, is whether one's actions are temporary due to coping with unusual circumstances, or if one is not in touch with their true self.

Motivation is very much interwoven with values. For massive motivation, we need to know ourselves. We need to know our limits, what we will and won't do. By knowing our values and what's most important to us in life, we can better understand ourselves and make productive choices. If you are trying to get all fired up and motivated to do something, but it's in conflict with your values, it won't work. If something is not important enough, it's not worth putting out large amounts of time, energy, and resources.

What if a goal is in perfect alignment with your values, and you're still not motivated? Remember, there are seven major aspects to consistently taking action, and values is only one element of the knowing ourselves component. Beliefs, another element, are often even more essential to having a passion about a particular outcome, which brings us to our next topic.

Beliefs

Our beliefs are extremely important. They form the boundaries within which we function, and shape the core essence of our experience of life. They filter what we perceive, and allow us to only be aware of what is consistent with them. Beliefs are what we think we can and can't do, which influences the actions we take, how we do them, and the results we produce. Beliefs not only define what we do and how we do it, but how we feel about it afterwards. They are what we expect of how things are and how they will be. Without the right beliefs, we might take a lot of action, but only in a halfhearted and ineffective manner.

Beliefs are not necessarily what is true, but what we accept and hold to be true. They can be so powerful, that they can create their own truth, even if they are false. Whether it's health, relationships, or earning power, beliefs could determine what is possible for someone to achieve. Since our beliefs come from our own limited experience, and the limited experience of our information sources (people, media, books, etc.), they may be inaccurate.

Beliefs can limit us, or enable us to fully utilize our abilities, resources, and faculties. They are like giant rubber bands. When we stretch beyond our boundaries, beyond our comfort zone of expectations, our beliefs tend to snap us back. How often do we see people achieve great success, and then they sabotage themselves for no apparent reason? It's because of their beliefs about who they are, about life, and about what's possible for them.

Everyone has a *BOSS*, a *Belief Operating System Structure*. This is made up of the accumulation of beliefs a human being has, which forms the programs that are unconsciously run by our brain. A computer can have a huge capacity, however the amount of capacity utilized is determined by the software programs that are installed, and how well the software is operated. With limited software, you can only use a limited amount of the power of a computer. The *BOSS* is the software for the human brain. A limited *BOSS* means an inability for a person to tap into their full potential. Before we can decide what software is necessary, we need to know what results we want, and what programming is already installed.

What kind of *BOSS* do you have? Is it kind, nurturing, caring, accepting, supportive, inspiring, loving, understanding, and cheerful, or is it critical, demeaning, resentful, discouraging, hateful, intolerant, mean, and moody? Does it applaud you and show appreciation for what you do right and help you to learn from your mistakes, or only comment on your flaws, call you names like stupid, and make you wrong? Is it perhaps time to reform your *BOSS*, or to get another one altogether? Part of managing your life, is to manage your *BOSS*, and the internal dialogue that it produces.

Life beliefs are the first ones we'll deal with. In general, what do you accept as true about life and people? Not about yourself, we'll deal with that subject in another section. To get you started, look at Figure 2-2, and underline or check off all the beliefs that you currently agree with. Then set up a page, title it "Life Beliefs," and list your beliefs from Figure 2-2, and add any additional ones. Write whatever comes to mind, regardless if it seems positive or negative.

Honesty is crucial in terms of listing your beliefs. Sometimes people in my workshops will only list beliefs that they feel are positive. Remember, conscious awareness of what's already wired into your mind, is one of the reasons for these exercises. Once you are fully armed with this information, you can then know yourself, and understand why you think, feel, and behave the way you do. This self-knowledge besides being an aspect of motivation, is also a part of self-confidence, self-esteem, and charisma. Awareness is the first step toward choice.

Charisma is something many people say can't be defined. Either you have it, or you don't. I feel that it's something that can be developed. Several things seem to be shared by most charismatic people. They have a goal, there is something specific that they want. They know themselves, appreciate what they like about themselves, and accept what they would like to be different. And they have an obvious driving passion and commitment to achieve their goal. Use the ideas and techniques in this book, and your charisma can be greatly increased.

FIGURE 2-2:
Possible Life Beliefs

• • •

Effective communication is crucial for maximum results.

Life is a gift to be enjoyed.

Life is a struggle, no pain, no gain.

You should always be the best that you can be.

You should only do what's necessary and no more.

What goes around comes around, and we eventually pay for our sins.

We are responsible for how we feel and for what happens to us.

Life is fated and that everything is predestined, so why bother working hard and killing yourself.

You should love your work and it should be fun.

Work is a struggle that you just accept and put up with.

People are basically decent and honest.

People are basically evil and can't be trusted.

People do evil things because they are weak and unaware.

Most people are selfish and greedy.

You need to take risks to succeed.

People must love themselves to be happy.

You need to prepare for the future and think before you act.

You should live life totally in the moment, as if you only have a few months to live.

We can always learn from everything that happens.

There's nothing new under the sun.

You need to be flexible and adapt to the situation.

You need to be yourself no matter what the circumstances.

Misery loves company.

Nothing good ever happens to me.

You need to take care of the details to be successful.

Only the big picture matters, and don't sweat the details.

Integrity is necessary to feel free.

Without growth you wither up and disappear, and that one must constantly improve.

Success is measured by a person's contribution to others.

Nice guys finish last.

Success is measured by how much money you make, and how much power you have.

You can be and have anything that you want, if you want it badly enough.

People are products of their environment.

I can't handle being criticized.

Traffic drives me crazy.

FIGURE 2-2:
Possible Life Beliefs (continued)

• • •

I can't juggle several tasks at once.
People like me never succeed.
High self-esteem is essential to reach one's full potential.
We should pay more attention to what's right than what's wrong.
The future will be better than the past.
I'm so worthless that I don't deserve to be happy.
We need to focus on solutions and not problems.
It takes a team to reach the top.
I have an obligation to take care of my parents.
We need to think of ourselves as human beings instead of identifying with
    nationalities.
All's fair in love and war.
Life is unfair, with the strong exploiting the weak.
You must be persistent to succeed.
I can never stick with anything long enough to make it work.
Relationships are a series of compromises.
If it's easy, it can't be good.
I'm very unlucky and never get a break.
Whatever comes up in my life, I can handle it.
I'm weak and I can't control my emotions.
Life is a series of ups and downs.
If you work very hard you will be successful.
If you come from a dysfunctional family, you'll always be a loser.
You have to be careful in revealing personal things about yourself.
People have a responsibility to maintain their own health.
I need other people to keep me sane.
Wealthy people have a responsibility to help others.
Most people are basically insecure.
People can always change and can become better.
Like a leopard's spots, people never really change.
People should not impose their values on others.
Life happens, and to always make the best of things.
If someone criticizes me, it means I'm no good.
Men have it much easier than women.
Women are really in control.
People won't like me if they know the real me.
I can overcome any obstacles or barriers that get in my way.
It makes me nuts to wait for anything.
I have the skills and traits necessary for me to succeed.

Once you've put together a substantial list of your beliefs, then examine each one. Is it positive or negative, optimistic or pessimistic? Does it free you to use your potential, or does it hold you back? Does a belief strengthen or weaken you? Which beliefs do you need to change or eliminate, and which beliefs do you want to make even stronger? For now, put a plus (+) in front of any belief that is positive, and a minus (-) in front of any belief that is negative. We'll be building on this list in other sections, and in later chapters we'll use specific methods for managing your beliefs.

Knowing, understanding, and directing your beliefs is one of the most vital skills you can have in regards to your level of success in life! Make a commitment right now to become belief conscious. Start to hear and recognize your own beliefs, as well as the beliefs of others. Some of the phrases that people use to communicate their beliefs are:

"I think . . . "
"I feel . . . "
"To me . . . "
"I conclude . . . "
"In my mind . . . "
"I expect . . . "
"I/you/they should (or shouldn't) . . . "
"It's important that . . . "
"I've determined . . . "
"What makes sense is . . . "
"I'm confident that . . . "
"In my opinion . . . "
"As I see it . . . "
"I accept . . . "
"I'm satisfied that . . . "
"I reason . . . "
"I'm convinced . . . "

Beliefs are being expressed all the time. Become aware of them, and increase your ability to control your life.

Learn to recognize the difference between a fact and a belief. When you find yourself saying a limiting statement, stop and ask yourself, "Is this a fact, or a belief, and where did it come from?" Facts can't change, but beliefs can and do. Remember, beliefs in a way create their own truths. If you believe you can't figure out how to work a computer or learn a foreign language or be happy, you're right, until you change the belief.

Understanding and accepting others, is an area where belief con-sciousness can be very constructive. Have you ever found yourself saying you can't believe so and so did or said something? Their behavior to you was completely ridiculous! As stated in the *Positive Language Patterns* chapter, the FACT that someone does something, means that from their point of view, from their reality, it made total sense, otherwise they would not have done it. It's all based on their beliefs.

Behavior is someone acting out their programming. So if anyone ever does you a wrong and you want to truly forgive them, learn what their beliefs are. What is their *BOSS*, their *Belief Operating System Structure*? Ask yourself, "What beliefs would cause this person to behave this way?" From this position of knowing and understanding, you can then really for-give and let go of any negative feelings toward them. It's like being upset with a computer for not being able to do spreadsheets, when it only has word processing software. The capacity is there, but all the required pieces are not in place, yet.

Anatomy of Beliefs

"A child's life is like a piece of paper on which every passerby leaves a mark," is an ancient Chinese saying. This idea can be very helpful in understanding where our beliefs come from. Are we born with them? Yes and no. Research has now shown that a human being's programming begins at conception, not at birth. A great deal of mental imprinting occurs during the term of pregnancy. Therefore, besides our genetic makeup, we arrive in the world with implanted tendencies derived from our environment.

Belief development has many layers. The process begins with a *stim-ulus*, or *stimuli*. In other words, something happens. We see something, hear something, feel something, taste something, or smell something, sin-gly or in combination. Our nervous system is stimulated, energy is gener-ated, connections occur in our brain, and we have an *experience*. As stated in the *Positive Language Patterns* chapter, we can only know and under-stand what we have experienced in one way or another. Either an actual mental or physical experience, or a mental experience of something through the communications of others, such as reading or listening. And if you step back and think about it, all life is, is a series of experiences.

From our experiences, we begin to form what we accept as true about the world, or our *beliefs*. Beliefs group together and create what we feel is important, or our *values*. Our values plus our beliefs form the script that we end up playing out. And many scripts need editing, massive editing. Some scripts need to be completely redone. We still want to do the project, but the script just doesn't work.

Attitude, or one's perspective and posture toward something, is the next layer after values. An attitude is how or the manner in which you do what you do. If someone asks you to do something, do you do it with a cheerful cooperative attitude, or do you do it with an irritated resentful attitude? What is the usual attitude you have when you do most things? As we all know, having a good attitude is critical for success. More people are fired from a job because of a poor attitude than anything else.

Behavior is the outward display of attitudes. We engage in, or don't engage in, certain actions. Then when we take an action, we get a *result*. We put out energy, and something does or doesn't happen. And remember, thoughts are things. Making a choice to do nothing, means that some activity, even though it might be subconscious, has taken place.

Once we have a result, we *evaluate* it, and the judgment of what the result means, is based on our beliefs. We determine whether the result is good or bad, or somewhere in-between. Then we have a *response* to the result, an emotion. We get a *feeling*, and this feeling can cause more action or giving up. This whole process can happen very quickly, and be simply experienced as stimulus response.

To recap, the Anatomy of Beliefs is:

- Stimulus
- Experience
- Beliefs
- Values
- Attitudes
- Behavior/Actions
- Results
- Evaluation
- Response/Feelings

Beliefs become the source. Everything comes from them, and goes back to them. The results we achieve reinforce the beliefs, and the beliefs all but predetermine the results, and the response to those results. To break out of a limiting cycle, to have different outcomes, to have different responses, the beliefs must be changed. Techniques for changing beliefs are handled in other chapters. Right now, understand the nature of beliefs, and get a grasp of your reality, as well as the reality of others.

Self-Concept

Another major part of knowing oneself, is the self-concept or the beliefs you have about yourself. Again we function in ways that are consistent with our identity. This is me and this is not me, therefore this is what I will do and this is what I won't do. These personal beliefs, can create a confining box that so often people put themselves in. In many cases, this box is very small and inappropriate. Once you know what your self-concept is, you can enlarge and modify the box, or perhaps do away with it altogether. There is tremendous power in consciously knowing who you believe you are.

Examine Figure 2-3, and underline or circle all of the traits on it that you feel are typically true of you. Then head up a piece of paper labelling it "Self-Concept," and list the traits, qualities, and characteristics you marked off from Figure 2-3. In most of the examples, the first trait is usually a negative one, with an opposite positive trait next to it. Whether it's positive or negative can depend on the situation. Being cautious, competitive, fussy, intense, and spontaneous, can be practical under some circumstances, or unproductive under others.

Figure 2-3 will give you a good running start. Add other traits, qualities, and characteristics that aren't on the list. Several others that often come up are rebellious, neurotic, petty, sneaky, impatient, perfectionist, versatile, resourceful, controlling, multifaceted, and personable. If you had people who really know you pick your traits, what would they say is true of you? Some of my clients have done this exercise with a trusted friend, and got a whole new insight into how they are being seen by others.

You'll gain maximum benefit out of doing this exercise by being totally truthful with yourself. Many times in my workshops, people are unwilling to face their real self, and they only identify with what they believe are positive traits. Be open and accepting of yourself. Get down on paper what your usual behavior indicates your traits are, and that represent what your self-concept is. Then as you analyze your traits, put a plus (+) in front of those that are strengthening you, and put a minus (-) in front of those that are weakening you and perhaps should be replaced. Just being conscious of and writing down your traits, helps to make the positive ones stronger, and the negative ones weaker. Awareness is the first step toward change.

FIGURE 2-3:
Self-Concept

• • •

Traits, Qualities, & Characteristics—"I'm . . .":

aimless • goal-oriented
aloof • friendly
amateurish • professional
anxious • patient
apathetic • ambitious
argumentative • agreeable
arrogant • down-to-earth
artificial • natural
average • special
awkward • poised
belittling • nurturing
blase • enthusiastic
boring • interesting
cautious • adventurous
changeable • loyal
chaotic • systematic
childish • mature
clumsy • graceful
cold • warm
competitive • cooperative
complex • simple
compulsive • controlled
conceited • humble
cranky • good-natured
crazy • sane
critical • accepting
cynical • idealistic
deceptive • sincere
destructive • constructive
detached • caring
devious • honest
dirty • clean
discouraging • inspiring
distasteful • likeable
dull • exciting
dull-witted • clever

eccentric • conventional
emotional • composed
erratic • disciplined
extravagant • prudent
a failure • a success
fanciful • realistic
fearful • brave
fickle • dependable
a follower • a leader
foolish • sensible
formal • casual
frigid • affectionate
frivolous • practical
fussy • easygoing
gloomy • funny
gullible • perceptive
hateful • loving
heavy • thin
helpless • independent
hesitant • decisive
hostile • peaceful
ignorant • educated
inaccurate • meticulous
indirect • straightforward
ineffective • productive
inferior • outstanding
insecure • confident
insensitive • sympathetic
intense • moderate
intolerant • understanding
intuitive • a planner
introverted • outgoing
irritating • pleasant
irrational • logical
late • punctual
lax • prompt

FIGURE 2-3:
Self-Concept (continued)

• • •

lazy • hardworking
liberal • conservative
limited • capable
a loner • people-oriented
loud • quiet
masculine • feminine
materialistic • spiritual
mean • kind
meek • aggressive
messy • organized
modest • proud
moody • cheerful
naive • knowledgeable
negative • positive
negligent • thorough
nervous • calm
nonchalant • conscientious
oblivious • attentive
offensive • charming
old • young
opinionated • open-minded
passive • dynamic
pessimistic • optimistic
phony • genuine
plain • sophisticated
poor • wealthy
possessive • lenient
private • communicative
prudish • sensual
a quitter • persistent
a procrastinator • self-starting
reckless • careful
resentful • forgiving
reserved • sociable
rigid • flexible
rough • gentle
rude • polite
sad • happy

secretive • open
selfish • giving
short • tall
shy • assertive
sickly • healthy
silly • serious
sloppy • neat
slow • fast
sluggish • energetic
somber • playful
spontaneous • predictable
stingy • generous
stubborn • adaptable
stupid • intelligent
submissive • dominant
superficial • analytical
suspicious • trusting
tacky • classy
talkative • concise
thoughtless • considerate
timid • a risktaker
unappealing • attractive
unconvincing • persuasive
uncoordinated • athletic
undiplomatic • tactful
unfaithful • trustworthy
unfair • decent
unfeeling • romantic
unimaginative • creative
uninterested • curious
unreliable • responsible
unskilled • competent
useless • worthwhile
volatile • stable
vulnerable • thick-skinned
wasteful • efficient
weak • strong

How can you know which traits are true for you? How do you know you are accepting or stubborn or trustworthy, etc.? You could ask a friend suggested above, but their opinions could be inaccurate due to their beliefs. Your behavior, how you feel, and the results that you are producing, are the most accurate ways to be sure. Actions do speak louder than words.

If you are giving to your family and friends, but are cutthroat and selfish with everyone else, are you a giving person? If you are accepting, patient, caring, and affectionate with your children, but not with other people, are these traits really true of you? Yes, we will be different in different circumstances, however, what is your real nature in most situations? Exhibiting a trait in a framework where there is a large personal gain, does not necessarily mean that someone has that trait at the core level.

Many of the examples in Figure 2-3 are extreme opposites, and you may fit somewhere in between, or it might depend on the situation. You may be stingy in some circumstances, and generous in others. You may be quiet at work, and loud at parties. Only list traits and characteristics that are usually true for you most of the time. The ones that are basically automatic regardless of the conditions.

Limiting Beliefs

A lot of the messages and beliefs we get during the early formative years, which can adversely affect us for our entire lives, might happen purely by accident. As mentioned earlier, we all have a script, unfortunately many of the authors, such as parents, siblings, relatives, neighbors, teachers, etc., are not professional writers. They don't intentionally want to mess us up, but through their process of coping with daily living, they could inadvertently insert limiting beliefs in us. They can end up giving us a script that's a dreadful drama or a horror show, instead of a romantic comedy. Some people have a script that's so negative, that they would be miserable if they were happy. They believe life is so painful, that happiness is uncomfortable for them. Joy does not fit their model of the world.

Women often during the last part of pregnancy, spend a lot of time at home. The television is on in the background, providing some company. What's on many channels during the day? Soap operas, talk shows, and news shows. What type of content makes up a large part of these productions? Anger, murder, cheating, stealing, lying, sadness, misery, hate, disease, fear, violence, greed, etc. Therefore, an unborn child can be programmed very negatively unintentionally.

As we said before, beliefs are what we hold to be true, not necessarily what is true. They form the boundaries within which we function, and therefore the range of our existence. Many beliefs can be limiting, and prevent us from utilizing all of our abilities and resources, and from reaching our full potential.

Words commonly told to a youngster are *no, bad, don't,* and *stop it.* Studies have found that on average, a child receives ten times as many negative messages per day as they do positive messages. This can translate into several hundred negative impressions versus a few dozen positive ones. Is it any wonder that people accept limiting beliefs about themselves, and have self-esteem issues?

Groucho Marx's saying, "I'd never want to join an organization that would have someone like me as a member," again comes into play. Does this ring any bells? Someone has such a low opinion of themselves, that if anyone would accept them, there must be something wrong with that person! There are many people that share this kind of negative thinking. A kind of thinking that leaves no winners. People who dislike themselves, are much more likely to take part in destructive behavior, than are people who truly like themselves. People who are genuinely strong, are more likely to sincerely help others, than are people who are weak due to limiting beliefs.

Achieving a feeling is the only reason a human being does anything. The power of positive feelings is explored in detail in *The Benefits* chapter. Unfortunately there are people that have such negative limiting beliefs about life and themselves, that they unconsciously cause problems so that they experience negative feelings. They do, or do not do, things that create situations where they will go through some form of conflict. They actually become uncomfortable when life is good because they believe life is filled with pain, and that they do not deserve happiness and joy. When you hear someone say, "Everyone wants to be happy," it may not be true for everyone. The program for happiness has not been installed, yet.

Many core beliefs are acquired when we are young and inexperienced. At an early age we have very little in the way of resources to make sense of things, and to make valid judgments. We are like sponges soaking up everything that we experience as true. We accept what we perceive from all around us during our early suggestible years, before we start to evaluate things for ourselves. Often we are labeled instead of our behavior. A child might be labeled as *bad, stupid, clumsy, ugly,* or *worthless,* instead of labeling their behavior. Consequently, many of our most basic beliefs are formed with limited and often false data.

Parents, teachers, and people do the best they can with the resources that they have, however, the child still pays the price for the limitations of others. Our initial beliefs may become self-fulfilling. If we are told we are bad, stupid, clumsy, ugly, or worthless, often enough, we can internalize these as true. Then it's likely we will engage in behaviors that cause these traits to be displayed. Our programming creates a script that contains the roles that we feel we can play, even though the roles may be unsuited to us. And unfortunately for many people, the scripts they are given are poorly written, very poorly written.

We must be very careful with what we feed our children mentally as well as physically. We need to nourish their minds with positive messages about themselves and life, just as we need to nourish their bodies with healthy food. As they say with computers, "garbage in, garbage out." Otherwise children could end up "paying for the sins of the parents." They could end up with all the fears, resentments, and limitations of those around them.

Beliefs are formed or accepted in order to help us make sense of and help us deal with the world. Having a grasp of ourselves, having an identity is a part of survival. Unfortunately too many people know themselves by their weaknesses and not their strengths. Limiting beliefs give us an opinion of ourselves that is consistent with and reinforces other beliefs. Since we also develop habits to simplify things, the limiting beliefs become self-generating and reinforced through repetition. Did you have anything happen growing up that formed limiting beliefs that you still have now?

We often go through life playing out our internal "script" and self-concept. We make evaluations and decisions based on "This is me," and "This is not me." When someone goes outside of their assumed boundaries, they usually experience great discomfort and tend to go back to their old patterns and behaviors.

What are some beliefs that you have that may be limiting? With little children, there's the concept of the *terrible twos*. By the age of two, children are usually very mobile, and begin getting into everything. Their curiosity is unlimited. For many adults, there are *terrible toos* which are beliefs that could be limiting in certain situations. Fears are included here, because often they are limiting beliefs about an assumed future problem. Of course *toos* could be accurate evaluations of behaviors that need to be altered. A salesperson could be *too* slow, lazy, awkward, uptight, stubborn, silly, sloppy, talkative, etc., to be successful.

The technique is to first be aware of your beliefs, and in later chapters we'll get into methods to adjust them according to your goals. Some frequently heard *toos* are, "I'm too . . .":

o	young	o	old
o	dumb	o	smart
o	tall	o	short
o	thin	o	heavy
o	honest	o	indirect
o	educated	o	ignorant
o	attractive	o	plain
o	wealthy	o	poor
o	aggressive	o	reserved
o	sloppy	o	neat
o	talkative	o	quiet
o	methodical	o	spontaneous
o	giving	o	selfish
o	crazy	o	sane
o	conservative	o	liberal
o	boring	o	exciting
o	proud	o	humble
o	energetic	o	tired
o	masculine	o	feminine
o	happy	o	sad
o	serious	o	silly
o	general	o	detailed
o	stubborn	o	cooperative
o	reckless	o	cautious
o	hardworking	o	lazy
o	friendly	o	detached
o	domineering	o	subservient
o	strong	o	weak
o	fast	o	slow
o	confident	o	self-conscious
o	healthy	o	sickly
o	optimistic	o	pessimistic

o uptight	o easygoing
o rigid	o flexible
o poised	o awkward
o emotional	o unfeeling

Circle or underline any of these "terrible toos" that you currently accept as true.

Limiting beliefs generally become self-perpetuating, even when untrue, and essentially make themselves true. When we're in the "I'm too . . ." mode, we can have limited expectations. We then get into a mindset of it's useless to take action, and if we do, we do it in a haphazard, halfhearted manner. Why bother when an outcome is outside of our sense of possibility? Consequently, limiting beliefs can destroy motivation and prevent us from moving forward.

Terrible toos type limiting beliefs might also apply to things outside of ourselves. Someone can believe that for their product there's *too* much competition, the price is *too* high, the quality is *too* low, the customers are *too* fussy, there are *too* many or *too* few options, the delivery is *too* slow, there is *too* little advertising, there are *too* many regulations, etc. Many of these type of *toos* could be accurate. However, they may be excuses for certain hidden personal issues, such as laziness and low self-esteem.

Challenge all limiting beliefs. Determine if they are valid appraisals of reality (*too* short to be a runway fashion model, *too* thin to be a professional wrestler, *too* simple to be a computer programmer, etc.), or smoke screens for other issues that need to be resolved. Is anyone else getting the results you want, despite the conditions? And if so, what beliefs do they have?

Head up a piece of paper, titling it "Limiting Beliefs." As in Figure 2-4, list any beliefs from your Life Beliefs page that are limiting, add the *terrible toos* from above, and any others that come to mind. SIMPLY WRITING DOWN ANY LIMITING BELIEFS, WEAKENS THEM. It sends a message to the subconscious that it's time to do something about them. For this exercise, we're looking for beliefs about life in general, as well as ones about yourself. In my workshops, I have people express their limiting beliefs and I write them on a poster. In just a few moments of doing this, you can see a positive difference in the participants, as their limiting beliefs are brought to the surface and acknowledged for what they are.

FIGURE 2-4:
Possible Limiting Beliefs

— — — — — — — — • • • — — — — — — — —

Life is a struggle, no pain, no gain.
You should only do what's necessary and no more.
Life is fated and that everything is predestined, so why bother working hard
    and killing yourself.
Success is just a matter of luck, either you have it or you don't.
Most people are selfish and greedy.
There's nothing new under the sun.
Misery loves company.
I'll never amount to anything.
No one will ever find me attractive.
All's fair in love and war.
Life is unfair, with the strong exploiting the weak.
If it's easy, it can't be good.
I'm very unlucky and never get a break.
Like a leopard's spots, people never really change.
I need other people to keep me sane.
I need other people for me to be happy.
I'm weak and I can't control my emotions.
If you come from a dysfunctional family, you'll always be a loser.
We all come from dysfunctional families.
I can never stick with anything long enough to make it work.
People won't like me if they know the real me.
If I lose my job, I'll never get another one just as good.
If someone criticizes me, it means I'm no good.
I'm so worthless that I don't deserve to be happy.
I'll fail, due to my: age, height, weight, gender, race, religion, nationality,
    family, past, appearance, lack of education, etc.

From now on, every time you hear yourself saying a limiting belief, especially about yourself, write it down as soon as you can, and make a commitment to challenge it. Consciously noticing any limiting beliefs is the first step to managing them. Anything that we pay attention to with a goal in mind, can change it. In the *Neutralizing Limiting Beliefs* chapter, we'll get into specific steps and techniques for handling limiting beliefs.

Victimization occurs all too frequently, and unfortunately, some people unintentionally bring it upon themselves. Having the belief that one is a victim, can cause someone to do things where they will be a victim. This occurs in many romantic relationships. There are people who regularly get involved with someone who is wrong for them, and treats them badly. And often if they find a person who is kind and treats them with respect, they find this person dull and boring.

Feeling sorry for oneself, is a common consequence of identifying with being a victim, and of having a negative self-concept. Feeling sorry for oneself is a very harmful thing to do. It isolates, limits, strains relationships, and depletes the immune system. Yes, there are people who have had horrible experiences. While some will respond with, "Oh poor me," others will respond with, "Okay, what can I learn from this, where can I go from here?" The difference is not ability, it's beliefs. Many addicts do not seek help because of an absence of "hope," and hope is based on nothing more than positive beliefs.

> *"We can't change the past, however we can change how we view, understand, and position it."*

What I'm suggesting here, is to be good to yourself, and to nurture yourself. It's bad enough that you may have gone through a lousy experience in the first place, so why continue to suffer due to someone else's limitations. Develop a *BOSS*, a *Belief Operating System Structure*, that will enrich and be supportive of you. Develop beliefs that cause you to choose to take care of yourself, and maximize your positive experience of life.

Empowering Beliefs

Motivation has many aspects, and having certain empowering beliefs is one of the most crucial ones. They are not always the opposite of a person's limiting beliefs. At this point, we'll talk about the four key empowering beliefs, the *Fundamental Four*.

The first core belief, is that you *can* achieve something, that you are able to do it. If you are applying for a new job, you need to believe that you can do the work that the job requires, and that you can get the job. You may not have done a type of work before, but because of your skills, traits, training, desires, beliefs, values, experiences, etc., you believe that you can do it. You must be sufficiently convinced before you can convince someone else. Rarely will a prospective employer or customer have more belief in you or your product than you do.

Worth is the next core empowering belief. If you do not believe attaining a particular goal is worthwhile enough, it's unlikely that you'll put out the time, energy, and resources necessary to make it happen. It must be of a certain level of importance to you, or you won't give it your all and bring it into reality. The fulfillment of particular values usually comes into play here. If an outcome isn't involved with a strong value, such as love, freedom, health, etc., it probably won't have a high worth or significance.

Another belief that can help you, is that you *will* fulfill an objective. You might deeply believe you can do it and that it's worthwhile, but for some reason it just doesn't seem like it will happen. This can be a good feedback mechanism for you. If you can't get a concrete sense that a goal will happen, this is possibly telling you that there are limiting beliefs that are unresolved and still need to be dealt with. Or it can be telling you that you have not done sufficient research and planning to form enough of a clear concrete vision of your final destination.

Deserving to have a goal, is the fourth and perhaps the most influential core empowering belief. If you don't believe you deserve to have something, it's doubtful that you'll be successful over the long haul. Without it, self-sabotage often comes into play. Just showing up is not enough to deserve to succeed. We must do something, whether it's taking certain actions or thinking certain thoughts, to deserve to have a result. Many other beliefs, especially the self-concept ones, can have a large bearing on you being able to believe you deserve to have what you want. Again, in later chapters we'll cover how to install and intensify the beliefs you need to have to use your full abilities.

Figure 2-5, lists empowering beliefs from Figure 2-2, and the four core beliefs. Using it as a reference, identify a new page as "Empowering Beliefs," and create a list of beneficial beliefs that will help you to attain your objectives. Write out beliefs that you already have, and ones that if you have them, would serve you.

FIGURE 2-5:
Possible Empowering Beliefs

● ● ●

Life is a gift to be enjoyed.
You should always be the best that you can be.
We are responsible for how we feel and for what happens to us.
People are basically decent and honest.
People do evil things because they are weak and unaware.
You need to take risks to succeed.
You need to prepare for the future and think before you act.
We can always learn from everything that happens.
You need to be flexible and adapt to the situation.
You need to take care of the details to be successful.
Integrity is necessary to feel free.
Success is measured by a person's contribution to others.
You can be and have anything that you want, if you want it strongly
     enough.
We should pay more attention to what's right than what's wrong.
The future will be better than the past.
We need to focus on solutions and not problems.
We need to think of ourselves as human beings instead of identifying with
     nationalities.
You must be persistent to succeed.
Whatever comes up in my life, I can handle it.
People have a responsibility to maintain their own health.
People can always change and can become better.
Life happens, and to always make the best of things.
I can overcome any obstacles or barriers that get in my way.
I have the abilities, skills, and traits necessary for me to succeed.
I can achieve the results that I want, which are to . . .
It's worth it to achieve my goal of . . .
I will achieve my goal of . . .
I deserve to achieve my goal of . . .

In many businesses, it's common to hear that you need to pay your dues before you can flourish. So and so was an overnight success, after 10 to 15 years of struggling. In many fields of endeavor, it often takes 10 years of experience to feel, and be considered, knowledgeable. Concepts such as "no pain, no gain," and "the greater the challenge, the greater the glory," often cause people to discount their accomplishments, when it was easy for them to achieve. Without the belief of deserving, there is little pleasure in the success, and again, the success is all too commonly destroyed through self-sabotage.

The four core empowering beliefs, *can*, *worth*, *will*, and *deserve*, are the beginning of constructing a belief foundation that will enable you to be motivated and to use your potential. Almost any potent belief will fit into one of these four categories, however, you want to make your list of enhancing beliefs as large as possible. The bigger the list, the greater the power it will have to move you forward, and to resolve any limiting beliefs.

Modeling Success

Learning something new, whether it's how to ride a bike, play a piano, or use a computer, is easier by modeling or studying someone who is already skilled at it. How exactly do they do what they do, so that they achieve the desired results? What are their beliefs, values, attitudes, behaviors, etc.? What are their traits and characteristics? What causes them to do what I call the *New Three R's*, the *Right Thing*, in the *Right Way*, and at the *Right Time*?

Asking yourself the *New Three R's* before and after an activity can be very functional in guiding you and keeping you focused. Before a meeting, ask yourself, "What's the *Right Thing* to do, what's the *Right Way* to do it, and what's the *Right Time* to do it, so that I obtain the results I want?" Then after the meeting, ask yourself, "Did I do the *Right Thing*, did I do it in the *Right Way*, and did I do it at the *Right Time*?" Three little questions that will give you big returns. If the answer is no, then ask, "What can I learn from this and do differently the next time, so that I achieve my objectives?" The right questions will help you to grow and improve, and move you toward your desired results.

Take out another piece of paper and label it "Modeling Success." Make a list of people you believe are successful, and why you believe they are successful. These can be people you know, know of, past and present. It could be a relative, a friend, a teacher, a member of the clergy, a celebrity, someone from history, etc. Leave three blank lines between each person's name. Then using Figure 2-6 as a reference, write out the main traits and characteristics that you feel made each person a success. Was it because they were dependable, persistent, outgoing, kind, adaptable, creative, communicative, honest, a risk taker, logical, persuasive, thorough, organized, trustworthy, etc.? What is different about certain people that enables them to achieve beyond the norm?

FIGURE 2-6:
Success Self-Concept

• • •

Traits, Qualities, & Characteristics - "I'm . . .":

accepting	cooperative	joyful	productive
adaptable	creative	kind	professional
adventurous	curious	knowledgeable	prompt
agreeable	decent	a learner	proud
aggressive	decisive	likeable	punctual
alert	dependable	logical	realistic
ambitious	determined	loving	receptive
appreciative	disciplined	loyal	respectful
approachable	down-to-earth	mature	responsible
appropriate	efficient	modest	a risk taker
assertive	empathetic	natural	sane
attentive	encouraging	neat	self-accepting
balanced	enthusiastic	nurturing	self-aware
brave	fair	objective	self-correcting
calm	faithful	open	self-starting
capable	flexible	open-minded	sensible
careful	focused	optimistic	sincere
caring	forgiving	organized	sociable
charitable	friendly	outgoing	spiritual
cheerful	generous	passionate	stable
classy	gentle	patient	straightforward
clean	genuine	peaceful	supportive
communicative	giving	people-oriented	sympathetic
compassionate	goal-oriented	perceptive	systematic
competent	good-natured	persistent	tactful
composed	happy	personable	thick-skinned
concise	hardworking	persuasive	thorough
confident	helpful	a planner	tolerant
conscientious	honest	pleasant	trusting
considerate	honorable	poised	trustworthy
consistent	independent	polite	understanding
constructive	inspiring	positive	warm
controlled	interesting	practical	worthwhile

As you put together this list, you may begin to notice that some traits keep coming up. The more you study success, the more you pay attention to it, the closer you'll come to your own success.

Success Self-Concept

Imagine that you have, and are, the success that you desire, what would your self-concept be? By establishing this awareness and mindset, it will assist you in reaching your goals. In the prior section, you've taken a look at examples of success. Now we want to develop a success profile for you.

Going over Figure 2-6 again, circle or underline every trait, quality, and characteristic on it that would be true of you when you are the success you want to be. Indicate all the ones you already have, as well as the ones you would have, that would help you to achieve and maintain your wishes and dreams. Figure 2-6 lists many of the same traits as in Figure 2-3, as well as a lot of new ones. Many of the traits in Figure 2-6 are similar in meaning, but since people define them differently, they are included for clarity. Then label a new page "Success Self-Concept," and copy the traits you chose, as well as adding any other useful ones.

An interesting point can come out through this exercise. Other than physical aspects and a particular level of intelligence, everyone can have just about every positive trait, quality, and characteristic in Figure 2-6. Everyone has the ability and capacity to embrace, embody, and exhibit the enriching and empowering attributes on the list. Therefore, everyone can have high self-esteem.

By being things such as accepting, attentive, caring, cheerful, decent, dependable, genuine, honest, kind, loyal, nurturing, patient, understanding, etc., you can feel good about yourself regardless of your intelligence, appearance, financial status, athletic prowess, or background. And no one can take this from you. Be proud of your worthwhile qualities and your worthwhile behavior versus any external elements. Look for ways to enhance others and notice how you are enhanced. Rise above the petty competitions of who is best and appreciate everyone's uniqueness. As discussed in the last chapter, stop playing the game of one-upmanship, and see how everyone can win.

Does anyone have all the admirable qualities in Figure 2-6? It might seem "too" ideal, and yet it is possible. The more we focus on and pay attention to what's productive, the more likely it will happen. By constructing a success self-concept, you'll have a beacon to guide you to your optimal self. You'll have a point of reference to create direction to how you think about yourself, and the choices you make.

It's probably safe to say, that at various times and under certain circumstances, most people have displayed most of these positive traits. Why might this only happen infrequently? It's the *BOSS*, the beliefs that dictate the boundaries of our thoughts and behavior. Because of the programming and the resulting script, large areas of our resources are rarely utilized, if at all. It's like having a one-million-acre farm, and only cultivating one acre, causing a bare subsistence existence. The capacity for self-esteem is there, but the beliefs required to use the capacity are either blocked or undeveloped.

Change is a topic that is useful to discuss at this point. Negative traits and characteristics need adjustment, or be eliminated. We know that to grow and advance, that we must change and have change in our lives, yet people often resist change even if it's good for them.

Fear of the unknown is one of the many possible reasons why change has been so difficult. For instance, many people will stay in an abusive relationship or job because the next one could even be worse, and the thought of being unattached can be overwhelming. They know they should get out, but they just continue to hang in there. Not being sure of the effects of changing, causes things to remain the same.

Security and survival are powerful human tendencies. We have habits to make it easier to do things. Changing what we do, and therefore what we understand and are able to predict, can upset a person's very existence. It can just seem better to stay with what we know even though it's painful, versus going out into unfamiliar waters.

Incompatibility with the self-concept is another potential reason for resistance to change. Everyone has beliefs about who they are. This is me, and this is not me. I have a sense of myself, I have an identity. New traits are not me, and if I adopt them, I might not be sure of who I am. If I change, I might not be sure of what to do, how to do it, and how to respond or feel about it afterwards.

Since many of the traits that make up one's self-concept are intertwined, changing one trait can create change, and possibly confusion, with other traits. If I believe I'm stubborn, a whole set of behaviors will follow this trait. If I now change to being adaptable, cooperative, or easygoing, most likely there will be changes throughout my entire life. And since we are complex beings, one part of the self-concept can maintain a negative trait, and prevent a positive trait from replacing it.

Relationships with people close to you, is an additional reason why change might be uncomfortable. Family, friends, co-workers, etc., can have a vested interest in you continuing the way you are. If you change, even for the better, the nature and quality of each relationship will be different. To an extent, you are predictable. People know you in a certain way, your likes and dislikes, your strengths and weaknesses, how you will respond in a given situation.

Reshaping yourself, no longer allows others to be sure of what you'll do, how you'll do it, and how you'll respond afterwards. If they can't be sure how you'll behave, it's tough for them to know how to behave. It could be hard for them to sense they really know you anymore. Although the new you may be a vast improvement, this newness could cause a high level of uncertainty in others. It is possibly so stressful, that they might unconsciously try to get you to go back to your old predictable ways. Net result, progress is halted, or a relationship can fall apart, or both.

Unfortunately, many times when someone is growing into their real capability, others due to their own limitations, may try to pull them back. When we learn and progress, it can be intimidating to those close to us. We move forward, and it can dramatize to others how stuck and limited they are. Instead of being happy and supportive of our improvement, they can be negative and destructive. Their influence can be so strong as to undue all our advancement, and bring us right back to our starting point.

Time and time again, we have seen people begin to blossom, and witnessed the impact of others cause them to wither and dry up. Remember, no one can know and understand something unless they have experienced it in some manner. Sometimes explaining to someone what you want and what you want to be, and why, is sufficient to enable you to grow, and still maintain a good relationship with them. If someone doesn't understand us, it's up to us to give them more information, and/or deliver the information in another way, so that they can comprehend us through their model of the world. We need to help others to understand us, so that they will be able to help us, or at least not stand in our way.

The conclusion, is that you must find a way to interact with the important people in your life in such a manner that they will either be encouraging of who and what you want to be, or at least be neutral. For them to only give their input when asked, or if they see you heading for an unseen disaster. This is a vital issue that must be addressed for maximum results.

Change is the only thing that we can be sure of. In our fast paced world, it's happening at an ever accelerated rate. To succeed, we need to know who we are, enhance our strengths, change what limits us, and accept what we can't or won't change, right now. Using change effectively requires knowing specifically what you want and why you want it. What will you, now and in the future, gain from changing something, and what will you lose by keeping it the way it is? More on these ideas in subsequent chapters.

Suggestion, on a daily basis invest a few seconds in looking at your "Success Self-Concept." Incorporate it into your thoughts and actions, as much as you find yourself being comfortable with. This will help to shape your thinking, and therefore influence your behavior in positive ways towards your goals. And as a final thought in this section, be a person of integrity. Integrity goes beyond being honest. It's about keeping one's word, being on time, taking initiative to do what's fair, right, and moral. It's about being whole, and being consistent. Integrity is a wonderful builder of self-esteem. *"What we concentrate on, we tend to create."*

Skills and Abilities Inventory

I often ask people, "What are your career skills?" Usually they are only able to put together a list of five to ten of them. This can be very limiting. Knowing what your skills and abilities are, is another part of knowing oneself, and being able to be motivated. It also helps to raise self-esteem. Too often, people know themselves more by what they consider their "weaknesses," and what they can't do, and they ignore or belittle their "strengths," and what they can do. It's much better to know ourselves by our strengths and what we can do, and to work on areas that we want to improve upon.

Skills are separated from abilities in this chapter, in that a skill is an ability that has been developed to a level of competency and expertise. For example, many people have the ability, capacity, and faculty to learn to use a computer, but they have not developed it yet into a skill. Just because someone is unable to do something now, doesn't always mean they can never do it.

Analyze Figure 2-7, and underline the skills that you currently have. Then put an 'X' in the box in front of each skill you need to develop or acquire to achieve your goals. Often people forget many of the skills they have that enable them to accomplish their objectives. This list will help to remind you of the many reasons you have been able to do things successfully in the past. The list is a starting point, so add whatever additional skills you have.

FIGURE 2-7:
Skills and Abilities

• • •

☐	Accuracy	☐	Efficiency	☐	Modeling
☐	Adapting	☐	Empathizing	☐	Motivating
☐	Advising	☐	Estimating	☐	Negotiating
☐	Agility	☐	Evaluating	☐	Organizing
☐	Analyzing	☐	Expediting	☐	Persuading
☐	Assembling	☐	Explaining	☐	Planning
☐	Auditing	☐	Financing	☐	Precision
☐	Budgeting	☐	Follow-through	☐	Prioritizing
☐	Calculating	☐	Forecasting	☐	Problem solving
☐	Clarifying	☐	Goal setting	☐	Promoting
☐	Coaching	☐	Hiring	☐	Public speaking
☐	Communicating	☐	Imagining	☐	Purchasing
☐	Compiling	☐	Implementing	☐	Recruiting
☐	Completing	☐	Improvising	☐	Reporting
☐	Computing	☐	Influencing	☐	Researching
☐	Concentrating	☐	Initiating	☐	Scheduling
☐	Coordinating	☐	Inspecting	☐	Selling
☐	Creating	☐	Interviewing	☐	Stamina
☐	Deciding	☐	Inventing	☐	Strategies
☐	Delegating	☐	Leading	☐	Summarizing
☐	Demonstrating	☐	Learning	☐	Supervising
☐	Designing	☐	Listening	☐	Synthesizing
☐	Detail oriented	☐	Logic	☐	Systematizing
☐	Developing	☐	Managing	☐	Team building
☐	Dexterity	☐	Marketing	☐	Team player
☐	Diplomacy	☐	Measuring	☐	Training
☐	Drawing	☐	Mediating	☐	Traveling
☐	Editing	☐	Memorizing	☐	Writing

What if you were good in a skill in the past but you haven't used it for a long time? Still put it on your list. For example, you were good at budgeting, however you haven't used this skill in the last five years. Add it to your list because it's the type of skill that with some review, study, and practice you could be good at again.

Some skills may have many other talents under them. Let's take managing as an illustration. Some of the possible skills involved in managing are adapting, analyzing, coaching, communicating, deciding, delegating, follow-through, goal setting, hiring, leading, measuring, motivating, organizing, planning, etc. The idea is to make your list as accurate and as large as possible.

Study and "own" your list of skills and abilities. Again, know yourself by your strengths and the things you can do, and by things you want to improve in. Your skills and abilities list, along with your self-concept lists, become resources to aid you in achieving all your goals. And as you learn and grow, change these lists to suit the changes in your life.

Success Inventory

Successful people primarily focus on their triumphs and learn from their mistakes. Unsuccessful people primarily focus on their mistakes as failures, and see their victories as temporary exceptions. Putting together a list of your successes, with the skills and traits you have that enabled you to achieve them, will help you to be motivated. The aim is to get you to have a successful outlook, and to put you in a resourceful, optimistic state. This list is a part of proving to yourself that you have obtained positive results in the past, and that you can do it again in the future. Life happens, and several unsuccessful events can cause someone to have a negative attitude. Having a "Success Inventory" gives you a lifelong resource helping you to maintain a positive perspective.

Label a new page "Success Inventory," and as shown in Figure 2-8, make a list of goals you've had that you've successfully completed, leaving several blank lines between each one. Then using Figures 2-6 and 2-7 for ideas, list the major skills and traits that you used to achieve each goal. This list will also show you that you can take your skills and abilities from one setting, and move them into another. You may have been persuasive with your family, and you can transfer that skill to your office. You researched a project at work, and you can use that skill in deciding where to go on vacation.

FIGURE 2-8:

Success Inventory

• • •

List 5-10 major skills and/or traits per achievement.

Finished school—discipline, improvising, self-starting, learning, memorizing, thorough, planning, completing, adapting.

Learned to swim—agility, stamina, patient, confident, persistent, concentrating, modeling.

Got driver's license—concentrating, learning, communicating, demonstrating, diplomacy, planning, persistent.

Bought a car—negotiating, researching, logic, understanding, thorough, imagining, clarifying, deciding, inspecting.

Got married—planning, forgiving, charming, imagining, communicating, cooperative, understanding, trusting, tactful.

Travelled to Europe—planning, organizing, persuading, budgeting, imagining, researching, coordinating, energetic.

Got a roommate—planning, follow-through, communicating, deciding, interviewing, negotiating, explaining.

Bought a home—analyzing, researching, negotiating, listening, influencing, evaluating, patient, follow-through, financing.

Promoted to manager—discipline, communicating, influencing, self-starting, understanding, leading, team player, initiating.

Become a nonsmoker—discipline, optimistic, imagining, researching, self-starting, follow-through, goal setting.

Learned to do my taxes—planning, accuracy, organizing, patient, computing, concentrating, researching, analyzing.

Achieved ideal weight—discipline, optimistic, self-starting, energetic, imagining, persistent, scheduling, independent.

Started a business—energetic, discipline, persuading, communicating, self-starting, imagining, flexible, tactful, enthusiastic, planning, budgeting, promoting, training.

Installed computer system—planning, scheduling, follow-through, listening, evaluating, expediting, logic, summarizing, mediating.

Become an accountant—concentrating, memorizing, planning, calculating, persistent, follow-through, goal setting, auditing.

Helped a friend—advising, prioritizing, trustworthy, nurturing, motivating, accepting, calm, creating, practical, positive.

Held job over 10 years—punctual, problem solving, implementing, writing, systematizing, researching, adapting, communicating.

FIGURE 2-8:
Success Inventory (continued)

• • •

Moved to Boston—adventurous, ambitious, deciding, planning, researching, self-starting, optimistic, sociable, mature.

Learned to use computer—listening, patience, concentrating, researching, learning, memorizing, discipline, curious, concise.

Learned to water-ski—optimistic, self-starting, persistent, confidence, follow-through, deciding, agility, stamina, outgoing.

Learned to dance—risk taker, aggressive, modeling, planning, stamina, imagining, goal setting, adapting, attentive.

Paid off credit cards—assembling, detail oriented, estimating, reporting, planning, budgeting, hardworking, prudent, proud.

Moved office—designing, compiling, organizing, supervising, purchasing, measuring, expediting, energetic, dependable.

Raised a child—caring, nurturing, accepting, planning, hiring, adapting, coaching, coordinating, problem solving, budgeting, scheduling, delegating, explaining, negotiating, inventing, etc.

Keep adding to your "Success Inventory" as you realize more and more outcomes in your life. Use small achievements as well as large ones. Especially useful are accomplishments that at first seemed impossible. It could be things such as riding a bike, learning a language, driving a stick shift car, skiing, playing an instrument, learning a computer program, etc. Glory in your wins, and learn from your non-wins.

What about projects that weren't total triumphs? Think about it, there could still be many successes in a venture that wasn't a hit. For instance, when I produced my film, it wasn't popular at the box office or with the critics. I could view the whole undertaking as a failure, or look at what was done successfully and learn from the rest of it. I successfully wrote the script, raised the money, put together the cast and crew, finished the film, and got it into the theaters. There can be many empowering victories regardless of the final outcome. Look for the successes in all your projects, even though you may not have reached your final destinations.

Wishes And Dreams

If you knew that you would succeed, what would your wishes and dreams be? If someone waved a magic wand and granted you all your desires, what would they be? What do you want to do, have, and be in every area of your life? This is more than just maximizing your potential. As mentioned in the preface, it's dealing with survival. Remember people are goal setting beings, and without rich rewarding future aspirations, we can shrivel up and disappear.

Use Figures 2-9 and 2-10 to get ideas for your goals. What do you want to do: travel, learn, have adventures, give to others, etc.? What do you want to have: a family, money, home, car, boat, clothes, a business, etc.? What do you want to be: healthy, honest, worthwhile, confident, liked, respected, secure, productive, spiritual, etc.? Keep in mind that moving along the path toward one goal provides learning to help you achieve other objectives.

Have a separate piece of paper for each goal category you are interested in, and write down your "Wishes and Dreams." Go all out, constantly aim for your "Ultimate End Results!" Since "we rarely get more than we ask for," ask for what you truly want. Not what someone else might want, but what you truly want. A lot of people talk about what they want, and yet they never take concrete, specific, persistent action to achieve their dreams. The first step, is to write out what you want in each area of your life, and get your thoughts planned on paper, *POP*.

Please note, the examples in Figures 2-9 and 2-10, are just starting points, they are NOT effectively worded or constructed goals. They are too general and vague. Notice all the "More/Less/Better" statements, and their cousins increase, improve, decrease, higher, closer, bigger, reduce, etc. They do not create a clear detailed picture, image, or visual representation. Wanting to get a job with a lot of travel, could have you going to places you don't want to go. Earning more money, could get you an increase of $1 per week. Doing something you'll be remembered for, could be for ruining something. Meeting your ideal mate, could be meeting someone who is happily married, or who lives 2,000 miles away. Sometimes beginning can be difficult, and getting something down on paper is what's important at this point. In the next chapter, we'll deal with how to specifically word your goals for the maximum benefit and effectiveness.

FIGURE 2-9:
Career Goals

• • •

Get a promotion.
Earn more money.
Improve my corporate image.
Relocate in the organization.
Get along better with people at work.
Increase production.
Get a raise.
Hire more staff.
Have better teamwork.
Get a job with a lot of travel.
Improve customer satisfaction.
Get a bigger budget.
Get a new ad agency.
Learn more about the competition.
Give my staff more training.
Set better sales goals for next year.
Develop a higher quality product.
Get a degree.
Own a restaurant.
Get a job closer to home.
Do some networking.
Become a consultant.
Install a new computer system.
Get a new job.
Have lunch with different executives.
Increase sales in the near future.
Get a job in a different field.
Receive some acknowledgement for my efforts.
Have more freedom in doing my job.
Write a book.
Be more involved in the decision making process.
Get a different territory.
Work less hours.
Reduce expenses and waste.
Work more efficiently.
Do less overnight travel.
Get a different office.

FIGURE 2-10:
Wishes and Dreams

• • •

HEALTH:
Lose some weight.
Start exercising.
Have more energy.
Learn to cook.
Be more healthy.
Live to a ripe old age.
Be able to sleep better.

FAMILY:
Communicate better with my spouse.
Do more things together.
Be a better parent.
Not fight as much with my mate.

COMMUNITY:
Do volunteer work.
Become involved in politics.
Get to know my neighbors better.

FRIENDS:
Improve my friendships.
Do more things with friends.
Be more sympathetic.
Get some new friends.

SPIRITUAL:
Be more in touch with my spirituality.
Attend services more often.
Become involved with my religious group.
Pray on a regular basis.

FINANCIAL:
Own real estate.
Have income producing investments.
Have a large net worth.
Be a good investor.

FIGURE 2-10:
Wishes and Dreams (Continued)

• • •

RECREATION:
Learn a new sport.
Learn to play a musical instrument.
Improve my golf game.
Go on weekend trips.
Read some books.
Learn to paint.
Go dancing.
Write poetry.
Do a lot of travelling.
Attend the theater often.
Be a better skier.

HOME:
Get new furniture.
Redo the kitchen.
Have the closets better organized.
Live in a different neighborhood.
Have a large house.

PERSONAL:
Learn a new language.
Buy a new car.
Be more relaxed flying.
Improve my vocabulary.
Be more comfortable meeting strangers.
Collect art.
Have higher self-esteem.
Be more persuasive.
Be more organized.
Have more inner peace.
Do something I'll be remembered for.
Get more schooling.
Change my wardrobe.
Be clearer thinking.
Improve my communication skills.
Have less stress.
Having people treat me better.

When you have your objectives written out, then you can compare them in various parts of your life and see if they are workable. If you want to be a globe-trotting journalist and have a strong family life, you may have a conflict. If you want to have your own retail business and be home for dinner at five, it may not be reasonable. If you want to be a politician and have a private life, it's highly unlikely. The mission is to look at everything objectively, and to create a balance between all your various ambitions. Otherwise you can satisfy one at the expense of another.

A question that often comes up, is how optimistic or realistic should your goals be? If there's a physical aspect such as strength, endurance, coordination, etc., there are certainly limitations as to what is possible for anyone. If you want to be a brain surgeon or dentist, but you are clumsy and your hands shake, you, and your patient, have a problem. If you want to be a jet pilot, but you have very poor eyesight and hearing, and you can't deal with stress, it would be impractical. If you want to be a professional football player, but weigh 130 pounds, are weak, and bruise easily, it isn't going to happen.

Fortunately, in many places the opportunities and possibilities are enormous. If you want to be the president of a company, you can work your way up. You may have to go to school nights and weekends, work overtime, join certain associations, socialize with certain people, etc. You'll need to work harder and smarter. If you willing to *WIN* to do *Whatever Is Necessary*, your potential can be unlimited.

Look at the stories of people who have come to this country with no money, no friends, no command of the English language, and yet become very successful. If you're not getting what you want, look at people who are. Look at the success stories. Find out how others have achieved what you want and learn from them. Most people have the ability, it's just that they don't know how to use it. This is where applying *Anatomy of Success* becomes so important.

Can you have too many pursuits at one time? The answer to this question is a very individual one. Many people do have too many "irons in the fire," and never get anywhere. They don't give enough time, energy, and resources to complete one project before they're off on another one.

History tells us that successful people in the early stages of their careers, often dedicated themselves to only one or two major goals at a time. Once those projects worked out, they then would tackle other ones. When they arrive at a certain level of accomplishment, they are able to follow many projects at the same time because they have the resources and people necessary to carry out their ideas. Therefore, have large lists of what you want, and continually add to them, but only go all out on two to four main goals at any one time. When one situation is sufficiently taken care of, then get involved in another pursuit from your lists.

Keep adding to your lists of wishes and dreams, and continually refine them. As a goal is accomplished, check it off and add it to your "Success Inventory." Since the only thing we can be sure of is change, keep monitoring your goals and adjusting them to keep them appealing to you.

What if you never get around to tackling certain projects? As long as no one else is let down, it probably doesn't matter. The key is to constantly have things in your life that you look forward to doing, having, and being. Excitement and aliveness in one area of your life, helps you to be more productive in other areas. All we know for sure, is that we have right now, an individual moment. Designing a wonderful future, contributes to having "wonderful now's." Be positive about your tomorrows, to gain the most out of today.

Life Purpose

Everyone has a purpose in life, although not everyone is consciously aware of what theirs is. Behavior is the bottom line, and behavior is tied into values and beliefs. Having a clear purpose supports a sense of self, an identity, and in some cases a reason to live. Many war prisoners survived when so many others perished, because they committed themselves to a purpose.

Questions to ask yourself to help you know your purpose, are:

- Why am I living, what gives meaning to my life?
- What is my ultimate goal in life?
- Where do I want to be in 10, 15, 20 years, and at the end of my life?
- What can I devote myself to that gives me the greatest satisfaction and fulfillment, and maximizes my positive experience of life?

Does a life purpose need to be a monumental mission, as in ending world hunger? No! A great idea, yet perhaps not suitable for everyone. What I'm suggesting, is having something that works for you. Whether it's being a great parent, taking care of your family, having a beautiful flower garden, helping others, promoting peace, creating works of art, or watching every rerun of your favorite television show, make it something that enriches you. Unfortunately I've worked with people who had such negative beliefs, that their purpose was to suffer and have conflict. Once they became aware of this, they were able to change it.

What has been your purpose in life to this point? Has it brought you the kind of experiences that you find worthwhile? If not, from now on, what is your purpose? And what do you need to be, and do, on a daily basis, to fulfill your life's objective?

Equipped with these lists of goals, values, beliefs, skills, and successes, you're now ready to work on an individual, specific goal. In the next chapter, we'll begin the goal setting process, with how to effectively word your goals for maximum results.

Chapter 3

WORDING
YOUR GOALS

● ● ●

DEFINING YOUR DESTINATIONS

Clarity is crucial to effective goal setting. As stated earlier, many people never reach their full potential due to weak, vague, unclear, indistinct goals. In the *Positive Language Patterns* chapter, we talked about the importance of always working for the *UER*, the *Ultimate End Result*. The key, is to be specific and detailed enough so that your goal is measurable. Specific and detailed enough so that you have created a picture, an image, a visual representation of what you want. A picture so clear, detailed, defined, and measurable that anyone can understand your desires and what you want.

Choosing between alternatives is something we are constantly doing. We're always making choices; doing nothing is a choice. The better the choices we make, the better the results we achieve. By setting explicit outcomes for ourselves, we can know what choices to make. We are giving instructions, directions, and focus to our thoughts, what to tune in to and give our attention to, and what to ignore. We can't pay attention to everything at once, it would be too much to process. Having effectively constructed objectives, causes us to notice certain things, and behave in ways that move us toward our objectives. It leads us as to what to do, how to do it, and when to do it, as well as what not to do.

Motivation is powerfully affected by clarity. To be motivated to the maximum, we need to specifically know what it is we're after. It's difficult to get excited about something when you can't exactly see what it is. Saying you want a new car will have one effect. Saying you want a new convertible sports car, of a certain brand, a particular model, color, interior, sound system, engine, suspension, wheels, etc., will cause a much different response. We must be able to see it to make it real and thereby establish a meaning to it. If things are blurred, if the image is in a fog, there will be little forward momentum. It takes a concrete definite precise picture, to generate excitement and action.

Delegating tasks to others, as mentioned in the *Positive Language Patterns* chapter, is also impacted by preciseness. Frustration occurs for many people when they are trying to do something for someone else, and they're not entirely sure what they are supposed to accomplish. This not knowing produces uncertainty and stress. It therefore limits a person's ability to use all of their talents. Subsequent results suffer. Whether it's communicating with others or ourselves, getting specific and being thorough, can be the difference between achieving your outcome or not achieving it.

Miscommunicating as said before, costs untold amounts of time, money, and resources. When assigning projects, let the other person know "WHY" something needs to be done in a particular way, and within a particular time frame. Only then can they know what to do, how to do it, and when to do it! Telling someone you need something done "as soon as possible," "when they can get around to it," "sometime next week," or "in the near future," will not help them to organize their work efficiently.

"I need this completed no later than Thursday at 3:00 P.M., for a meeting with the president to discuss next year's budgets," is the type of information that will assist someone in fulfilling their responsibilities. If you're the one being given an assignment, simply ask, "When's the latest that this project can be completed by?" This question establishes the target date and a timetable, and allows you to schedule your work productively.

Begin working on an individual outcome by giving it a title. This will be broad and general, topics such as excellent health, great wealth, or being married. It needs to be stated in the positive. The idea is to get started with something, and to keep adding to it and refining it for greatest impact. Sometimes what one doesn't want comes to mind first, such as low pay, stress, long commutes, being single, poor health, etc. This is fine to get the ball rolling and to narrow the field. But remember, the technique is to ask after every don't, what is it's opposite, "What do I want?"

Health, mental and physical, is a good pursuit to use as an example. As discussed in the *Positive Language Patterns* chapter, some people are constantly stuck in focusing on what they "don't" want, and therefore cause a negative reality. Step one is recognizing, identifying, and being aware of a need, want, or desire. Then turn it around to the positive of what you "do" want. What kind of pictures do the following statements generate?:

"I don't want to be unhealthy."
"I don't want to crave sweets."
"I don't want to be sad and depressed."
"I don't want to be weak and frail."
"I don't want to be clumsy and awkward."
"I don't want to be confused."
"I don't want to be tired all the time."
"I don't want to have high blood pressure."
"I don't want to be flabby."
"I don't want to have a 40-inch waistline."

Stopping with these types of images can keep someone stuck in an unhealthy state. *"What we concentrate on, we tend to create."*

Wording your health goal has many possibilities. What is the *UER* that you wish to have? The following is a sample of constructing a health target:

"I (your full name), ALWAYS want (or 'choose') to be completely healthy, mentally, physically, emotionally, and spiritually, feel great, be strong, coordinated, athletic, clear thinking, youthful, have all the energy I want, blood pressure 120/80, resting pulse 50, weigh _____ lean, fit, and toned pounds, with (neck, chest, arms, stomach, hips, thighs, and calves) measurements."

Now you have the start of a specific vision to guide all your actions. Now you've given instructions and directions to your brain so that a plan can be designed to fulfill your wishes. In another section, we'll get into even greater detail as we'll explore how you know you have achieved a given goal.

Using your full name in your goal statements, after the "I," is usually a good idea. It helps to establish ownership and commitment. It helps to make a goal real, and to install it within your consciousness.

Time is an element that is very significant. If you just say you want to be healthy, the instructions to your brain are temporary. If you give commands that you "always," now and forever, want to be healthy, you now have a standard to measure all your actions against. You now have something that will affect all the choices you make.

"Always" establishes a directive that you must take steps today, tomorrow, and everyday on a consistent basis. This take charge approach enables you to continually have something. If you "always" want to be completely healthy, constantly eating fried foods, highly processed meals, sugar filled sweets, and thinking negative thoughts, will not be appropriate selections. If you "always" want to be completely healthy, exercising, eating nutritious and nutritiously prepared foods, and thinking positive thoughts, would be compatible and suitable actions based on your instructions.

There seems to be a human tendency to leave doing tasks until the last minute, until right before they have to be done. When did so many of us usually finish doing term papers in school? If you were like me, it was right before I had to hand it in. And even if I had three months to do it, I would only get serious about it the day before it was due. When do a lot of people finish packing for a trip? When the cab driver arrives to take them to the airport.

We need to give our brains target dates of when we want a result to occur, when it's not "always." Specific dates help us to organize our time as well as our energy on a daily basis. When I was producing films, we started with the completion date, and then worked backwards as to what we had to do each day to be finished by that date. When we get into the time management chapter, we'll explore how each step toward your goal, needs its own target date. For now, write down the specific date of when you want to have each goal accomplished.

What happens if your target date arrives and you still haven't achieved your outcome? Set another specific date. Continue setting new target dates until you accomplish your goal or decide to go down a different path. The key is to have time consciousness so that you use your time productively. Without doing this, there might be an inclination to procrastinate, or to use time inefficiently, since tasks tend to take as long to complete as we allow for them.

Different types of goals require different time intervals when establishing target dates. Experiment with time frames that make sense in each situation. If you want a new job, reset the dates in three to seven day increments. If it's a weight issue, monthly targets could be sensible. If it's increasing sales, daily, weekly, monthly, or quarterly spans could be practical, depending on the type of business.

Figuring out how long you want to have a particular goal, can be another important factor. It's usually best to position having a goal longer than you probably want it, because you can always change your mind and shorten a time frame, but it can be very difficult to extend it. First determining the length of time something is desired, will help in deciding if a choice is the right one. Whether it's a job, a relationship, a home, a car, a vacation, or a piece of furniture, calculating how long you want it, will help to guide your selections and what actions to take.

Producing functional time frames, whether it's always, by a certain date, or in certain situations, is an essential part of effective goal setting. Besides health, for things such as wealth and relationships, I recommend using the concept of "always." The quality of our future is largely determined by what we do today. If you always want something, there's a greater tendency for you to do something for it now and on an ongoing basis. At this point, the concept is to be aware of, and to determine, what your time boundaries are for each of your objectives.

How high should you make your aspirations? What are realistic targets to work for? "We rarely get more than we ask for," and if we do, we may be suspicious of it. You can always lower your expectations, but it's hard to raise them once a path is chosen. Having high hopes for a bright tomorrow, positively impacts the quality of today. And again, all we know we really have for sure, is this moment, in this day.

As mentioned in the *Building a Foundation* chapter in the "Wishes and Dreams" section, some goals, especially of a physical nature, can be unrealistic. But, you'll go a lot further if you aim for the sun than if you aim for the moon. Especially if you are prepared sufficiently, in terms of skills, resources, and plans. What is possible for each person to accomplish, is dependent on many factors. Use the concepts and techniques in this book, especially the belief work, and who knows what you might achieve.

Career ambitions have many types of issues to decide upon, depending on the circumstances. In the *Career Checklist* chapter, there is a detailed list of questions to help you determine what job or occupation to pursue. At this point, as another illustration of constructing goals, we'll focus on the wording for a business situation. Some people will have a target to make a certain amount of sales in a year. This could be ineffective because regardless of how much is sold, the expenses or cost of doing business, could be greater, and you can end up with a loss. And just having a goal that people want your product could be ineffective. The desired outcome is for people to want, purchase, pay for at a certain price and within a certain time, enjoy, keep, reorder, and refer your business to others.

Structure goals in terms of the *UER* that you want. The elements in this example for a business owner, are the amount of net profit, doing what with whom, and the nature of the relationship. Possible initial wording could be:

"I (your full name) ALWAYS want to have a minimum net profit of $_____ per year, providing (*type of product or service*), to friendly satisfied profitable loyal repeat long-term customers, who always refer other desirable customers to my company, who also become satisfied profitable loyal repeat long-term referring customers."

This is a good start, and now needs more specifics as discussed in this chapter.

To have a certain minimum net profit, there needs to be a certain amount of sales, a certain type of sale, a certain amount of expenses, and within a certain amount of time. Also, by stating a minimum net profit, there's no limitation on earnings. And at some point, it would probably make sense to up the minimum as each level of net profit is achieved.

Customers in and of themselves, do not guarantee that a business will be successful. They must be the right kind of customers. Pursuing having over 100,000 consumers could cause a company to breakdown and collapse. There are companies that lose money because they have too many customers. Customers that pay late or not at all, that take too much time in relation to the sales that they generate, that return products, that do not do repeat orders, etc., can put a business out of business.

Defining the type of customers depends on each individual company. The goal statement above provides some universal elements that could apply almost anywhere, especially the idea of referring. One of the best ways to get new buyers is through referrals. Having this point in the goal, will affect how an organization is run. The mission to get ongoing, constant, consistent referrals, will impact the decisions that are made, and the way that everything is done.

The focus becomes, "What do we need to do, so that each customer is so happy with us, that they continually give us their business, and that they continually recommend us to others?" Human beings usually enjoy bragging about the great people with whom they do business. "My doctor is the best," "My accountant is wonderful," "You have got to use my tailor," etc. It's also similar to when you see a movie, read a book, or go to a restaurant that you think is so outstanding, that you tell everyone about it.

Make your company so outstanding to your customers, that they are compelled to tell everyone about you.

Affirmations

Some people suggest that goals should be stated as if they've already been completed, in the form of affirmations. "I have $10,000,000," "I am married to my ideal mate," "I am completely healthy," "I am the president of my company," etc. This is fine if in front of the affirmation, there is an opening statement or title such as, "MY GOALS ARE . . ." Otherwise, when it's dealing with things of a material or physical nature, it is fiction.

No matter what you run through the conscious mind, the unconscious knows the truth. Inappropriate affirmations can actually cause someone to be unmotivated, and create problems. I've had many unemployed people end up in my job interviewing workshops, that had affirmed themselves into poverty. Yes, there are stories of some people who talk about using affirmations and eventually achieving them. But when you investigate, you usually find that these people took massive action, constantly learned, and were dedicated to accomplishing their vision. They didn't stop with wishful thinking. Affirmations for them, helped to clarify their thoughts and boost their motivation.

Someone can pump themselves up to feel they have something or that they can do something, and then due to not knowing what they are doing, they can get into trouble. Then, since they "should" be able to have or do something, they feel even worse about themselves because they did not succeed. It's great to always look to learn from each experience. Yet with some endeavors, such as tuning a car, making a speech, or using a computer, without a certain amount of knowledge, very little or no learning will take place. Just "doing" an activity without some level of understanding, information, and skill, can be very ineffective and actually cause backward momentum. Many times people become expert at doing something the wrong way.

What if you actually did make yourself believe untruths? There would be no reason to take action to obtain something that you already have. No action, no result, no change. When we're uncomfortable, have a need, a want, or a desire, then we act! There need to be reasons to change. If someone has everything they want, then why alter the status quo?

If you have no money, you are deep in debt, and your creditors are hounding you, telling yourself you have $10,000,000 will not help. Why bother working or being conservative with your money if you have great wealth? If you're alone and frustrated, telling yourself you already have your ideal mate will not assist you in getting connected. Why bother going to parties and making yourself available to meet new people, if you're already in a great relationship? If you have a chronic illness, repeating that you are healthy could keep you from getting the necessary help. Why bother resting and doing things to heal yourself if you're already healthy?

Dangers of using affirmations can occur in many situations. For example, "I am an incredible salesperson, I can sell anything to anyone, customers come to me effortlessly." With enough repetition, someone could raise their confidence when selling. But they could be too confident. If "I can sell anything to anyone," why bother to plan, prepare, practice, and prospect? Why bother to constantly develop and improve? Why bother to get feedback and help from others? Why bother learning what the customer's needs are, what the competition is doing, and what the trends in an industry are?

Overconfidence can happen in a variety of areas. To be successful in an undertaking, a certain amount of factors such as training, education, information, experience, and skill, are necessary. Having a potential and a capacity is one thing. Having developed the potential into a skill, is a whole other matter. Most people have the ability to use a computer, however they may not have trained, learned, and practiced enough to where they are competent using one. To say, "I am a brilliant investor, everything I invest my money in is profitable," can produce some unfortunate losses. This I know from personal experience, and I've had several unprofitable investments to prove it.

Whether it's communicating, managing, selling, investing, parenting, or exercising, learn what you want to be great at from the best people you can. Trying to fool yourself into believing you have a mastery that you don't, could have unpleasant consequences. I have a multitude of scars to verify the potential hazards of engaging in physical activities with confidence, but without proper competence. Skiing down a steep, icy, bumpy mountain slope without knowing how to do it, provided me with memorable pains, but no new skill or expertise.

Affirmations can make sense if your goal is to achieve certain mental states. Positive self-talk can help to fulfill this end. "I am happy, calm, excited, satisfied, secure, tranquil, blissful, enthusiastic, etc.," are feelings that you can have whenever you wish. Remember the importance of physicality or physical pattern, as related in the *Positive Language Patterns* chapter, when we talked about anger and depression.

Physical patterning can be so useful, it's worthwhile to review the concepts. Get in the physical pattern (posture, breathing, facial expression, muscular tension, and manner of movement) of a desired emotion. How would you look and move when experiencing the emotion? What is the muscle memory linked to this state? Sense how you would feel physically and where the sensation would be most intense in your body. And use your voice (rate, volume, tone) in ways that would be in sync with the emotion that you want. You can do all these steps very quickly, and choose how you feel just about anytime and anyplace.

Getting It on Paper

Write out your goal statements, in the positive, of "WHAT" you want, "WHERE" you want it, "WHEN" you want it, "HOW LONG" you want it, and "WITH WHOM" you want it, as specifically as possible. Consider all the possibilities of what you want to do, have, and be. Would the behavior of others be involved? What results do you want to have happen? What feelings do you want to have? Are money, size, shape, quantity, quality, color, location, etc. involved? Remember we rarely get more than we ask for. If you want eternal life, you may also want to add eternal youthfulness, health, and a certain quality of life.

Just get something down on paper using the examples below as a guide. Once you've gotten started, then you can keep refining your goals to your satisfaction. In part II of this chapter, we'll explore ideas on how to add greater reality to a goal. We may not fully accomplish all that we want, but the journey plays a major part in developing us and what we become.

The following are some samples and illustrations of how to possibly word your goals, and develop them into effective outcomes. The purpose here is to provide you with ideas and starting points, that you can modify and edit to suit your particular desires. Try constructing your statements with and without your complete name after the "I," and see which style works best for you with a particular goal. Remember, if you have in front of your goal statements "My goals are . . .," you would word them as if they had already been fulfilled. "I always want to have," becomes "I always have," "I always want to be," becomes "I always am."

Also, as shown in several of the examples, experiment using "choose" to instead of "want" to. In some goals where you can have a great deal of immediate control over what happens, "choose" can be more effective.

Use each one, and see which is strongest for you with each individual goal.

Financial

"I always want to have a minimum of $10,000,000 net after taxes and debts, all mine to do with whatever I wish, and to achieve this no later than _____."
vs. Have a large net worth.

"I always want to be a brilliant investor, always buying and selling the right investments at the right time for maximum profit for me, at least doubling the net value of my investments every _____ years, for the rest of my life."
vs. Be a good investor.

Career

"I always want (or 'choose') to have a mutually respectful, nurturing, honest, pleasant, compatible, understanding, cooperative, harmonious, accepting, trusting, productive, fulfilling, growing relationship with my boss, co-workers, staff, suppliers, customers, etc."
vs. Get along better with people at work.

"I want to have a job as a _____; for a successful computer graphics software company; that has sales of over _____ per year; that is growing at least 15% per year; located within 30 minutes from where I live; earning and receiving a minimum salary of _____ per year; receiving full medical benefits; working with honest, responsible, upbeat, intelligent, healthy, respectful people; for a minimum of _____ years; from _____ to _____, or until I decide to leave."
vs. Get a new job.

"I always want (or 'choose') to be completely organized, instantly knowing where everything is located, and use my time efficiently and productively, easily, competently, and successfully completing all my projects ahead of schedule and under budget."
vs. Work more efficiently.

"I always want (or 'choose') to be an outstanding salesperson, always exceeding my quotas, earning and receiving a minimum of $_____ per year, easily and effectively connecting with and selling my product to anyone who can use it, who are happy with and keep my product, reorder on an ongoing repeating lifelong basis, on mutually satisfactory terms of price, quantity, delivery, payment date, etc., who buy additional products, and who always refer other desirable profitable satisfied lifelong referring customers to me."
vs. Earn more money.

"I only want to travel overnight, within three hours of my home, a maximum of one night per week, and no more than one week in a row every six months, starting _____."
vs. Do less overnight travel.

"I want a corner office on one of the top four floors, a minimum of 400 square feet, with a clear view over the city, an eight foot mahogany desk, full leather high back chair, and two inch thick beige wool carpeting, at corporate headquarters in Chicago, no later than _____, for as long as I want it."
vs. Get a different office.

"I always want (or 'choose') to have and be a part of completely effective, cooperative, and harmonious teams, where all projects are successfully completed on or before schedule, on or under budget, and where everyone involved learns, grows, prospers, and is entirely satisfied."
vs. Have better teamwork.

"I want to write a fantastic, irresistible, best-selling book about _____, finished and in bookstores no later than _____, that is so outstanding, everyone on earth reads and recommends it, that I receive a minimum of $_____ for, no later than _____, and it becomes a standard textbook in all schools, no later than _____."
vs. Write a book.

Family

"I always want (or 'choose') to be a wonderful parent, helping my children to be the best that they can and want to be; for them to be completely healthy, happy, safe, fulfilled, and for us to be mutually loving, caring, respectful, nurturing, honest, and trusting with each

other."
vs. Be a better parent.

"I always want (or 'choose') to have a mutually loving, caring, nurturing, respectful, cooperative, harmonious, accepting, honest, understanding, sensual, pleasurable, fun, growing, intimate, sharing, trusting, compatible, supportive, and satisfying relationship with my mate."
vs. Not fight as much with my mate.

Recreation

"I always want to be an excellent skier, easily and safely skiing all types of terrain and conditions, including ice, moguls, chutes, powder, trees, slushy crud, fog, cold, and white out."
vs. Be a better skier.

Home

"I always want (or 'choose') to have my closets be totally neat, clean, and organized, and to where I know exactly what's in them, where everything is, and have everything easy to get to."
vs. Have the closets better organized.

"I always want to live in a healthy, safe, clean, beautiful community, surrounded by friendly, kind, supportive, honest, loving, healthy, fun, intelligent people, with an excellent educational system, that has a lot of friendly, healthy, and decent children the same age as mine."
vs. Live in a better neighborhood.

"I want to own free and clear, no later than _____, and live in, from _____ to _____, a 5,000 square foot ranch style home, with 5 bedrooms, 5½ baths, a full finished basement, skylights in every room, brick construction, 4 car garage, on two wooded acres, with a large front yard and long driveway; in a small suburban town, within 30 minutes from a University, 20 minutes from a large shopping center, within 1 hour from a lake, and within 45 minutes from Atlanta."
vs. Have a large nice house.

Personal

"I always want to communicate with everyone easily, effectively, and efficiently, so that there is full mutual understanding, cooperation, and respect, and so that I connect with anyone, anytime, and anywhere."
vs. Improve my communication skills.

"I always want to have things in proper perspective and be in total charge of my emotions, so that I choose how I feel and respond to anything and anyone, anytime, anywhere, and under any circumstances, and that all my thoughts and responses are beneficial, pleasurable, and healthy for me, giving me ongoing contentment and satisfaction."
vs. Have less stress.

"I always want people to treat me with kindness, courtesy, respect, caring, fairness, politeness, trust, openness, patience, cooperation, nurturing, acceptance, consideration, understanding, integrity, and love."
vs. Having people treat me better.

"I always want to think in a clear, logical, focused, efficient, creative, and practical way, so that I make the right decisions and choices, and so that I effectively achieve all my goals in the time frames that I set for them, and in the best manner possible."
vs. Be clearer thinking.

"I always want (or 'choose') to have high self-esteem, truly like and love myself, feel secure, confident, worthwhile, and in control, and constantly think and behave in positive ways that support, maintain, and enhance my sense of self-worth."
vs. Have higher self-esteem.

"I always want (or 'choose') to feel great, focus on what I love and find beautiful, live every second of every day in total loving bliss, and to enrich myself by enriching others."
vs. Have more inner peace.

Wording goals when it's dealing with people, can have many similar characteristics. Whether someone is an intimate family member, a business associate, or a total stranger, certain helpful attitudes will be appreciated. Things such as kindness, trust, honesty, acceptance, respect, fairness, patience, and cooperation, are welcomed in any situation. When we treat each other in positive ways, everyone benefits.

Part II

Deciding and choosing the *UER* is the first step in wording and getting specific about a goal. Next, is further development and refinement of your criteria and guidelines for each objective. In other words, how will you know you have achieved your desired results? How do you know you have it? How will you be convinced that you have obtained your outcome? What is the evidence and proof that you have what you want? What will you see, hear, feel, taste, and smell? Imagine you've achieved your goal, how do you know that it works for you, and that you are happy with it?

Some of the above goal statements have part of the details fleshed out, but more defined information can be identified and added to them. Having a clear set of requirements gives you a way to measure the results you are creating. This gives you the feedback necessary to make adjustments to keep you on track to your destination.

Buying something, making a decision, or going somewhere without enough complete specifications, can cause unhappy conclusions. Have you ever taken a job, started a business, or entered into a relationship where it proved unsatisfactory? By developing checklists, and determining what is ideal, and what is acceptable beforehand, we can make gratifying choices.

Using all of the five senses, we can make your ambitions come alive. Set up a sheet with your name at the top and with your goal statement written out as fully as you can. When you do this part, start with the easiest sense first. For instance, when buying a new car, some people will be most aware of the appearance. Other people focus on what can be heard. They open and close the doors and trunk, tune in the radio, and listen to how the engine sounds. And others get into the feel of the seat and need to go for a test drive to sense the handling. Begin with the most noticeable sense, and then fill in the next most obvious.

You may not have every one of these senses working consciously for every goal, however go ahead and ask anyway and see what happens. As with all the questions in *Anatomy of Success*, you might not receive an immediate answer, but by merely asking the questions you become more directed and achieve better results.

See

What would you see to be certain that you have realized your goal? What people, places, and things are present? How are other people affected? How do you look because you have succeeded—your posture, your facial expression, your energy level, your movements, your clothing? Is there a particular color that seems to represent your success?

Look beyond the obvious. What other things might you see that are proof of your accomplishment: your picture in the paper or a company magazine, a television interview, a diploma or license, an airplane ticket, a smile of appreciation, a certain place, a particular activity, etc.? Have some fun, make the dream as detailed and real as possible.

Let's use the goal of you having over $10,000,000 net after taxes and debts, all yours to do with as you wish. What might you see as proof of you having this goal?

- blueprints for your new 5,000 square foot home
- pictures from your trip around the world
- new 20 bed hospital wing you donated
- closets filled with your favorite clothes
- the smiling faces of people you help
- your new car at the car wash
- people dancing at parties you give
- your tax return with huge interest income
- statements showing your vast investments
- your 90' yacht docked in the harbor
- taking a group of 200 people to a concert

Allow your mind to look at and see all the wonderful things that occur because you have obtained an objective.

Let's use another example for what might be seen. The career goal of:

"I always want (or 'choose') to be an outstanding salesperson, always exceeding my quotas, earning and receiving a minimum of $_____ per year, easily and effectively connecting with and selling my product to anyone who can use it, who are happy with and keep my product, reorder on an ongoing repeating life-long basis, on mutually satisfactory terms of price, quantity, delivery, payment date, etc., who buy additional products, and who always refer other desirable profitable satisfied lifelong referring customers to me."

Some of the things that might be seen as confirmation of this objective being accomplished are:

- receiving unsolicited orders from clients
- smiles of appreciation from sales manager
- receiving award for sales achievement
- name in company newsletter as top salesperson
- clients introducing you to referrals
- thank you cards from customers
- 10% bonus check from company president
- product being delivered to client
- having dinner with company president
- driving new company car
- clients businesses improving by over 25%
- audience of your peers listening to you speak

What would you see that verifies you have acquired your outcomes?

Hear

Now let's investigate what you might hear when you've fulfilled a goal. What words, sounds, and music would you hear? What do you say to yourself, and how do you say it? What tone does your voice have? Are there sounds of nature or machines present? What kind of conversations are going on? What do people say to you? What do you say to others? Is there any special music or a certain sound that represents your accomplishment?

Again use your imagination about other possible things you might hear that confirm you've gained your outcome. Perhaps you hear people talking about your success, or giving you compliments. Maybe someone interviews you about how you attained your goal. Or you hear your achievement announced at a meeting or on the radio. What are the possibilities? Do you hear the wind, birds, crashing waves, people cheering, splashing into a pool, the roar of a sports car engine, etc.?

Feel

When we get into what you would feel when you've reached your destination, there are two aspects. One is the physical sensations, the other the emotional feelings. What would you experience in terms of textures, temperature, muscular tension, etc.? What would your clothes feel like, the furniture you're sitting on, the comfort level of your body? What are you actually doing? What kind of movements do you have? What is your overall sense of your physical being?

Emotional feelings are the main reasons why we do anything. They are our most powerful motivators. What wonderful mental sensations are you experiencing because you have achieved a particular outcome? Do you feel happy, free, proud, secure, excited, worthwhile, and so on? In *The Benefits* chapter, Figure 4-1 provides you with a list of major feelings that can be desirable. Which of them does fulfilling each goal provide?

Taste and Smell

Taste and smell may not be obvious for a given goal, but ask anyway. Are there any foods, beverages, colognes, flowers, plants, or items that provide any savory or aromatic elements that you associate to having your objective? Whether it's a new car, an island vacation, a trip to the mountains, or a special restaurant, there are tastes and smells that can have positive associations. Ask the questions, and experience the "taste of victory" and the "sweet smell of success."

Knowing Through the Senses

Let's look at the possible wording for a romantic relationship again:

"I always want (or 'choose') to have a mutually loving, caring, nurturing, respectful, cooperative, harmonious, accepting, honest, understanding, sensual, pleasurable, fun, growing, intimate, sharing, trusting, compatible, supportive, and satisfying relationship with my mate."

How would someone know that they had achieved this goal? What would they see, hear, feel, taste, and smell? What would actually happen so that they know they have what they want?

SEE: sharing certain activities, smiles, having their full attention, certain facial expressions, gifts, romantic cards, they dress in a certain way, greeting you at the door when you come home, they do certain things for you.

HEAR: praise, compliments, asking your opinion, concern for your well-being, laughter, acceptance of your ideas, an interest in you, understanding of your feelings, encouragement of your ambitions, a certain tone of voice, playing your favorite music.

FEEL: affection, holding hands, cuddling, massages, intimacy; safe, secure, free, energetic, proud, at peace, worthwhile, valued, trusted, connected, fulfilled.

TASTE and SMELL: certain foods, beverages, flowers, candles, colognes, incense, etc.

What would it take for you to believe that you are satisfied with what you have in your relationship?

Health is another objective worth examining using this viewpoint. Some of the points that could be a part of a health goal are: energy, blood pressure, heart rate, cholesterol, immune system, digestion, assimilation, sleep, dreams, skin, body fat, muscle tone, elimination, sensuality, hair, breathing, stamina, teeth, gums, nails, hearing, eyes, bones, healing, flexibility, strength, internal organs, blood vessels, feet, circulation, coordination, measurements, mental states, etc.

Restating the health goal from the early part of this chapter:

"I (your full name), ALWAYS want (or 'choose') to be completely healthy, mentally, physically, emotionally, and spiritually, feel great, be strong, coordinated, athletic, clear thinking, youthful, have all the energy I want, blood pressure 120/80, resting pulse 50, weigh _____ lean, fit, and toned pounds, with (neck, chest, arms, stomach, hips, thighs, and calves) measurements."

How would someone know that these health objectives are being reached? What is possible evidence that these outcomes are a reality? Some things could be:

SEE: a report stating excellent health, a sparkle in the eyes, clear smooth skin, a glowing complexion, fitting into a certain size of clothing, smiles of admiration, beautiful dreams, plates of nutritious and nutritiously prepared foods, glasses of pure water and healthy beverages, healthy teeth and gums, the view from the top of a mountain just climbed, video of self dancing energetically at a party, exercising in a health club.

HEAR: doctor and dentist saying how great your checkups are, getting compliments, full smooth breathing, someone asking you how you stay so healthy, the noise of a boat water-skied behind, the sound of a golf club connecting with the ball, saying out loud how great you feel, water splashing as you swim 50 laps.

FEEL: energy to work and play as long as you want, dancing all night, walking 10 miles easily, perfect digestion, upright posture, easily falling asleep, waking up refreshed and energetic, lifting heavy objects with ease, free and comfortable movements; a sense of happiness, easily handling pressure and stress.

TASTE and SMELL: sweet breath, fresh fruits and vegetables, pure water, nutritious foods; pine trees on a mountain trail, sunbathed skin, the aromas of nutritious foods.

What would you be experiencing at all levels when you have the health that you want?

As you move toward the fulfillment of your goals and continue to learn, keep adding to and refining your guidelines for success. Again, strive for the *UER*, because "We rarely get more that we ask for." Consider all the possibilities and be thorough, so that you can make choices that you find rewarding. Gain the clarity that is a critical component of motivating yourself on a consistent basis.

Knowing clearly and specifically what you want is the first step. Once this is reached, "how" and "what" type questions will move the process to the next level. They presuppose and assume there is a way. Keep asking yourself, "How can I (your goal)?," and "What do I need to do to (your goal)?" For example, "How can I always be healthy mentally, physically, emotionally, and spiritually, . . .?," and "What do I need to do to always be healthy mentally, physically, emotionally, and spiritually, . . .?" The better the questions, the stronger the focus, the better the answers. Subsequent chapters will be dealing with the details of "how" and "what" questions, and will guide you to be prepared and to set up your action plan to achievement.

In the next chapter we'll get into the benefits you'll receive from obtaining a goal, and charging up your motivation.

---- *Chapter 4* ----

THE
BENEFITS

---- ● ● ● ----

MAJOR KEY TO MOTIVATION

Motivation, taking action, and staying persistent have seven elements. We've covered two of them, clarity of purpose or how to specifically word your goals, and knowing yourself or your values, beliefs, abilities, skills, and self-concept. We also began the process of managing any limiting beliefs, and establishing the necessary empowering beliefs. We will get into much greater depth on beliefs in future chapters.

Benefits that you will gain by achieving your objective, is the next major aspect of motivation we'll explore. To have maximum sustained output, it's important to be in the state of mind that you absolutely positively totally must have a particular goal. Only then, as mentioned in the preface, will you be willing to *WIN*, to do *Whatever Is Necessary*, to be successful.

What will having a goal do for you? Why do you want it? How will it improve your positive experience of life? How will it affect your family, career, friends, health, finances, etc.? Why is achieving it so worthwhile, that no matter what happens, you will be unstoppable until you succeed? What is it that will drive you to reach your destination?

EVERYTHING WE DO in life, we do to experience a sense of being, TO HAVE A FEELING. We do things and buy things so that we can ultimately own certain emotional states. Even sought after physical sensations, such as warmth, comfort, and relaxation, could end with emotional components such as security, contentment, and pleasure. Again by being an active listener, you will hear the feelings that people desire to obtain. Figure 4-1 gives you examples of feelings that are often strived for. Which of these are strong motivators in your life? Underline or circle the feelings that you want to have on a daily basis. Also, add any other ones that aren't on this list. Many of these feelings may seem similar, however they can have different levels of meaning to different people.

Discovering the feelings that will motivate you, begins with questions such as:

"What are the benefits to me of reaching this goal?"
"What will this goal allow me to do, have, and be in all areas of my life?"
"How will I be better off because I've achieved this goal?"
"What's really important to me about this goal?"
"Why do I absolutely positively totally need to make this goal a reality?"

Head up another piece of paper with your name and a goal at the top. Then write out all the benefits this objective will provide for you. Look at the career goal example, Figure 4-2 (for more detail on job aspirations, see the questions in the *Career Checklist* chapter). It's important that you allow yourself to write down whatever comes to mind. Just let your thoughts flow spontaneously.

FIGURE 4-1:
The Feelings of Motivation

• • •

accepted	decent	informed	relaxed
adventurous	decisive	in love	respected
appreciated	desired	inspired	responsible
athletic	ecstasy	intelligent	right
attractive	educated	intimate	romantic
aware	efficient	invigorated	safe
balanced	elated	involved	sane
belong	energetic	joyful	satisfied
blessed	ethical	kind	secure
bliss	excited	loved	self-respect
brave	fair	loving	sensual
calm	feminine	masculine	special
capable	focused	mature	spiritual
caring	free	motivated	strong
cared for	friendly	natural	successful
challenge	fulfilled	needed	superior
charming	generous	noble	sympathetic
classy	gentle	nurtured	tenderness
clean	genuine	nurturing	thorough
closeness	good	organized	thrilled
closure	great	passionate	trusted
complete	growing	peaceful	trusting
comfortable	happy	playful	understood
companionship	harmony	pleasure	upbeat
competent	healthy	poised	warmth
confident	helpful	popular	wealthy
connected	hopeful	positive	whole
contentment	humble	powerful	wise
control	important	productive	wonderful
coordinated	independent	proper	worthwhile
creative	influential	proud	youthful

FIGURE 4-2:
"Goal"

• • •

"I (your name) have a job as a _____; for a success-ful computer graphics software company; that has sales of over _____ per year; that is growing at least 15% per year; located within 30 minutes from where I live; earning a minimum salary of _____ per year; receiving full medical benefits; working with hon-est, responsible, upbeat, intelligent, healthy, respectful people; for a mini-mum of _____ years; from _____ to _____."

- What will this goal allow me to DO, HAVE, and BE, in all parts of my life?

BENEFITS:
Money

Help people

Feel successful

Freedom

Feel proud

Self-esteem

Challenge

Control

Learning

Provide for family

Creativity

Companionship

Belonging

Feel productive

After you list out as many benefits as you can think of, we go to the next step. Take each benefit separately, and to find out what each one really means to you, ask "What's the benefit of this benefit?" Continue asking what is the benefit of each subsequent benefit, until no more answers come to mind, and a final feeling surfaces. See Figure 4-3 (note: these examples are combined from different people to illustrate the process). Remember, there are no right or wrong answers for these exercises. Only what's important to you, now. This is about self-discovery. Just let the ideas flow without restriction.

If a feeling comes up as a benefit, or a benefit comes up more than once, keep asking, "What's the benefit of this benefit?," or "What's the benefit of that?" It's common for some benefits to come up several times. Often a benefit will be linked to other ideas when it appears again. Sometimes an answer will not seem to make any sense, or have nothing to do with the prior thought. The key is to not evaluate your answers, and to continue with the questioning until your brain stops! A string of benefits might be five or fifty-five. Just keep asking with an open mind. Bottom line, the more benefits the better it will work for you.

Some people may try to get through this section quickly by getting to the ultimate final feeling of each benefit as soon as possible. That could be limiting. The point of using this technique is to find and construct as large a list of benefits as possible, with the motivating feelings. The more reasons you have for obtaining something, the more valuable it is, the more energy and resources you'll put into getting it. And the more likely you'll do what's necessary to do the right thing, in the right way, at the right time.

Remember to keep focused on the positive of what you "do" want. If a benefit is that you won't be "stressed out," what's the opposite of that? That you'll be "calm and relaxed." If a benefit is that you and your spouse won't "argue" anymore, the opposite is that you'll have "harmony and cooperation." If the benefit is that you won't be "sick and tired," the positive is that you'll be "healthy and energetic."

When doing this process, you only need to write down the key words or phrase that represents a benefit. For instance, if an answer is, "So that I can take care of my wife and children," just write down "take care of family." If a benefit is, "To move up the corporate ladder and become the V.P.," just write "become V.P." What is the essence of each statement? The target is to get as much information as possible condensed into a small space for greatest impact. Again there are no right or wrong answers. Just let your thoughts flow freely. Allow your mind to reveal to you what is stored at subconscious levels. Some people receive powerful insights about themselves when they do this questioning.

FIGURE 4-3:
Benefit of the Benefit

• • •

GOAL: "I (your name) have a job as a _____."

- What will this goal allow me to DO, HAVE, and BE, in all parts of my life? What are the ultimate FEELINGS it will provide for me?

BENEFITS: Money; Help people; Feel successful; Freedom; Feel proud; Self-esteem; etc.

Money: buy what I want—have a five-bedroom home—take care of my family—feel good—happier—do more things—fun—more friends—(won't be lonely)—companionship—feel confident—do more things—learn—grow—be productive—satisfaction—higher self-esteem—healthier—live longer—pleasure—live life to fullest—feel fulfilled—have a good life—feel satisfied—*feel at peace.*

Help people: I made a difference—make world a better place—people happier—people kinder—better place raise my children—children happy—children reach full potential—proud of them—I did right thing—feel worthwhile—be upbeat—better relationship with spouse—proud—self-confidence—more open—try new things—added opportunities—learn more—greater success—freedom—*feel secure.*

Feel successful: sense of achievement—feel good about myself—communicate with others—better relationships—achieve goals—self-esteem—feel good—be happy—self-confidence—take risks—get involved—be productive—accomplish more—feel worthwhile—(not be afraid)—feel safe—(less stress)—be calm—feel relaxed—pleasant to be around—people like me—get more done—be efficient—save time—get more done—*feel successful.*

Freedom: do what I want when I want—face challenges—know myself—feel great—be energized—enjoy things fully—feel alive—motivate other people—people happy—pleasant to be with—joy—happiness—I'm motivated—experience new things—travel around the world—have adventures—meet new people—learn—understand things—satisfy curiosity—be informed—*feel self-respect.*

FIGURE 4-3:
Benefit of the Benefit (continued)

• • •

Feel proud: sense of excellence—do quality work—recognition—sense of value—feel qualified—confidence—feel capable—feel good about myself—feel worthwhile—security—be loving—create love—world is better—everyone wins—people like themselves—treat each other better—everyone happier—everyone healthier—more fun—joy—feel connected—*feel safe.*

Self-esteem: feel worthwhile—confident—feel comfortable—friendlier—get along with people—trust—harmony—cooperation—work well together—get more done—feel capable—enjoy what I do—feel good—feel secure—feel I belong—be focused—organized—in control—decisive—power—freedom—feel special—feel wonderful—*feel at peace*

Pairing up to do this process can be very helpful. Doing this section with someone you trust and are comfortable with, can enhance your experience. Get in a relaxed posture and possibly close your eyes, and have your partner guide you through the questions and jot down all your responses. By doing this, you can freely associate without analyzing your answers. Working this way can yield high quality information, and feel like a mental massage.

Give this technique your full attention and all the time that it requires. It's vital to do it now to get and maintain your motivation in gear. I've worked with private clients as long as 90 minutes fleshing out this exercise. These benefits and feelings will act as magnets pulling you forward toward your goal. These are the "carrots;" in a later chapter we'll deal with the "sticks," the consequences of not completing a mission.

Another useful aspect of doing this exercise, is that your values as they relate to this goal, will show up. You may notice that several benefits and feelings appear often, which can reveal what's very important to you now. Once certain fundamental values are satisfied, there's more opportunity for other higher purpose values to be fulfilled.

When you've written out all your answers, compare the values that come out of this process, with your life values. See if they are basically in harmony. For example, if companionship is one of your top life values, and your career value of challenge keeps you traveling 70 percent of the time, dissatisfaction is sure to follow. There's tremendous power in knowing oneself and being true to that identity, and these exercises will assist you in gaining that knowledge.

Motivation can require encouragement to maintain. Keep adding to your list of benefits. Keep refining and enriching it to make it as powerful as you can. As time goes on, your answers may change. Daily, in the morning and before going to sleep at night, briefly look at your benefits list for all your goals, as in Figure 4-3. Use them as a constant reminders as to why it's so meaningful for you to achieve your goals. Use it to start and end your day on a positive note. *"What we concentrate on, we tend to create."*

Into The Future

Time frames can play a significant role in developing the benefits that will move you to act. A future orientation affects current behavior. The bigger the perceived payoff down the road, the greater the motivation to do something now.

Imagine you have achieved an objective, and then project yourself into that future time. What has having this goal helped you to do, have, and be six months, one year, and five years after its attainment? How has this goal helped you to achieve other goals? What are the benefits for yourself and others? Put together a page as in Figure 4-4, going through time with the benefits of having produced this result. What is different, and what have you gained, in the various parts of your life?

Let's take one time frame at a time. Envision you've accomplished your objective and it's six months later. What are all the advantages you've experienced? If your goal is involved with money, what will you have done and bought because of your achievement? Did you do or buy something for someone else? Have you become more as a person? Do you have more self-esteem, confidence, stature, health, contentment, etc., or just feel good?

Now go out one year after fulfilling your pursuit, and apply the same questions. Twelve months later your responses to the questions might be different or the same. A meaningful future helps to form a meaningful present. To have long-term change, you need a perspective on long-term benefits.

Dealing with five years after achieving a goal, there are two aspects. First apply the previous questions of what you have been able to do, have, and be because of this goal. Then ask yourself where you want to be in five years. What do you want your life to be like? What do you want to be doing, and with whom? Where do you want to be living? What do you want to be as a person mentally, physically, spiritually, socially, and so forth? Will fulfilling this goal and the other things that you're doing, help you get to where you want to be? Remember that you may change direction at any time, and that it's the quest for one thing that can put us in touch with who we are, and the possibilities life has to offer.

The positive effect some goals might have on your future, may not be clear cut. If your intention is to get a new car, the benefits in the future may not seem obvious, but ask yourself the questions anyhow. A new car may help you to be more relaxed, thus have more energy, be more productive, think more clearly, have greater self-esteem, and therefore be in a better position to achieve other goals. Each individual action now, can play a major role in forming your future. A sense of a bright future, establishes hope and optimism, which leads to being productive in the present.

When I was producing my film, every week there were new challenges. Investors would drop out, the budget would increase, an actor or crew person would quit, locations would fall through, a distributor would cancel a contract, to name a few. But I kept focusing on the future, on what I wanted years down the road, and I kept on going until I made my dream come true.

Challenges became even larger after the film was completed. I had one distributor as a "friend," tell us that the film was hopeless, and that we should just dig a hole and bury it. Suggesting that I take two years of my life, all my money, and all my ambitions and throw it all away, was not what I wanted to hear. And as with so many motion pictures, others had given their all to the project and were equally disappointed.

Fortunately I had wonderful people that helped to keep me going and to look for other answers. We eventually raised more money, re-edited the entire movie, and did achieve a limited worldwide release of the film. The project was not a success, but the experience and the learning it provided, enabled me to be successful in other projects. I used what I had achieved (such as wrote the script, raised the money, put the deal together, completed the filming, finished the editing, sold it to a distributor, and saw it in theaters), to empower me, versus positioning the whole project as a failure. Even though an ultimate objective is not reached, the completion of any step is the successful achievement of a goal. Look at each result as something to learn from and to nurture yourself.

In the next chapter we'll delve into special techniques on visualization, and on how to conceive and compose a clear image of your success.

FIGURE 4-4:
Into the Future

● ● ●

GOAL: "I (your name) have a job as a _____."

● What will this goal allow me to DO, HAVE, and BE in the future?

Six months after attaining the goal: I paid off 2 credit cards, weekend trip to the beach, dinner with friends twice a month, better relationship with my family, blood pressure down 5%, fixed up car, feel good.

One year after attaining the goal: I bought new living room furniture, paid off all credit cards, one week vacation in the Rockies, volunteer work one day per month, great relationship with my family, feel close to friends, finished all projects on or ahead of schedule, obtained a 10% raise, high self-esteem, started saving for retirement, got weight to where I want it, get along great with co-workers and clients.

Five years after attaining the goal: I received several raises to where my salary has doubled from 5 years ago, promoted to V.P., bought new car, bought new 6-bedroom home, travelled to Europe for 2 weeks on second honeymoon, learned scuba diving, raised money for charity, received commendation in company newsletter, received praise from clients, acted as mentor for new employers, have solid retirement fund, made profitable investments that more than doubled, health and energy level excellent, learned a new language, wrote first half of a novel, wake up each morning thrilled to be alive.

Chapter 5

EFFECTIVE VISUALIZATION

● ● ●

SEEING IS BELIEVING

Visualization is the activity of forming mental images or pictures. People have used imagining their wishes for everything from curing an illness, to excelling in athletics, to having self-confidence. All with varying degrees of success.

Why does it work so well in some cases and not in others? It could have to do with one's values, beliefs, and self-concept. Sometimes it's because people are unaware of how to do it for maximum results, which is what this chapter is about.

Since visualization is a powerful tool used by so many successful people, we'll cover how to use it productively for yourself. As we know "seeing is believing" in most situations. In the case of accomplishing goals, it's hard to hit a target if you can't see what it is. When we have a picture of our end result, this contributes toward a positive expectation of success. What we see, we are more likely to do. It helps us to employ all of our resources and abilities. We tend to take action with greater poise and confidence, which can yield better outcomes.

Effective visualization helps to make the unknown known. It's a method for taking a test drive, a dress rehearsal, trying something on before you buy. It allows you to safely practice before it counts. Deeply using the imagination can in fact activate the muscles and provide an experience of an accomplishment even though it has not happened, yet. Research has shown that visualizing something with enough emotion, creates essentially the same brain patterns as actually doing it. Learning can occur during visualization that can assist the realization of something in tangible terms. And using full visualization on a regular basis, can actually strengthen your mental powers by forming more connections between your brain cells!

"Practice makes perfect," is an old saying, but perfect what? If we keep practicing doing something incorrectly, all we do is perfect error and imperfection. This is illustrated in sports. How often do we get into the habit of doing things one way in a sport, and we are unable to progress. When we learn the right way, it can be difficult to get rid of the old habits, but when we do, our performance improves dramatically. Visualization can be an important part of the process.

Nikola Tesla, a famous inventor and electrical engineer, was reported to be an expert at visualizing. He would conceive of an invention only in his mind, with as much detail as he could. Then he would put the idea away for a period of time. When he came back to his mental invention, he was able to see what worked and what didn't, and how the invention needed to be changed. And he did this all in his mind.

Modeling is a concept we talked about in the *Building a Foundation* chapter. One way to use visualization, is to think of someone who has achieved what you want, or you feel could do it, and imagine how they would go about attaining your objective. What would they think, believe, and do? How would they behave? Who would they seek for help? What knowledge, skills, and experience would they need? Seeing on your mental screen how someone else would succeed at something, can give you an insight and outlook that will assist you in succeeding.

Everyone can increase their ability to visualize through practice and special techniques. In life "use it or lose it," is usually true. One way to improve your imaging ability, is to look at a photo, study it for a moment, and then close your eyes. Picture as much of the photo as you can mentally, while recording your observations into a tape recorder. Open your eyes, look at the photo again, listen to your tape, and see what you missed. Repeat the process until you can form a clear image of the photo in your mind. A few moments of daily practice will give you many benefits. Remember, not everyone sees crystal clear color images when they visualize. Doing the best you can, should yield positive results.

What data should be in your visualizations? Start with the information that you put together for your criteria in the "Wording Your Goals" chapter. What specifically do you want, and how will you know you have it?

To have a powerful vision, imagine the input you receive from all of your five senses. What would you see, hear, feel, taste, and smell when you have achieved your goal? Again, use things that are evidence that you have your desired result. Envision and feel your success as vividly as possible, with as much detail as you can. See yourself doing, having, and being what you want. Continually give directions to your brain of what you want it to produce. Using photos, videotapes, and drawings of your goals, is also highly recommended.

An exercise that can be useful, is to visualize people who are important to you, watching television. What they're watching is you being interviewed about how you accomplished an objective. See them delighting in your success and in the fact that they know you. Through association, your triumph becomes their triumph. This can be an effective way to make your imaging dynamic and tangible.

As with anything new, there might be an adjustment period before you're comfortable using the following techniques. Keep in mind the many ways that visualization can be worthwhile to you. It helps to make your goals concrete and real, enhancing your belief that you can have a goal. It assists you in recognizing any obstacles and preparing to handle them. It boosts morale and motivation, by giving you a means to constantly focus on what you want. And it strengthens your capacity to fully apply all of your potential and abilities. Understand your peak performance by experiencing your outcomes successfully beforehand.

Photography, motion pictures, and videotaping supply some of the elements that you can adjust to make your internal representations stronger and more effective. When you take photos, notice what changes you make as you arrange things to make them attractive to you. When taking motion pictures or videotaping, some of the things that can be adjusted are:

- lighting—level of brightness in the scene
- contrast—difference between light and dark areas
- color—the intensity and tint, or black and white
- camera angle—straight on, from the side, high, or low
- image size—distance from the camera
- image movement—freeze frame, or moving pictures: regular, fast, or slow speed
- focus—how blurred or sharp and defined the image is
- composition—what is seen in the scene, and where it's placed
- camera movement—stationary or moving, and at what speed

In addition, with film and tape, we can control the sounds through volume, tone, rate, and the types of sounds including voices, music, machines, and nature.

While you do your visualizations, you can also regulate physical feelings such as the temperature and bodily sensations, what you smell, and any tastes that enhance your experience. And lastly, you can manage and sense the emotional feelings (such as joyful, secure, and content) that you would have as a result of reaching a goal. Adjust all the possible variables to make your dreams come alive at a level that is most desirable and enjoyable for you!

There are certain methods to developing effective visualizations. First, let's get you in a resourceful receptive state of being. Refer back to your list of successes that you put together in the *Building a Foundation* chapter. As you recall all your achievements, form images of them in your mind. Also remember the sounds, feelings, tastes, and smells that come into your memory as you think about your accomplishments.

Your eyes can help to tap into the part of your mind that is used for visualizing. By moving our eyes in a certain way, we cause specific parts of the brain to be activated. Have you ever watched good spellers, where do their eyes go? They usually go up. Since so many words in English cannot be spelled phonetically, a good speller must memorize the way that words look. When they look up, they are tapping into the visual channel of their brain. They literally see a picture of a word in their mind's eye, and read what they see aloud.

When people are making pictures in their head, their eyes basically go into one of two positions. Either the eyes go up or they have a unfocused stare, and sometimes the eyelids will flutter rapidly. Ask someone a question about remembering how something looks, and watch what happens with their eyes.

To begin your visualization session, first determine the goal that you want to work on. What is the *UER*, the *Ultimate End Result* that you want? Achieve clarity before doing anything else. Then sit in a comfortable and supportive chair, in a quiet place where you won't be disturbed. Take a diaphragmatic breath, pushing your stomach out as you inhale, and pulling your stomach in as you exhale. Do three of these breaths allowing yourself to relax more and more with each movement. It's meaningful that you do this at an intensity that is easy and pleasant for you. Just focusing on, and noticing your breathing is beneficial.

Next, while keeping your head stationary, look up with your eyes only, as high as you can comfortably (it is very important to ONLY move your eyes up to a comfortable level and no farther). Take another deep breath and as you exhale let your eyelids slowly close. With each breath you take, and with each sound you hear, allow yourself to become more and more relaxed.

Begin relaxing your body starting with your face and jaw, then your eyelids, your forehead, your scalp, and on down through your neck, shoulders, arms, hands, back, chest, stomach, hips, legs, and feet; your whole body. The face is the key. Relaxing your facial muscles sends a message of relaxation to the whole system. Allow a wonderful, comfortable feeling of relaxation to flow through your entire being. If something distracts you, let it pass, and as you refocus, allow yourself to become even more relaxed.

After you're relaxed, see a mental picture of yourself doing, having, and being what you want. Create an image that represents and illustrates the achievement of your goal. This is the objective position, with you in the picture as in a photograph, or being filmed. Again remember to use all of your five senses, and to use as much detail as possible. If you have some difficulty in seeing crystal clear images, it's okay. Regardless of the quality of your images, the more you practice these techniques, the greater the benefits. Your conscious mind may currently not have a full vision, but your unconscious mind still receives the message.

Explore using all the elements in different ways. Vary the angle from straight on to a side view, from very low to way up high, and everything in between. Experiment with placing yourself in different parts of the frame. Alter your image size by moving it farther away and then closer in. Shift the lighting from dim to bright, and from low contrast to high contrast. Change the focus from soft to very sharp, for greatest clarity. Is there a color that you associate with this achievement? Bathe the scene, or parts of it, with this color. Modify the sounds you hear, louder and softer, more or less bass and treble, faster and slower. Then sense all the wonderful physical and emotional feelings that you are experiencing.

When you are able to observe yourself having what you want, examine another perspective. Move to a subjective viewpoint. In other words, see the evidence of your success without you in the scene, through your own eyes, the way you normally see the world. In this subjective outlook, get deeper into the pleasurable feelings of having fulfilled your desires. Fully experience and lock-in the positive emotions of accomplishment. After you are able to get into the sense of being successful, return to the objective position where you again see yourself in the scene.

"Full Spectrum" Visualization

There are unique methods to pack power into your visualizations. These ideas are sometimes seen in films and videotapes. As if looking through the lens of a camera, see yourself as the star of your own production. Start off the scene by seeing yourself successfully having your goal. What kind of expression do you have on your face? How do you move? What kind of clothes are you wearing? Where is this taking place? Who else might be there? What things (furniture, stereos, artwork, etc.) are there? What's the lighting like? What do you talk about? What qualities does your voice have? What do other people in the scene talk about? What other sounds are present? How does your body feel, and where are the sensations the strongest? How do your clothes feel on your skin? What is the air temperature? What do you smell? What kind of taste do you have in your mouth? What emotional feelings do you have?

Begin recording with the camera seeing you from the front. Then have the camera move completely around you in a clockwise rotation, ending where it began. Have the camera see and record you and everything that is there, from all different viewpoints. Make it as real as possible.

Once the camera has moved all the way around you going clockwise, do the same thing in a counterclockwise direction. Then one more time, have the camera go all the way around you in a clockwise rotation. Each time the camera goes completely around you, see and hear things that you didn't notice before. Perhaps rearrange, add, or subtract things. Change the speed at which the camera moves around you. Zoom out and zoom in. This is a place to really experiment, and to continually enrich the images.

Keep making adjustments (lighting, focus, distance, composition, sounds, feelings, etc.), designing a three-dimensional portrayal of you having and enjoying your goal. The idea is to fine-tune the scene, just like you do with your television and VCR, until it's the most appealing to you. "Full Spectrum" Visualization, is a tool to make your desires real and to move you closer to them.

"Reflection Realization" Visualization

Another special approach to assist you in constructing effective visualizations, is "Reflection Realization." Begin by seeing yourself having and enjoying a particular goal. Then imagine there is a huge mirror in the scene. Face the mirror and see a crystal clear reflection of you appreciating the realization of your objective. At this point, you are seeing two images of yourself, from two distinct perspectives. You are seeing yourself from behind, and a mirrored reflection of the front of you, at the same time.

Mirrors placed in several places at different angles, is an additional variation on this technique. Imagine watching yourself viewing yourself in three mirrors set at separate angles, as in many clothing stores. Some people will take this even further, by mirroring the entire setting. All the walls, the floor, and the ceiling have mirrors, and they show every aspect of the scene. Experiment with various quantities and positions of mirrors, that are the most powerful and effective for each of your goals.

Seeing yourself seeing yourself, could require a lot of focus and attention. This causes involvement, and contributes to developing your visualizations. As with the "Full Spectrum" formula, adjust all the possible variables (lighting, focus, angle, and so on) until the vision is the most desirable to you.

When you are able to see two viewpoints of yourself, add another step. As if looking through a camera, move in or zoom in, so that you now only see one image of yourself, the reflection of you in the mirror. This is essentially what you see anytime you look in a mirror. After you've done this, change the composition by moving the camera back to where you again are seeing yourself seeing yourself in the mirror. Shift back and forth several times between these two perspectives for maximum benefit.

"Full Spectrum" Visualization and "Reflection Realization" Visualization, can employ a great deal of concentration and imagining. They will strengthen these skills as well as increase the power and influence of your visualizations. This helps you to be in control of staying motivated, and bolstering your beliefs in what is possible. Habits are created and reinforced through repetition. By practicing these techniques a few minutes a day, you should be able to use them whenever and wherever you wish, to assist you in obtaining all your objectives.

Negative stimuli can bombard us on a daily basis. It's up to us to choose what we pay attention to, and how we respond. Having the ability to change your internal channels, allows you to determine your emotional state and therefore the quality of your experiences. Effective visualization can be an important part of tapping into this ability.

Anticipating, mentally rehearsing, projecting what might happen, can drain us, or charge us up so that we can be at our best. How often do we become afraid or excited before an event happens? We learn how to respond as we grow up. To be in a specific state of mind, we make certain pictures in our head, think certain thoughts, have a particular posture, breathe in an exact manner, etc. Learning to manage your internal pictures, will provide you with many external gains.

Once you have the visualization of attaining your goal in the future, look back toward now, and see all the things that you did to be successful. See how you did it. What did you do, how did you do it, and when did you do it? Was anyone else involved? See yourself enjoying the actions you took to make your dream a reality. If you need to do something, you may as well enjoy it.

Locking in the positive feelings you have of your success, is the final part of the visualization process. Enjoy how good it feels having what you want. Once this is completed, take another deep breath. If you are doing this as you go to sleep, as you exhale smile and allow yourself to go into a wonderful, restful, rejuvenating night's sleep. If you are visualizing first thing in the morning or during the day, as you exhale slowly open your eyes, and tell yourself that you are fully awake, alert, and aware.

When you're familiar with these techniques, you can reach a point where you can do them very quickly and easily, anytime, anywhere. Often before a meeting, a speech, or a difficult ski slope, I'll do a visualization for only a minute. That's all it can take to get focused for the task at hand. By visualizing in the morning, you get yourself centered and ready for the day. By visualizing at night, you're giving instructions to your brain as to what it's to cultivate while you sleep. The mind is always working. Use these methods to control that you're the one who decides what it works on.

Another useful way to increase this skill, is to describe your visualizations into a tape recorder. Verbalize whatever is seen, heard, felt, tasted, and smelled, as you mentally experience your wishes. Make it as detailed and specific as possible. Say it in a confident, caring, committed tone. Put strong positive emotion into your voice. After you listen to what you've said, think of what else you could add or change, and do it again. Constant efficient repetition leads to understanding and improvement.

Return, Revise, and Resolve

"Return, Revise, and Resolve," is a visualization exercise that can yield very pleasant results. Get into the visualization mode, and then drift, at a pace that is comfortable for you, back to the beginning of your existence. Drift all the way back to your conception. Based on what you know now, go back and imagine all the people in your life getting in touch with their values, beliefs, and self-concept, and healing the issues in their lives.

Picture them managing their beliefs, and constructing positive self-concepts.

Imagine them being nurtured and loved from the time of their conception, so that they reach their full potential, and so that they are understanding, accepting, and truly loving of themselves, and of others. Now imagine how they behave in loving ways toward you, from the time of your beginning until now. Perhaps see, hear, and feel yourself assisting them in having self-love. Feel all the positive feelings. Enjoy the sensations. Then when you're ready, come back to now. Come back with all the wonderful experiences that result from all the loving people throughout your lifetime.

"Return, Revise, and Resolve," is an exercise that can support a beneficial way to think about and remember what has already happened. It can promote being able to understand, empathize, and accept someone else enough to forgive them, and being able to remedy past situations. It can promote being strong enough to rise up above the shortcomings of others, and therefore to nurture oneself.

*"We can't change the past, however we can change how we
view, understand, and position it."*

Figure 5-1 lists the steps for effective visualization. As you practice them you'll find that they can flow very smoothly and easily. Have fun with them and enjoy the positive results you receive from using these techniques. Clearly seeing your desired outcomes contributes to a sense that you will succeed. And this sense reinforces the motivation to take action, which in turn yields greater results. Visualization is a part of the success cycle, and if it hasn't been, it can now be one of your habits.

In the next chapter we'll work on putting together the resources necessary for you to succeed.

FIGURE 5-1:
Steps for Effective Visualization

• • •

OUTLINE:

- Get in a receptive state of mind using past successes.
- Determine the *UER* that you want.
- Sit in a comfortable supportive chair.
- Take several easy gentle diaphragmatic breaths.
- Look up with your eyes only, keeping your head stationary.
- Exhale and allow your eyelids to close.
- Progressively relax your entire body beginning with your face and jaw.
- See yourself doing, having, and being what you want. Perhaps describe it out loud.
- Adjust the elements (lighting, focus, angle, sound, etc.), using all five senses.
- Use "Full Spectrum" and/or "Reflection Realization" techniques.
- Look back to now from the future time when you have achieved a goal, to see how you accomplished it.
- Lock-in the positive feelings you have of fulfilling your *UER*.
- Instruct your brain what to do after you finish your visualization session, (such as sleep, being alert, confident, creative, coordinated, or relaxed).

Chapter 6

READYING YOUR RESOURCES

● ● ●

BEING PREPARED TO ACHIEVE

Efficiently completing a project will require certain resources. As part of constructing your action plan, you need to figure out what is necessary for you to accomplish a goal. What do you need to have to enable you to reach your objective and get the result you want?

Resource categories we'll deal with in *Anatomy of Success* can be represented with the acronym "SIMPLE." All of them might not be fully needed for every project, but by asking you can be sure to cover all the bases. The major categories are:

- S—skills & traits
- I—information
- M—money
- P—people
- L—location
- E—equipment

SKILLS

In the *Building A Foundation* chapter you constructed lists of your skills and traits, and a list of some of your successes with the skills and traits you used to fulfill them. To achieve an objective, what skills and traits will you use that you already have, and are there any others that you might need to acquire? Think of someone who has or who could achieve a particular outcome. What type of person are they? What are the skills, traits, and qualities that would make them successful at accomplishing a

135

goal? Which of them do you already have, and which might be helpful for you to develop?

What are some general qualities that are useful in most pursuits? Ones that come up often are planning, analyzing, communicating, persuading, learning, adapting, persisting, and enthusiasm. Another is energy. The famous football coach Vince Lombardi basically said, "Fatigue doth make cowards of us all." When we're tired and exhausted, things can become distorted, they can lose their meaning. So taking care of oneself mentally and physically can be essential.

To accomplish a goal you'll need a particular level of vitality and stamina. What is the level of intensity, passion, and commitment required to fulfill your wishes? Where would you rate it on a scale of one to ten? Where is your intensity now, and does it need to be changed?

Head up a piece of paper titled Resources, write out the goal you are working on, and form a subsection for Skills and Traits. Then list the skills and traits that you'll need to complete this goal. As an example, Figure 6-1 lists characteristics that could be useful in getting a job. Certain skills and traits will be necessary to enable you to fully obtain and use other resources. Next, put a mark in front of those that you need to work on and need to acquire. At first you may not be totally aware of the qualities that are essential, but whatever you get down on paper will assist you.

Communicating effectively, within oneself as well as with others, is often the most critical skill required to be successful. Very few things can be realized without being in the right frame of mind, and without the input of other people. How you present yourself determines the perception others have of you, and can affect what they will agreeably do for you. We are always communicating something by our posture, energy, facial expressions, voice, and language patterns. Is your communication style appropriate for a given situation, or do you need to change it? Does it encourage others to want to work with you and to help you? Utilizing the methods and techniques in this book, will assist you in presenting yourself purposely.

FIGURE 6-1:
Resources Needed

• • •

Skills and Traits

Goal: To get and have a job as _____.

SKILLS:
Analyzing
Communicating
* Concentrating
* Deciding
Empathizing
Evaluating
Explaining
Follow-through
* Goal setting
Improvising
Learning
* Listening
Marketing
* Negotiating
Persuading
* Planning
Researching
* Writing

TRAITS:
* Adaptable
Aggressive
* Attentive
Cheerful
Clean
* Concise
Confident
* Dependable
Enthusiastic
Friendly
Healthy
Honest
Loyal
Optimistic
* Organized
Persistent
Polite
* Self-starting

*Marked items need to be worked on or acquired.

Information

Success on a project will require certain data so that you know what to do, how to do it, and when to do it. Also, certain data is needed to be able to evaluate and know if what you're getting is what you want. Have you ever bought something, gone somewhere, or undertaken a task without adequate information and ended up with less than perfect to destructive results? Whether you're buying a computer, traveling to the South Seas, or choosing a restaurant, certain information and knowledge can be crucial for satisfactory outcomes. To make the right choices, we need the right facts.

Paralysis of analysis may come into play here. One can forever be accumulating facts and figures, and be preparing to such an extent, that nothing ever gets done. How can we know how much information is sufficient to begin taking the right actions so that we attain our desired results? The answer is experience. But, the experience doesn't need to be only your own. It can be from others. Books, videos, databases, seminars, and consultants, to name a few, can provide a wealth of understanding and enhance efficiency. Using these sources taps into other resource categories, such as people and equipment, which will be discussed later in this chapter.

Securing useful information usually calls for asking the right questions, in the right sequence, at the right time. Figure 6-2 lists some of the questions someone might need to ask themselves to get a job. Also see the checklist in the *Career Checklist* chapter, for developing a job criteria. In subsequent chapters, there are checklists on running an organization and relationships. They can give you ideas on creating your own checklists and lists of questions, to assist you in getting the type and amount of information that you require in various parts of your life.

FIGURE 6-2:
Resources Needed

• • •

Information and Knowledge

Goal: To get and have a job as _____.

Possible questions to guide collecting the required information:

What skills am I best at and enjoy the most?
What are my key traits?
What type of jobs are most suitable for me based on my skills and traits?
What types of products or services am I interested in?
What industries or organizations have the types of jobs, products, and services that appeal to me?
Where do I want to be career wise in 5, 10, and 15 years?
Where can I find out about appropriate companies or organizations?
What do I need to learn about a prospective employer?
What kind of education, training, experience, skills, and traits would make me appealing to a prospective employer?
How can I get an interview with a prospective employer, and how do they usually hire?
What should my resume contain?
Should I use a cover letter, and what should it say?
How should I dress to an interview?
What's the best way to negotiate the salary and benefits?
What questions should I ask, and not ask?
What's the best way to answer the interviewer's questions?
How many references should I have, and who should they be?
Who should I send a thank-you note to, and when?

Money

Breakdown often occurs due to inadequate money, capital, credit, or financing. Many businesses will have a great product and get huge orders, but are unable to generate enough cash flow at the right time to pay their bills, to fulfill their orders, and they collapse. Being able to pay for things including salaries, rent, shipping, raw materials, warehousing, or marketing, makes capital the lifeblood of most organizations. Constantly expand and grow, or decline.

Time is a major element of the money equation. Usually the longer it takes to do something, the more dollars are involved. Using the example of getting a job, does someone have enough savings or borrowing power to have sufficient time to get a position that is really suitable for them? In my job interviewing workshops, this issue comes up repeatedly.

Someone once said that a key to success is that, "You have to be there." To get a job, being able to be there and to be ready, can cost money. Whether it's going to networking events, mailing out resumes, or commuting to interviews, money enters into the picture. Does someone have the means to go back to school and get additional training? Do they have enough of a budget to obtain all the tools and coaching they need, to make the kind of impression that will get them the job offer they want?

People

As we said before, most goals in life require the input and cooperation of other people. Who can help you, whether it's information, introductions, training, references, capital, or emotional support, to achieve a goal? Who can help you to know what resources you'll need to accomplish a particular project?

Compile a list of people who can be beneficial to you, as in Figure 6-3, which is for getting a job. On your list write down people you already have a relationship with, and those you want to enlist in your campaign. When asking for assistance, it's usually beneficial for there to be an exchange of value. Someone gives you help, you give them something in return. This does not necessarily mean a gift or something of a material nature. A verbal or written thank-you could be adequate. A simple expression of gratitude, serves everyone.

FIGURE 6-3:
Resources Needed

• • •

People

Goal: To get and have a job as _____.

family: Brian, Mary, Tony
friends: Sue, Phil, Janet, James
co-workers: Jack, Barbara, Bill
past employers
employment counselor
* career counselor
* librarian
clergy
* support groups
* fitness trainer
accountant
lawyer
* business references: Don, Helen
* personal references: Vicki, Michael
* image consultant
mechanic
doctor
* dentist
financial advisor
insurance agent
day care teacher
* computer consultant
* chamber of commerce

* Marked items need to be arranged.

In *The Benefits* chapter, we dealt with the idea that people are moved to action because of the desire to have certain feelings. It's the same when you want to get someone to agreeably help you. You need to find out what feelings are worthwhile to them. If you ask a librarian to help you do some research, what might be appealing? Some possibilities are feeling trusted, wise, needed, helpful, appreciated, satisfied, powerful, respected, accepted, important, capable, and special. The thought is to create win/win scenarios in all interactions, with something favorable in it for both parties.

Model the beliefs, attitudes, and behavior of people who have accomplished what you desire. Keep looking for examples of people who have succeeded. Read inspirational stories of people, who against all odds, hit their target. In addition to learning what to do, you can learn what not to do. Know what mistakes others have made, so that you can avoid them.

It's very advantageous to have the support and encouragement of others in your pursuits. If you get negative feedback about your ideas, if people constantly find flaws, it can be harder to go forward with the right attitude. Prepare for the possible responses you might receive. Have reasons ready why a goal is so significant to you. Have proof of the validity of your plan. Help them to understand your wishes, and what they mean to you. Then ask for their assistance in reaching your destination. Show respect for what their viewpoint is, to be able to get respect for yours.

Location

Succeeding in a outcome, requires a place to do the work. To operate at peak efficiency, you need to have a physical environment that's favorable to an activity. You need a place where you can effectively have the availability of, and use of, the necessary tools and equipment. Lighting, noise, interruptions, space, layout, furniture, colors, temperature, smells, air quality, and people, could affect how we are able to function.

Environment can greatly enhance or diminish one's capacity and productivity. Whether it's a room at home, an office, or a corner in a park, create the best location that you can for your intended purpose.

Equipment

Have you ever tried to do something and you didn't have the right equipment, tool, or supplies, and it tied up the whole project? When we produced the film "Everyday," we had a 29¢ prop, a squirt gun, that eventually cost over $2,000. We were shooting a scene on an airplane, filled with extras, at LAX, Los Angeles International airport. The airplane was a commercial jet, and to film many of the shots, we had to remove some of the seats, which took a tremendous amount of time. This was a situation where the saying "time is money," comes alive.

In one scene, a little girl used a squirt gun on the lead character. Later after rearranging the seats, the little girl was to use the squirt gun in another shot. But when she tried to fire it, it didn't work, and due to poor planning we didn't have another one. So we sent someone out to buy a duplicate squirt gun, while we gave everyone a short break. Well, a short break turned into a long and costly one. The cast, the crew, the equipment, the airplane, all sitting idle while we waited and waited.

Hours, and several thousands of dollars later, a replacement squirt gun arrived, and we finally were able to resume filming. Ironically, we edited out the entire squirt gun sequence. Moral of the story, always have the availability of backups for everything. Constantly asking questions such as, "What else do I need?" and "What else could happen?" will help you to be prepared, and to stay on target.

Set up a page for the equipment, tools, supplies, instruments, materials, etc., that you need, as in Figure 6-4, which is again for getting a job. List everything that is required for you to fulfill a goal, and mark what you still need to obtain.

In the next chapter we'll deal with what could in many cases, be your most important resources, beliefs. The ones you need to build in others, as well as the ones you need to own yourself.

FIGURE 6-4:
Resources Needed

• • •

Equipment

Goal: To get and have a job as _____.

* new resume
* copies of resume
  map book
  library
* library card
  answering machine
* extension cord
* two new car tires
  change for parking
* lamp for desk
* new business cards
  pens
  stationery
  postage
  large envelopes
* mailing scale
  return address labels
* fax modem
* shoe polish
  dictionary

  thesaurus
* pad for chair
  daily planner
  note paper
  calculator
  computer
  computer printer
* printer paper
* reference letters
* mailing labels
* pocket daily planner
  file box
* file folders
  address book
  telephone book
* sample application form
  briefcase
  notebooks for letters
* 3-hole punch
* newspaper subscription

* Marked items need to be acquired.

Chapter 7

EMPOWERING BELIEF MANAGEMENT

● ● ●

MANAGE BELIEFS, MANAGE YOUR LIFE

When we work with beliefs, we are dealing with what is basic, integral, and fundamental to a human being. As discussed in the *Building a Foundation* chapter, they shape our reality, setting the boundaries of our comfort zones of mental and physical activity. Beliefs are what we hold to be true, and therefore determine what we perceive, and what we do and how we do it. Since our filtered perceptions are our reality, beliefs can be the most powerful determining factors in what our life is, and what it becomes.

Persuasion is a critical skill in being able to accomplish an objective. In almost any situation, the efforts of other people are required to complete a project. Have you ever "tried" to persuade someone about something? Whether it's what to watch on television, what to have for dinner, where to go on Saturday night, etc., convincing others to do or not to do something, is an everyday occurrence. And beliefs are essentially what persuasion and influencing is all about.

Certain beliefs need to be installed in other people, so that they do what you want and help you, because they want to. For optimal results, the beliefs need to build understanding and beneficial experiences for both parties. To effect this, a primary question to ask yourself is:

*"What beliefs do I need to establish in this person, so that
they willingly help me, and do what I want?"*

What are some beliefs that could be useful for others to have about you and your goal? Some might be that:

- you are worthwhile
- your goal is worthwhile
- they will benefit in some manner (fulfill their values, achieve certain feelings, accomplish their goals, etc.)
- you are capable and know what you're doing
- you can be trusted
- you are persistent and will follow-through
- other people will benefit, etc.

Career pursuits can help to illustrate this concept. When I present my job interviewing workshops, I created the acronym, *ICSEXY*, as a means to help participants remember some of the beliefs that they need to construct in a prospective employer. *IC* stands for *Inspire Confidence*. This is a way of saying, that you must make the employer believe that you are the best suited for the position. *SEXY* represents the beliefs that determine who gets hired and who doesn't.

Skills is what the *S* stands for. You must inspire confidence in the interviewer that you have the skills, experience, training, education, health, abilities, etc., that indicate you "can" do the job. You may not have done it before, but you can still make them believe you are capable of doing the tasks you are responsible for completing.

Energy and Enthusiasm is what the *E* represents. In other words, that you have the right attitude and that you "will" do the work. They might need to believe that you're:

- self-starting
- hardworking
- dependable
- loyal
- trustworthy
- cooperative
- optimistic
- decisive
- persistent
- thorough

There are a lot of capable, talented, educated, and trained people in the world, that unfortunately are lazy and unproductive.

The *X* symbolizes *X* amount of dollars. An employer needs to believe that you are okay with the overall payment package, if they don't, it's unlikely that they will hire you. If an employee is unsatisfied with their earnings, it's highly probable they will quit for more income, they will constantly complain about the money, do minimal work, or all of the above. The hirer needs to believe that you feel the total compensation (salary, medical, expense account, pension, profit sharing, tuition reimbursement, perks, etc.) is valuable enough to you, so that you will give the best that you are capable of, to your work.

You is what the *Y* illustrates. Will you fit in. Will you be compatible not only with your boss and co-workers, but with customers, vendors, suppliers, civil servants, etc. Due to technology, it takes fewer people to do the work, and therefore there are fewer links in the productivity chain. This means that each link is more important than ever. One weak link, one inappropriate employee, could cause the whole process to fall apart.

Other beliefs that may be useful to implant in a prospective hirer:

- That you'll stay with the company a long time.
- That you have a happy home life.
- That you'll enjoy the work.
- That you'll make your supervisor look good.
- That you want to work for this company.
- That you live within your means.
- That other companies want you.
- That you are the best choice for the position, and that they will be happy that they hired you.

Achieving certain goals is what an employer wants, that's why a job exists. There's a perceived need and/or problem. Something is or isn't happening the way that they want it to. You need to build beliefs in their mind that you are part of the solution, and will help them to have the results they want, how they want them, and when they want them.

"How will I establish the necessary beliefs in this person?" is the next question to be answered. When I teach public speaking, we have a section on how to apply evidence and proof to verify what a speaker says, so that their listeners will believe them. There are many ways to do this. Deciding on which one or one's to use, is determined by the nature of the topic as well as of the audience. It's usually best to prepare as much evidence as is practical. This will enhance confidence, which has persuasive qualities in and of itself.

The following is a list of possible ways to support your ideas, and to generate positive beliefs in people, the *PROOF MENU*:

- facts and figures
- past experience
- testimonials
- examples
- comments by an expert
- skills and abilities
- traits
- education and training
- polls and surveys
- seen and/or heard in the media
- analogies, similes, and metaphors
- values, benefits, and feelings
- future actions
- consistency of presentation

Often there's overlap when using different forms of proof. For instance, facts and figures may come from an expert who's interviewed in a magazine article. Regardless of whether or not this is the situation, the more of a case you build to make your point, the stronger it will be. Also, the order of the above forms of proof, are not related to their level of importance or influence. What will work best is dependent on each circumstance. And some proof, might validate more than one belief.

"Facts and figures" are usually best when they are very specific. "I increased sales last month 17.64%," versus "I increased sales recently." Being detailed suggests that an actual measurement was made, and that the data is based on real research and analysis. Also, the sources for the information, and the manner in which the information was processed, must be felt to be reliable by each particular audience.

"Past experience," and a second ago is the past, can establish credibility. Logic is, that if a human being was able to do something before, they can do it again. Resumes are based on this type of thinking. If someone has a certain background in a certain arena, then it's probable the person has certain skills, abilities, and knowledge. Longevity, such as a store being in business a long time, also implies a level of competence. Seeing a demonstration or taking a test drive, would fit under this category. If we have a personal experience of something, we tend to believe it.

"Testimonials" can be very powerful since they are from people's personal experience, which can be the next best thing to our own. They are a form of referral. Someone else has already risked buying or doing something, and is risking their reputation to sing its praises. Even when we know it's an actor in a commercial saying how great a product is, it can still have an influential effect.

"Examples" or the experiences of others, may work well in some situations. If another person or organization is able to do something, then perhaps we can too. If something is similar enough to our situation, it's reasonable to feel that if it worked there, it can work here. Someone else has already proved something can succeed. If XYZ company switched software (phone service, location, hiring, advertising, compensation, training, etc.) and profited, then it can help us too. If somebody used a certain type of diet or exercise or herb to get healthy, then it could work for others.

"Comments by an expert" are useful, especially if the person is known and accepted as an expert by the people you're dealing with. What would make this person an accepted authority? Is it education, training, experience, testimonials, authorship, etc.? Or is it simply the style and confidence in which they present themselves? You might actually be an expert, yet so often, a stranger, the "expert" from afar, has more authority and believability.

"Skills and abilities" are critical in certain belief situations, especially in business. As stated above, these are why you can produce certain results. Sometimes observation is the main way in which they are known. In a job interview, if an applicant says their skills are listening, communicating, concentrating, organizing, persuading, diplomacy, deciding, goal setting, writing, etc., their actions must demonstrate these abilities, to be believed. Many people can talk a good game, however behavior is still the bottom line.

"Traits" are qualities and characteristics a person has. They are how we do what we do, and what we choose to do or not do. Many people have skill and ability, but will they use it? As with many skills, the observation of behavior is the bottom line to trait believability. If someone says they are friendly, cheerful, dependable, accepting, giving, calm, confident, cooperative, persistent, sincere, etc., do their actions prove it?

"Education and training" can be effective, especially when it's from well-known institutions. If a person has received certain learning, it's assumed that a particular knowledge has been acquired, and certain skills developed. Therefore, it's expected that certain results can be produced by this person.

"Polls and surveys," or the opinion of others, could be very influential. When many people seem to agree on something, it tends to be more believable. Since as an individual we have a limited perspective, the apparent agreement of the masses can be very powerful. The opinion of just one person, might change someone's feelings about a topic. Peer group pressure fits into this category. Who conducts a survey, how it's conducted, who's in it, and how it's analyzed, can all be elements that could make or break the legitimacy of the conclusions that are drawn.

Anything that's "seen and/or heard in the media," tends to be more convincing. When something is in the public eye, it can be vulnerable to intense analysis and examination. There can be legal risk, as well as the risk of loss of reputation. Therefore, it could take on an assumed truthfulness, whether the medium is newspapers, magazines, books, radio, television, the Internet, etc.

"Analogies, similes, and metaphors" can create understanding through the use of comparison or illustration. They are often interwoven into our speech, such as:

- The brain is like a computer, garbage in, garbage out.
- Without goals you're like a ship without a rudder.
- Too many cooks spoil the broth.
- A smooth sea does not make a skillful sailor.
- If you can't stand the heat, get out of the kitchen.
- A rolling stone gathers no moss.
- Each crop will only fully blossom in a particular type of soil.
- He was a tiger in battle.
- It's like riding a bike, you never forget.
- To hit a home run, you have to swing the bat.
- It's like closing the barn door after the cows have run away.
- Where there's smoke there's fire.
- You can lead a horse to water, but you can't make him drink.
- The time to fix the roof is when the sun is shining.
- It's like driving with one foot on the gas and one foot on the brake at the same time.
- You're comparing apples to oranges.
- It's like the blind leading the blind.
- Without the right beliefs, it's like trying to build a house on quicksand, and wondering why it keeps falling down.

To work, the comparisons and illustrations need to be suitable and sensible within the situation where they're being applied. Well used, they can be a very effective part of making your point.

"Values, benefits, and feelings," are often the determining factors in being convincing. As we know in sales, people make buying decisions emotionally, and justify them afterward logically. As discussed in other chapters, learn what is important to someone. What do they want to do, have, and be? Then present your information in a way that ties into terms that are meaningful to them. "By doing . . ., you will be able to . . ." What benefits and ultimate feelings will happen due to taking, or not taking, a specific action?

"Future actions" is relating to things someone commits to doing at some specified or unspecified later date. In some cases, this is one of the main things you've got to implant a belief in. Say you're in a job interview, and you don't have the experience, skills, or education they want. Yet, you still can make them believe that you will be an asset to the company, and the best person for the job. You can make them believe that you will work hard, learn quickly, get along great with your co-workers, be dependable, etc. You can make them believe that you have ability, and the traits to develop your ability into the required skills. You need to paint a picture of what you'll do, and how you'll do it, in a manner that makes sense to the listener, and in terms of fulfilling their criteria and guidelines.

"Consistency of presentation" can be a part of, and relate to all the other forms of establishing beliefs. Things need to be delivered in a believable fashion. Eye contact, attire, neatness, body English, voice quality, product packaging, etc., need to be done with appropriate poise, polish, and pacing. A presentation needs to be planned, prepared, and practiced, to be its most effective. Someone can be telling the total truth, and yet not be believed because of the manner and style of their communication. The old adage, "It's not what you say, but how you say it."

Keep in mind that other issues can be involved, such as frequency and repetition, and time intervals. Is there a certain quantity of exposures to something before it is believed? Does it need to happen over a particular period of time before it is accepted? Whether it's deciding on an investment, if a person is honest or competent, or who to vote for, how many impressions does it take to convince someone?

To understand how to use these ideas, analyze several large and small choices you've made to buy or to do something. List the beliefs you had that influenced your decisions. What caused and planted the beliefs in you? Start to notice and be aware of, how you are persuaded. Knowing how you've been convinced of something, will help you to know how to convince others, as well as yourself.

Buying my car, several forms of evidence motivated me. The media (magazine articles, television advertising, brochures), testimonials (meeting people who owned the car), facts and figures (the price, resale value, insurance), values, benefits, and feelings (comfort, safety, security), and consistency of presentation (quality of construction, handling, ride). Which factors had the greatest impact is hard to say. It became a combination of ingredients verifying and confirming each other, that led to the final selection.

Deciding to attend an expensive workshop, nine forms of proof caused me to commit to invest the money. Skills and traits (the speaker's poise and control of the audience), consistency of presentation (things were organized and ran smoothly), examples (stories of people that had benefited), testimonials (speaking with former attendees), future experiences (what I would receive from the training), values, benefits, and feelings (freedom, knowledge, control), past experience (other workshops the speaker had done), training and education (research this speaker had done), and the media (articles about the speaker). In this instance, the key factors were clear. Skills and traits, testimonials, and values, benefits, and feelings were the main motivators.

Again the primary questions to ask yourself are:

"What beliefs do I need to establish in this person, so that they willingly help me, and do what I want?"

"How will I establish these beliefs in this person?"

"What do I need to do to establish the necessary beliefs, in this person?"

These three questions are powerful organizers of the type of thinking that will assist you in accomplishing your goals. Just asking these questions, without reaching any immediate answers, causes connections in the brain that focuses your actions, and improves your results.

Your Beliefs

"Either we control our beliefs, or they control us!"

Winning over someone else provides you with important skills for your own enrichment. What I'm talking about, is influencing and motivating yourself in ways that are beneficial to you. I'm talking about establishing the necessary beliefs in yourself, so that you willingly do the right thing, in the right way, at the right time, to achieve your objectives. I'm also talking about being in charge of your feelings, by being in charge of your beliefs. How we respond emotionally, other than due to physical imbalances, is essentially caused by our beliefs.

Repeating a previous section, notice how you come to believe something. What happens, or how does someone get you to accept something as true? As you learn how you are persuaded, use the same procedure to install the necessary beliefs within yourself. This is the essence of self-management.

Belief influence dramatically showed its power to me when I was a teenager working out at a health club. I was always trying to lift heavier and heavier weights. One day, there were some new dumbbells that were bigger than all the others. I took them off the rack, and positioned them to use on the incline bench press. I noticed in the mirror a weightlifter, who was a professional wrestler, watching me. Wanting to look manly, I started to press the dumbbells. They felt heavy but manageable.

After two repetitions, while holding the weights high above my head, the wrestler asked me if I knew how much the dumbbells weighed. I said no. He then told me that they weighed 90 pounds apiece, a total of 180 pounds, and that he couldn't believe I was pressing them on the incline bench. Neither could I! Upon hearing his words, the dumbbells became too heavy, and went crashing down to the ground. I was never able to lift them in the same way again. My beliefs did not support what I was actually capable of doing.

What beliefs do you need to have to empower you to succeed? What beliefs will get you to take enough of the correct type of action on a consistent basis to reach your target? What beliefs will keep you unbiased, so that you can evaluate feedback and make ongoing adjustments to keep you on course? What will it take, in terms of proof and evidence, to set and maintain the required beneficial beliefs within you?

How many beliefs are required for best results? It depends on the goal. Remember the core beliefs, the "Fundamental Four," from the

Building a Foundation chapter that usually support any outcome. Again, they are: I "can" have the goal, it's "worth" having, I "will" have it, and I "deserve" to have it. These four convictions promote taking effective action. Without them there can be a tendency to hesitate, to hold back, to perform indifferently. Even if success occurs, without the right beliefs, self-sabotage or dissatisfaction can too often follow.

Because

Establishing and strengthening empowering beliefs within yourself, is accomplished in the same way as it's done in other people. To assist this process, the use of the word and concept "BECAUSE" is very valuable. A way to state it, is believing in a belief, and basic cause and effect. It's crucial to get acceptance of a belief at the conscious and unconscious levels. There needs to be a way for a belief to exist, for it to be adopted, installed and productive.

"BECAUSE" gives reasons WHY something is acceptable. By using this technique you assemble credibility for a belief. Begin by writing out beliefs that will assist you in achieving an objective. Figure 7-1 gives some examples for someone seeking a new job. Then take each belief and put it on a separate piece of paper. Now write out, in great detail, why the belief is possible using "BECAUSE" and all the suitable proof you can come up with. See Figure 7-2.

FIGURE 7-1:
Getting A New Job

• • •

Possible Beneficial Beliefs:

"I can get the job that I want as a . . ., and I can do the work."

"It's worth it to me to get a job as a . . ."

"I will have a job as a . . ."

"I deserve to have a job as a . . ."

"It's easy for me to get a job as a . . ."

"I'm always a very effective (job) . . ."

"I'm excellent at handling job interviews and getting the job offers that I want."

"I'm able to effectively juggle many tasks at the same time."

"I will get a job at $— salary."

"People enjoy working with me."

"I adapt easily to new situations."

"I'm effective at presenting my qualifications and abilities."

"I'm effective at researching companies."

"I'm excellent at networking and getting people to willingly help me."

"I'm persistent and keep going until I achieve my outcomes."

"I'm effective at knowing whether a job is suitable for me."

"I'm effective at managing my time and setting priorities."

"I'm effective at seeing and uncovering job opportunities."

FIGURE 7-2:
Getting A New Job

• • •

Validating and Establishing Beneficial Beliefs:

"I can get the job that I want as a . . . and I can do the work, BECAUSE I have over 5 years experience in the field; I'm excellent at analyzing, communicating, goal setting, and persuading, I'm aggressive, confident, and persistent; other people with less ability, such as . . ., have gotten this kind of job; I have the training in . . . and education required; people such as . . ., have told me that I can do this work; belonging, winning, and security are very important to me; everyday I will make at least 20 cold calls, every week network at 3 events, and I will contact everyone I know for job leads; and I will practice for 30-60 minutes daily on my interviewing techniques."

"It's worth it to me to get a job as a . . ., BECAUSE other people who have done this work such as . . ., have prospered; I will be able to use my skills such as analyzing, creating, negotiating, and planning; I can fulfill my values such as accomplishment, adventure, belonging, challenge, excellence, growth, knowing, prestige, and security; I can take care of my family; and I will feel proud, joyful, safe, successful, energized, competent, and worthwhile."

"I will have a job as a . . ., BECAUSE I can do the work very effectively and I would be an asset to any company that I choose to work for; the job I want is available to me even if I have to create it; I plan out my activities for everyday; I will get the help of others such as . . .; I do everything to the best of my ability; I'm persistent and follow-through; I will take care of my health by exercising daily and eating healthy foods; everyday I will make at least 20 cold calls, every week network at at least 3 events, and I contact everyone I know for job leads; and I will practice for 30-60 minutes daily on my interviewing techniques."

"I deserve to have a job as a . . ., BECAUSE I'm hardworking, quick learning, do everything to the best of my ability, get along great with others, I'm very competent, I'm flexible, handle pressure well, I'm energetic, and dependable; I have many years experience doing . . .; I love the product and think it's great; and I'm willing to do 'Whatever Is Necessary' to be an outstanding employee."

FIGURE 7-2:
Getting a New Job (continued)

— — — • • • — — —

"It's easy for me to get a job as a . . ., BECAUSE I'm persistent and organized; I've gotten similar jobs before, such as . . .; other people such
as . . ., who are less experienced than I am, have gotten this type of job; I'm
trained and knowledgeable in my field; people who put out the effort that I
do in the way that I do, usually get hired; and a lot of people such as . . .,
have said that they will help me."

"I'm always a very effective (job) . . ., BECAUSE I'm excellent at analyzing,
communicating, explaining, and persuading, and I'm aggressive, cheerful,
confident, enthusiastic, and persistent; I have over 5 years experience and
specialized knowledge in . . .; I have advanced training in . . ; I consistently
exceed my quotas and produce results more quickly than my peers; I've
received excellent reviews from several companies such as . . .; and I value
accomplishment, caring, challenge, excellence, growth, honesty, knowing,
loyalty, and responsibility. "

"I'm excellent at handling job interviews and getting the job offers that I
want, BECAUSE I'm good at analyzing, communicating, diplomacy, empathizing, explaining, listening, persuading, researching, and writing, and I'm
adaptable, attentive, cheerful, enthusiastic, friendly, genuine, likeable, loyal,
perceptive, tactful, and thorough; I've gotten many offers before such
as . . .; I've taken classes in interviewing and studied the process; several
people such as . . ., have told me how well I interview; I know and believe in
myself; and I constantly practice and improve my interviewing skills, and
get feedback from others."

"I'm able to effectively juggle many tasks at the same time, BECAUSE I'm
good at analyzing, compiling, concentrating, coordinating, deciding, delegating, estimating, explaining, follow-through, improvising, planning, prioritizing, and scheduling, and I'm assertive, concise, disciplined, energetic,
and punctual; I've handled many complex projects such as . . .; other people such as . . ., have successfully dealt with difficult situations; I've taken
courses in organizing and time management; it's important to me to accomplish a lot and to have control; and I will plan specifically what results I
want to fulfill for each day."

FIGURE 7-2:
Getting A New Job (continued)

• • •

"I will get a job at $— salary, BECAUSE I'm good at clarifying, influencing, logic, memorizing, motivating, negotiating, and summarizing, and I'm assertive, competent, creative, hardworking, optimistic, productive, responsible, self-starting, and tactful; I've received similar wages in the past; other people with a similar background have gotten this salary; surveys have shown that I should be worth this salary; and so that I'll feel I'm being paid fairly and to be able to fulfill my responsibilities."

"People enjoy working with me, BECAUSE I'm skilled at analyzing, communicating, diplomacy, empathizing, follow-through, goal setting, initiating, listening, mediating, organizing, planning, and team building, and I'm accepting, adaptable, attentive, calm, capable, caring, cheerful, clean, conscientious, cooperative, dependable, enthusiastic, friendly, generous, genuine, hardworking, honest, inspiring, loyal, patient, persistent, polite, and trusting; I've always made long-term friends wherever I've worked; I have testimonials of how easy I am to work with from 3 employers; I was featured as employee of the year in the company newsletter; I value belonging, compassion, fairness, giving, and respect; and I always work to be the best that I can be."

"I adapt easily to new situations, BECAUSE I'm good at analyzing, clarifying, communicating, diplomacy, empathizing, explaining, goal setting, imagining, learning, listening, memorizing, prioritizing, and researching, and I'm adventurous, agreeable, aggressive, assertive, attentive, cheerful, curious, disciplined, energetic, flexible, friendly, open, optimistic, patient, perceptive, polite, sincere, and thorough; I've easily fit in at former jobs such as . . .; I've taken courses in communication skills and understanding human behavior; and I appreciate challenge, change, creativity, growth, and winning."

"I'm effective at researching companies, BECAUSE I'm good at analyzing, communicating, compiling, concentrating, evaluating, imagining, initiating, interviewing, learning, memorizing, persuading, planning, stamina, summarizing, and writing, and I'm concise, curious, efficient, fast, friendly, logical, meticulous, open-minded, patient, perceptive, persistent, and trustworthy; I've researched many projects such as . . .; my last supervisor praised my researching abilities; and closure, control, excellence, knowing, understanding, and wisdom are very important to me."

FIGURE 7-2:
Getting A New Job (continued)

● ● ●

"I'm excellent at networking, and getting people to willingly help me, BECAUSE I'm good at analyzing, clarifying, communicating, demonstrating, diplomacy, empathizing, evaluating, explaining, follow-through, goal setting, improvising, influencing, initiating, interviewing, leading, listening, memorizing, organizing, planning, recruiting, and I'm accepting, adaptable, adventurous, attentive, cheerful, clean, considerate, dependable, enthusiastic, forgiving, generous, good-natured, honest, humble, inspiring, loyal, open, patient, persistent, polite, a risk taker, trusting, and trustworthy; I'm effective with people and have gotten 2 prior jobs through networking; and I believe in compassion, contributing, friendship, and sharing."

"I'm persistent and keep going until I achieve my outcomes, BECAUSE I'm adventurous, aggressive, ambitious, competent, creative, curious, disciplined, goal-oriented, optimistic, patient, productive, proud, and self-starting; I completed many projects such as . . ., when others told me to give up; successful people such as . . ., are very persistent; surveys show that the most successful salespeople are the one's who keep going and knock on the most doors; and accomplishment, closure, control, growth, honor, and purpose are very important to me."

Complete the proof for each belief before going on to the next one. Keep in mind that the same proof may come up and be used to validate more than one belief, and that these examples are broadly written to give you ideas.

For many people, doing this procedure produces a totally different feeling in their whole being. Confidence levels go way up, as does motivation and results. The significance of writing out the "BECAUSE'S" is enormous. It's what makes the beliefs real. The beliefs can then become ongoing resources that you can draw upon at anytime. One belief can be a stepping stone for many others. Of course a useful belief needs to be safe and sensible. For someone to try to believe that they can jump off a building and fly by flapping their arms, is a dangerous fantasy.

Without enough "BECAUSE'S," you may learn a whole new truth about how you feel concerning a particular goal. You may learn the real reasons why you thought something was so important, and why it's really not. At some point you might receive an understanding that a situation is inappropriate for you, and that a change in direction may be in order.

What if there isn't enough evidence to confirm a belief? Sometimes "future actions," and tying into your "values," are the most potent forms of proof you've got. For instance, a person has gone through a tough time for the last five years, and they want to get a new job with potential. How could they affirm the belief that they can succeed? They could set up a plan, brainstorm with a mentor, make commitments that a friend coaxes them to fulfill, and do visualizations every morning and night. They could pledge to read the want ads daily, make 20 cold calls per day, attend at least two networking events per week, take computer classes, practice answering interviewing questions everyday, and so on.

Someone could also tie into their values such as accomplishment, belonging, freedom, health, security, and self-esteem. They could make it so important to themselves, and in such alignment with who they are and who they want to be, that the belief takes hold.

In Figure 7-3 we move to the next plateau, the exploration of belief consequences. The purpose of this is to strengthen beliefs, and to uncover if there are any potential problems to having them. Imagine a time in the future when an empowering belief would come into play. Experience that time with the belief and notice your feelings and behavior. What kind of results do you have due to this belief? Remember that the examples are for illustrative purposes and are not from any one individual.

Take each belief and find out if it's suitable for you by asking, "Is there any possible or likely downside or loss from having this belief?" Fully consider the answer (ideally the answer is NO) to this question before going to the next one. Then ask, "What are the ways I gain by having this belief? How do I, as well as others, benefit?" We want to end on the benefits and stay resourceful. These questions can be very illuminating. Sometimes great insight occurs as someone will realize why things have turned out the way they have, due to their beliefs.

Every time we repeat a thought, it reinforces it. As you learn and grow, keep adding to your list of empowering beliefs. Continue to add "BECAUSE'S" to them. We'll build on this in a later chapter, when we'll use techniques for neutralizing any limiting beliefs. Each day through belief management, you can make yourself stronger and increase your effectiveness.

"What we concentrate on, we tend to create."

In the next chapter we'll deal with what could cause you "not" to achieve a goal.

FIGURE 7- 3:
Getting a New Job

• • •

Beneficial Beliefs—Potential Negative and Positive Consequences

"Having the belief that I CAN get the job that I want as a . . ., and that I can do the work, a possible downside is that I might get lazy and overconfident, and not prepare and do everything I can to get the job; and the gain of believing that I can get the job, is that I feel confident, optimistic, and hopeful, and therefore it helps me to stay motivated, resourceful, and perform at my best."

"Having the belief that it's WORTH it to me to get a job as a . . ., a possible loss is that I could get too aggressive and pushy and turn people off, and that I get so compulsive about getting the job that I ignore my family and friends, and lose balance in my life; and the gain of believing the job is worthwhile to me, is that I will stay motivated, take appropriate risks, and take massive action until I have the job."

"Having the belief that I WILL have a job as a . . ., a possible difficulty is that I perhaps will be disappointed if I don't get the job that I want, I might get discouraged, and I may not be as hardworking as I need to be to get hired; and the gain of believing I will get the job, is that my spirits will stay high, I'll feel good, and I'll be in a positive state of mind and able to get people to help me."

"Having the belief that I DESERVE to have a job as a . . ., a likely negative is that I may become impatient, and arrogant, and I might be resentful if I don't get the job I want, and that I will make things tougher for myself; and the gain of believing I deserve to have the job, is that I do a realistic appraisal of my strengths and prepare them properly to effectively present them to a prospective employer, and my self-esteem is enhanced."

Chapter 8

WHY NOT?

● ● ●

COULD ANYTHING LIMIT YOUR PROGRESS?

Awareness and focus can often be enhanced by looking at the opposite of something in order to understand it. As said earlier, by knowing what you don't want, it can help you to know what you do want. In the same vein, investigating what could cause you *NOT* to achieve a goal, gives you insight as to what you need to do.

Helpful questions are, "What, under your control, could cause you *not* to obtain your objective?" and "What could prevent you from having it?" The key here is, under your control. You can make choices to take action, and in a certain way, or *not* to take action. Only you are ultimately responsible for producing your *Ultimate End Results*. Some people try to put responsibility on everyone and everything else, the economy, the government, other countries, the weather, etc. No matter what's going on out there in the world, it's still up to us to make decisions, take action, and be accountable for what happens in our lives.

Using the example of wanting to increase sales, what could cause this target to be missed? Some answers might be: *not* contacting qualified prospects, *not* calling on enough prospects, *not* doing enough advertising, *not* using the best distribution channel, *not* having enough appropriate salespeople, *not* having the right product elements (features, quality, warranty, price, packaging), and *not* having good customer service. Figure 8-1, is a list of "not's" concerning getting a new job.

Write down a goal, and set up a piece of paper as in Figure 8-1, and list as many "not's" as you can think of. It often helps to get ideas from others as to what could cause you *not* to accomplish a project. Remember to only write things down that are under your control.

FIGURE 8-1:

Getting a New Job

—————————————— • • • ——————————————

- What, under your control, could cause you *NOT* to achieve this goal?

Not: thoroughly knowing my skills, traits, and achievements, and being prepared to prove them.

Not: having a clear criteria of the job and career that I want.

Not: knowing the trends and people in the industry that I want.

Not: having an appropriate resume for the job that I want.

Not: setting clear specific goals for each day, month, and year.

Not: taking care of my mental and physical health.

Not: rehearsing answering interviewing questions out loud.

Not: reading the want ads everyday.

Not: sending out resumes promptly.

Not: sending a tailored cover letter with each resume.

Not: following up after sending a resume.

Not: having business references.

Not: having personal references.

Not: having all the information for a job application.

Not: knowing what minimum salary I'll accept.

Not: being aware of and neutralizing any limiting beliefs.

Not: installing and reinforcing helpful empowering beliefs.

Not: contacting every employment agency.

Not: networking wherever I can, and asking everyone for possible leads.

Not: researching a company before an interview.

Not: cold calling potential employers, with a prepared benefit for them.

Not: being dressed appropriately for each interview.

Not: carrying a clean well organized briefcase.

Not: being on time for the interview.

Not: being friendly and polite to everyone at a company.

Not: neatly and completely filling out the job application.

Not: standing to greet the interviewer and their associates.

Not: having a dry hand for the handshake, and giving an appropriate handshake.

Not: establishing rapport with the interviewer.

Not: asking suitable questions of the interviewer.

Not: finding out what the interviewer is looking for.

Not: finding out the duties and responsibilities of the position.

Not: being appropriately enthusiastic and optimistic.

Not: communicating how I fit the interviewer's criteria.

Figure 8-1:
Getting a New Job (continued)

• • •

Not: relating how I can help the employer achieve their goals.
Not: letting the interviewer talk and having a two-way conversation.
Not: being respectful of former employers and co-workers.
Not: being objective when discussing the salary and benefits.
Not: ending the interview telling them that I want the job.
Not: thanking the interviewer for the meeting.
Not: sending a customized thank-you note to everyone that was helpful, immediately after the interview.
Not: following up after an interview, when appropriate.
Not: keeping the door open by sending another thank-you note even if I don't get the job.

After you've completed your list, cover up the "not's" column, and usually every statement that remains, is something that you need to do to have maximum achievement. This exercise is another means to uncover the required steps to be taken to reach a destination.

Beliefs you need to establish in others and in yourself to attain an outcome, were covered in a prior chapter. On the other side of the coin, there might be beliefs you have that could cause you *not* to be successful. We touched upon general limiting beliefs in the *Building a Foundation* chapter. This is such a crucial topic, that a subsequent chapter is devoted to recognizing limiting beliefs attached to a particular goal, and to the process of neutralizing them.

An interesting concept comes up in this area of what could cause you *not* to succeed, and that is "asking." Asking in two arenas, *not* asking for the order, and *not* asking for help. Many surveys have been conducted regarding salespeople. It's been found that a large percentage of the time, there are salespeople who do *not* ask for the order. They do their prospecting, set an appointment, make a good presentation, and yet fail to actually ask the customer to buy.

Fear of failure and fear of success, seem to be two of the main reasons why salespeople do *not* ask for an order. If they never ask for the order, they can't be rejected and can't fail. Also there's the secondary benefit of always having hot prospects. And strange as it may sound, the fear of success, of going beyond one's believed limits, can be a huge inhibiter. If a person thinks they can only earn a specific amount of money and they go beyond that amount, conflict and confusion can occur.

Asking for help is the other type of asking. Too many times people will *not* ask for help when they need it. Have you or someone you know, stubbornly tried to get somewhere and *not* asked for help with directions, and become lost? Most people like to be helpful when asked, especially when asked in the right way. Helping others gives us a good feeling, when we feel they deserve to be helped. So utilize the talents and abilities of others by inviting them to assist. If one person doesn't have what you want, then ask them if they know of someone else who does. When you ask with politeness and respect, the results could be very rewarding.

People

In the *Building a Foundation* and *Readying Your Resources* chapters, we talked about how the people in your life can affect you in the pursuit of your goals. This can be so important, that some of the concepts are worth discussing again. What impact will your actions and achievements have on other people? Will they be supportive of your success? Many dreams fail because people did *not* give enough attention to this matter. Without the genuine support of the people close to us, it may be difficult to have and maintain our goals.

Great care, on a consistent basis, must be given to how others are responding to the changes in our lives. Stay aware of how they feel and deal with it immediately. If they have trouble with your growth, respect their position and explain why you are pursuing the course you are on. Help them to appreciate your goals based on their model of the world. Remember, people can only understand what they have had an experience of, whether it's directly or indirectly.

After you've realized an objective, will relationships with others (such as family, friends, and co-workers) change? See Figure 8-2. Would anyone want you or things to stay the same? When you lose weight and get in shape, will your spouse become insecure and jealous of the new attention you get? Will your spouse feel less self-esteem because you improved and they didn't? Will your friends feel intimidated by your glowing health? Will they feel you are *not* one of them anymore because you choose to eat healthy foods? Will your co-workers be irritated by your increased energy and productivity, which could make them look bad?

FIGURE 8-2:
Getting a New Job

● ● ●

● Will RELATIONSHIPS with others CHANGE in a way that could hold you back?

"When I get the new job that I want, I'll be working more hours, entertaining clients at night and on weekends, and I'll be doing more overnight traveling."

Family: I'll have less time for my mate, children, parents, siblings, and other family members. I'll be unavailable for some family functions, and therefore the quality of the relationships will diminish. My mate will have to handle more things alone, and experience extra stress. Without sufficient guidance and nurturing, my children could suffer. My parents will not get all the attention that they require at their stage in life.

Friends: I won't be able to socialize with my friends as much. I won't be able to be there for them when they need it, and I could lose some of their support and encouragement. I'll probably get some pressure from them that I'm taking on too much responsibility.

Co-workers: I won't be able to interact with them in the same way, and be as open and candid with them. Two of them might be envious and become difficult to work with.

Part of the issue is that people know us in a certain way. There's a certain amount of predictability to us. They have a sense of how we will respond to things and what they can rely on us for. This knowing helps them to relate to us more easily. The probability of what they can expect from us is a major component of trust. When we move to another level of accomplishment in our life, others may feel that they do *not* know who we are, and who they are in connection to us. Many relationships suffer due to this lack of communication and understanding.

How others feel is their responsibility, but, over time a pattern of behavior is formed between you and them. So for optimal results for everyone, take their requirements and feelings into account. It's like the old adage, "We won the battles, but lost the war." Without accepting and dealing with the needs of others that matter to you, you may find yourself saying "I've become more, and yet my life is worse." The bottom line, is that we need to work out a way to interact with the people in our lives, so that they are supportive of who and what we want to be, or at least neutral. Interact in such a way, so that they are *not* obstacles or barriers to our final destination.

Benefits of *Not*

Figure 8-3 examines the question, "Are there any benefits of *NOT* achieving a goal?" In other words, are there any benefits to staying the same? Have you ever heard of someone winning or receiving a huge amount of money, and yet they choose to keep their job and live in the same residence? Or where they give the money away? This can be difficult to grasp, however these extreme examples show that for some people there are benefits of *not* having an extravagant lifestyle, and keeping things the way they are.

We've already talked about how your outcomes can affect your relationships with others, which could certainly be limiting. What are some other reasons why people actually prefer to *not* fulfill their ambitions? First off, success means change, and as discussed in the *Building a Foundation* chapter, with change we may be entering the unknown. In a new territory, we might *not* be sure of what to expect and how to respond. Have you ever gone to a new vacation spot where it took you so long to get used to it, that you had a lousy time? I had a lifelong dream of going to Tahiti. When I finally got there it took so much time to get comfortable with the heat, mosquitoes, and way of doing things, that when I returned home, I needed a vacation from my vacation.

Risk is another issue. If we just talk about a goal and never take realistic action, there's no risk of failing. It gives us a carrot to always be striving for, and can create a false sense of purpose. There can definitely be the fear of reaching the top and being disappointed, feeling "is that all there is." For some people the dream is more valuable than the reality. And what if you believe "no pain, no gain?" Without the struggle of the quest, would your life have less meaning and excitement? Have you ever noticed how some people's lives seem to always be filled with preventable, self-inflicted drama? How when they get close to real success, they engage in self-sabotage? How they seem to thrive on the crises they have created? How they seem to need conflict to give stimulation and importance to their existence?

FIGURE 8-3:
Getting A New Job

• • •

•   Are there any benefits of *NOT* achieving this goal?

I keep my current job that I'm very good at, and where I'm very comfortable.
There's no risk of not getting the new job and feeling that I've failed.
There's no risk of losing my current job due to pursuing a new one.
I keep my relationships as they are with my family, friends, and co-workers.
I continue working with the same clients that know and trust me.

Sometimes people know themselves mostly through their fears and limitations, by what they can't do versus what they can do. If we achieve "prosperity" there's a risk in *not* being sure of and knowing who we are. If our life is different (money, health, love, prestige, responsibility, power, knowledge, etc.) our self-image and identity might change. Our beliefs of what is possible for us changes. We respond differently, and therefore others around us respond differently. All this can lead to confusion and wondering, "Who am I?"

If there are any benefits of *not* achieving your goal, write them down and think about all their various aspects. Are these benefits likely to inhibit your progress? How can you work with them so that they can be put in proper perspective? Where did they come from? Are they giving you insight into the possibility that this particular goal is really *not* suitable for you at this time? You may arrive at the realization that it's "O.K." to be just where you are. There is enormous power in truth and integrity.

Using the visualization techniques from a previous chapter, is very useful in working with the benefits of *not* reaching an outcome. Project yourself out into the future in one- and five-year time periods. Imagine how your life will be with and without having attained a goal. How do you feel about the quality of your life? Which scenario gives you better results? Visualization can help to give you an understanding of the future that your current actions will cultivate. This can assist you in knowing what decisions and choices to make.

Loss Through Success

Another major consideration is the question, "Could anything be lost by achieving this goal?" What are some of the possibilities to this concept? See Figure 8-4. Let's take the example of someone getting a promotion. They might gain more money, opportunity, control, and perks, with the accompanying feelings of security, prestige, satisfaction, belonging, trust, respect, confidence, and excitement. So far, so good. Is there any conceivable loss? Hopefully the answer is no.

In some circumstances there might be loses with the success. They could be things such as: longer work hours, less freedom to act, more responsibility, more stress, new location, longer commutes, earlier hours, more overnight travel, unhealthy conditions, new staff, new co-workers, new supervisor, or rising to a level of incompetency. All of this could net out to less free time, less energy, poorer health, no time for friends, and less quality time for the family. Do any of these ring a bell? Again use visualization as a tool to think things through with all of the potential consequences.

These questions and exercises are designed to clear the path so that you can make evaluations and judgments that work for you. So that you can acknowledge and become aware of what's inside of you, putting you in the driver's seat. So that you can remove any "obstacles," enabling you to fully utilize your capabilities, design your life the way that you want it, and to achieve your goals.

The next chapter deals with limiting beliefs, and begins the process of neutralizing them.

FIGURE 8-4:
Getting a New Job

• • •

- Could anything be lost by achieving this goal?

I'll be working longer hours and have less time for my family, friends, and
   myself.
Greater responsibility, greater scrutiny, and therefore more stress.
Managing people versus the satisfaction of doing the work myself.
Moving to new offices where I don't know anyone, which is awkward and
   can be lonely.
Longer commutes that are stressful and tiring.
Business social obligations with people I am uncomfortable with.
More overnight travel and being alone.
Unhealthy conditions of travel and eating out so often.
Losing the support and friendship of former co-workers.
Feeling less than totally competent, and insecure about my abilities.

Chapter 9

NEUTRALIZING
LIMITING BELIEFS

● ● ●

UNTYING BELIEFS THAT BIND

In the *Building a Foundation* chapter we discussed how beliefs become programmed into us by the experiences we have and the people we encounter. Essentially we are not responsible for the initial beliefs we grow up with, but as adults, we are responsible for changing those that limit us, and for installing new ones that strengthen and enable us.

Protection can be the reason for some limiting beliefs. They might be a defense from what we perceive to be physical or psychological dangers. They might give us an excuse for not taking responsibility for our lives, and taking a risk. We're not getting what we want, so we blame it on someone or something else. Therefore there may be a positive intention behind our accepted limitations or fears, but it still binds and restricts us.

Limiting beliefs are memories that often have no basis in reality. Have you ever known anyone who was stick thin, and yet felt they were too heavy? Or a person who has wealth but still feels poor? How about an intelligent person who holds the idea that they are dumb? And the classic cases of a beautiful woman or a handsome man, who continue to think they are unattractive? Fortunately over time, with enough information and experience, beliefs can and do change.

How often do we make judgments about other people that turn out to be mistaken? What about the shy person that we thought was stuck up? Or the person we assumed to be ignorant who is actually wise? And have you ever believed someone was selfish, to discover they are very giving? We are constantly making evaluations based on our past experiences and beliefs, about ourselves and others. Now is the time to challenge your limiting beliefs, and to commit to replacing them with one's that are suitable and beneficial for you.

173

Have you ever had something that was very useful at a particular time in the past, and later it became useless? Have you ever thought something was true, and then later found out it was false (the stork brought you, Santa Claus, the tooth fairy)? Have you ever thought you couldn't do something, and yet later you were able to? Just as we outgrow our clothes during childhood, we can also outgrow our initial restricting conclusions about ourselves and the world.

Assemble on a new piece of paper, a list of former limiting or negative beliefs that were transformed into positive ones. It could be a habit, a fear, a trait, a behavior, etc. What caused these beliefs to change in the past? How did it happen? Through mental and/or physical action, you had an experience and a belief was changed. Use the following examples to give you ideas:

Past Negative or Limiting Beliefs	Changed to Positive Beliefs
○ I'll never have my own car	• I've owned my own car for 5 years
○ I can't use a computer	• I'm good at using a computer
○ I can't ride a bike	• I ride a bike effortlessly
○ I never win anything	• I've won many things, including . . .
○ I need others to motivate me	• I motivate myself and others
○ I'll never learn to swim	• I swim like a fish
○ I'll always be over/ underweight	• I'm now my ideal weight
○ I'll never get to travel to . . .	• I've travelled to . . .
○ I can't persuade anyone	• I'm very persuasive
○ I'm lazy	• I'm very hardworking
○ I'll never have a job as a . . .	• I've had a job as a . . .
○ I'll always be a critical person	• I'm accepting and understanding
○ I'm worthless	• I have high self-esteem
○ I can't drive a stick shift car	• I drive a stick shift easily
○ I'll never own a home	• I've owned a home for 7 years
○ I'm terrified to fly	• I love to fly
○ I'm afraid of (snakes, deep water, cats, heights, dogs, insects. etc.)	• I'm very comfortable with . . .
○ I'll never have endurance	• I can walk over 10 miles
○ I'm always late to everything	• I'm very punctual
○ I'm a terrible cook	• I'm a very good cook
○ I'm a loner	• I love being with people

○ I have a terrible memory	• I have a very good memory
○ I can't learn another language	• I'm bilingual
○ I'll never have close friends	• I have several great friends
○ I'll never change	• I'm learning and changing regularly
○ I'll never graduate	• I have my degree
○ I think reading is boring	• I love to read
○ I'll never get married	• I've been married 12 years
○ I'll always be shy	• I'm outgoing and friendly
○ I can't stand kids	• I love children
○ I'll always be dependent on others	• I'm very independent
○ I can't control my anger	• I choose what emotions I feel
○ I have to do everything myself	• I use delegation effectively
○ I'll always live in my hometown	• I've lived in many places
○ I'll never kick the habit of (nail biting, smoking, bed wetting, etc.)	• I no longer have the habit of . . .

Writing out your changed beliefs, firmly, concretely, and absolutely confirms that beliefs can and do get replaced. This list that you put together, clearly establishes and PROVES that your BELIEFS can and do CHANGE! Like other lists that you constructed in earlier chapters, this list of beliefs that have changed, is a resource that will be helpful to you with many goals. As stated before, many core limiting beliefs are created from incomplete and often inaccurate information. Continue adding to and enriching your list, to increase its value to you of proof that negative beliefs can be removed and erased. And as you may have experienced, when one belief is replaced, others might also change.

Seeking a new job provides examples of limiting beliefs that often become self-fulfilling, as in Figure 9-1. If someone believes they are "too quiet," "too aggressive," "too talkative," or "too argumentative" during a job interview, they're probably right. Remember, our beliefs create our behavior, and our behavior needs to conform to our beliefs. Therefore, the belief remains intact as long as it's accepted as a truth. It produces an undesirable result, and the result reinforces the belief. Beliefs are intertwined with other beliefs, and the *BOSS* as discussed in the *Building a Foundation* chapter, is in charge. Again, if your *BOSS* is critical, demeaning, and destructive, it could be time to get a new *BOSS*.

FIGURE 9-1:
Possible Limiting Beliefs

• • •

Career: Getting a New Job

o   I can't learn new skills required to get a job.
o   I can't get along with co-workers.
o   I'm always too argumentative.
o   I'm too old.
o   I'm too quiet.
o   I'm too inexperienced.
o   I'm too frank and outspoken.
o   I can't decide what job to pursue.
o   I'm too slow thinking.
o   I always procrastinate.
o   I have a lousy past employment history.
o   I've failed in the past, so I'll fail in the future.
o   I have no self-confidence.
o   I'm too unfocused.
o   I'm too cautious.
o   I'm too scared.
o   I'm too serious.
o   I can't handle rejection.
o   I'm too shy.
o   I'm too insecure to present myself effectively.
o   I'm too uneducated.
o   I'm too stubborn to get the help I need.
o   There's too much competition for the job I want.
o   They'll never hire someone like me.
o   I'm too loud.
o   I'm a perfectionist.
o   I'm too emotional.
o   I'm too aggressive.
o   I distrust anyone who's in management.

Can there be some limiting beliefs that are accurate and that cannot be neutralized and replaced? Yes. But they are more facts than beliefs. We talked about having realistic goals in the *Building a Foundation* chapter. Having the limiting belief you could never be a brain surgeon, is more of a fact if your hands shake, you can't stand the sight of blood, you have very poor eyesight, you have no money, you're a lousy student, you dislike detail, you're impatient, and you're allergic to brain tissue. If you only have a high-school diploma and you say you're too uneducated to be a college professor, that's a fact. If you say you can't get an advanced degree, then that's a limiting belief.

In this system, a limiting belief is defined as something that can be incorrect, and therefore can be changed. We're dealing with a memory or memories, that basically have false or incomplete information, and that blocks someone from being able to use their full abilities.

List out a goal, and any limiting beliefs you have concerning achieving this goal, as in Figure 9-1. Whether or not these beliefs are true for someone, by accepting them, makes them real for that person. Again, beliefs filter our perceptions, and only allow us to be consciously aware of things that are consistent with them. They therefore determine our behavior, and cause us to produce results that are compatible with the belief. The cycle is never ending, until the beliefs are changed. And some form of experience, brought about through mental and/or physical action, is the way to change beliefs.

Figure 9-2 gives examples of beginning the process of replacing beliefs that may or may not have had a purpose in the past, with what is best for you now, in the present, and in the future. Since nature seems to dislike a vacuum, it's important to work with your beliefs in pairs, and to have an empowering belief already setup to fill-in for the former evaporated old belief.

FIGURE 9-2:
Neutralizing Limiting Beliefs

● ● ●

Career: Getting a New Job

Limiting Belief: "I can't learn new skills required to get a new job."

Exceptions:

   I learned how to drive a car.
   I learned how to play a musical instrument, the . . .
   I learned how to use a camera.
   I learned how to use and program a VCR.
   I learned how to use a typewriter.
   I learned how to use a fax machine.
   I learned how to fix . . .
   I learned how to write a resume.
   I learned how to use a computer.
   I learned how to do each job that I've ever had, such as . . .
   I learned how to do term papers.
   My friend Joe, who is less experienced and no more intelligent than I
      am, learned new job skills and got hired.

Empowering Belief: "I can always easily and effectively learn whatever I need
to, to get a job that I want, and to achieve my goals."

Limiting Belief: "I can't get along with co-workers."

Exceptions:

   I got along with my friend Jane, who I did a project with.
   I got along with my supervisor on my first job.
   I got along with two of my co-workers, . . . and . . ., on my second job.
   I get along with co-workers, such as . . ., when we're at a party.
   I get along with people, such as . . ., at my club when we work on
      projects.
   I get along with my neighbors, such as . . ., when we do a project.
   I get along with my customers, such as . . ., and our suppliers, such
      as . . .

FIGURE 9-2:
Neutralizing Limiting Beliefs (continued)

• • •

Empowering Belief: "I can always get along with anyone I want, anytime, anywhere, and have harmonious, cooperative, and mutually satisfying relationships."

Limiting Belief: "I'm always too argumentative."

Exceptions:

>I don't argue with my cousin . . .
>I'm open and agreeable with my friends, such as . . .
>I'm open and accepting of children.
>I'm open and accepting of my grandparents.
>I don't argue with my cleric.
>I'm agreeable with people I respect, such as . . .
>I'm open and agreeable with people I have sympathy for, such as . . .
>I wouldn't argue with my celebrity idols, such as . . .
>I have harmonious discussions with . . .

Empowering Belief: "I can always be tactful, and have productive, supportive, and respectful communications with everyone, and learn from other's point of view."

Limiting Belief: "I'm too old."

Exceptions:

>Many famous artists, writers, and business people, such as . . ., first became successful in their later years.
>My friend Bob started a new career at my age.
>Many people at my club, such as . . ., started new careers at my age.
>I see people my age working at places such as . . .
>I read in the newspaper about people my age getting jobs.
>My friend Mary told me how her brother, who is older than I am, got a new job that I'd like.

Empowering Belief: "I have the experience, knowledge, and skills that enable me to be very effective in the jobs that I choose, and many jobs are more suitable to a more experienced person, such as myself."

FIGURE 9-2:
Neutralizing Limiting Beliefs (continued)

• • •

Limiting Belief: "I'm too quiet."

Exceptions:

> When I talk about things such as . . ., I'm very talkative.
> When I feel strongly about something, such as . . ., I openly express myself.
> I'm talkative with certain people, such as . . .
> When I'm in charge of a project, such as . . ., I express myself fully.
> Bob got a job I'd like, doing . . . at . . ., and he's as quiet as I am.

Empowering Belief: "I can always be as outgoing and communicative as I need to be, to achieve my goals."

Limiting Belief: "I'm too inexperienced."

Exceptions:

> Bob and Mary got jobs where they had no prior experience.
> There was a program on television about three people with no experience, who got the type of job I would like.
> My doctor told me about his brother who got a job without having experience.

Empowering Belief: "I have the abilities, traits, skills, and desire, to be able to handle the job that I want, I'm an asset to any organization that I work for, and everyone needs to start somewhere and is inexperienced at some point in their career."

FIGURE 9-2:
Neutralizing Limiting Beliefs (continued)

• • •

Limiting Belief: "I'm too frank and outspoken."

Exceptions:

> When I'm with my spouse's parents I'm very diplomatic.
> When I'm with children, I'm very careful about what I say.
> When I'm with my religious leader I'm very tactful.
> When someone is in trouble, such as . . ., I'm very supportive.
> With someone I admire, such as . . ., I'm very nurturing.

Empowering Belief: "I can always be tactful and respectful, and only say what is appropriate in every situation."

Limiting Belief: "I can't decide what job to pursue."

Exceptions:

> Other people, like Bob, have been more confused than I am, have chosen satisfying jobs.
> I accepted jobs such as . . ., that were worthwhile.
> I help other people such as . . ., decide what jobs to take.
> I listened to a radio show about people who couldn't decide on a job, but with help, found jobs that worked for them.
> Many famous and successful people such as . . ., went through uncertain times and made mistakes, before they knew what they wanted.

Empowering Belief: "I can always decide what is best for me, and make career choices that are rewarding, satisfying, and productive for me, and there's an appropriate job and career for everyone."

FIGURE 9-2:
Neutralizing Limiting Beliefs (continued)

• • •

Limiting Belief: "I'm too slow thinking."

Exceptions:

> When I help other people such as . . .,I have ideas quickly and easily.
> I'm very quick to know what I don't want, such as . . .
> When I know what I'm doing and I'm prepared, such as . . ., my mind works quickly.
> When I discuss something I'm interested in, such as . . ., I think quickly.
> I think quickly when deciding what to eat.
> I think quickly when deciding what to do on the weekend.

Empowering Belief: "I can always think at a level that is effective and appropriate for whatever I'm doing and want to accomplish."

Limiting Belief: "I always procrastinate."

Exceptions:

> When the workday is over, I'm quick to be on my way home.
> When it's time for lunch, I'm out the door immediately.
> When I'm hungry, I get a snack right away.
> When I'm invited to a party, I accept promptly.
> When it's a sunny day, I get outside as soon as I can.
> When I'm tired, I take a break immediately.
> When . . . calls me, I return the call straightaway.
> When I see something I want to buy, I buy it immediately.
> I know what I want to eat in a restaurant, as soon as I look at the menu.
> When my favorite television show is on, I sit down to watch it immediately.

Empowering Belief: "I can always be motivated, self-starting, and take action at the right time on a consistent basis, to achieve my goals."

FIGURE 9-2:
Neutralizing Limiting Beliefs (continued)

• • •

Limiting Belief: "I have a lousy past employment history."

Exceptions:

Many successful people, such as . . ., had tried many things before they found their true calling.

I read a newspaper article about a homeless person who turned their life around and got a good job.

There was a program on television about three people who had drifted from job to job, and who finally got jobs that they liked and prospered in.

My neighbor's sister has a history similar to mine, and got a job that I would like to have.

Empowering Belief: "I have gained valuable skills, such as . . ., from the choices I've made in the past, which enable me to be effective in what I do now, and in the future."

Limiting Belief: "I've failed in the past, so I'll fail in the future."

Exceptions:

Many successful people, such as . . ., failed many times before they finally became productive.

I've succeeded at many things, such as getting a driver's license, graduating from school, getting married, getting jobs as . . ., travelling to Europe, buying a car, learning a musical instrument, getting my own apartment, learning to use a computer, etc.

Empowering Belief: "The past doesn't have to equal the future, I've learned . . . from the experiences that I've had, and I now have skills, talents, and attitudes, such as . . ., that enable me to succeed in the future."

FIGURE 9-2:
Neutralizing Limiting Beliefs (continued)

───────────────   • • •   ───────────────

Limiting Belief: "I have no self-confidence."

Exceptions:

> I'm confident when I am involved in things that I know and enjoy, such as . . . (sports, politics, music, etc.).
> I'm confident in knowing who I am, and what I like and don't like (food, vacations, people, fun, movies, etc.).
> I'm confident in giving people advice about . . .
> Many successful people, such as . . , worked extra hard and proved themselves, because they didn't have self-confidence, until they achieved their goals.
> I'm confident in evaluating my job performance.
> I'm confident in knowing my body, and if I'm healthy.
> I'm confident when I'm driving a car.

Empowering Belief: "I can always be self-confident, and I will constantly learn and grow, and work on my skills, traits, and beliefs, and have the self-confidence that I want and need to achieve my goals."

Limiting Belief: "I'm too unfocused."

Exceptions:

> I was totally clear about who I wanted to marry.
> I was totally clear about what car I wanted to buy.
> I'm totally clear about where I want to go on vacation.
> I'm totally clear about what I want to do this weekend.
> I'm totally clear about what behavior I want from my children.
> I'm totally clear about what kinds of clothes I like.
> I'm totally clear about how much money I want to have.
> I'm totally clear about the type of house that I want to live in.
> I'm totally clear about what area I want to live in.
> I'm totally clear about the types of food that I like to eat.

Empowering Belief: "I can always know what I want, and have total clarity about my goals, and what I want to do, have, and be."

FIGURE 9-2:
Neutralizing Limiting Beliefs (continued)

● ● ●

Limiting Belief: "I'm too cautious."

Exceptions:

Many successful people, such as . . ., are cautious at certain times.
When I participate in sports, I go all out.
When I play a game, I'm very spontaneous.
When I dance, I do it with total abandon.
When I cook, I'm very experimental.
When I write, I'm very free flowing.
When I travel, I'm very adventurous.
When I date, I'm very bold.

Empowering Belief: "I can always do the right thing, in the right way, at the right time, and take, and be okay with, the necessary amount of calculated risk to achieve my goals."

Limiting Belief: "I'm too scared."

Exceptions:

When I got my last job, I was very comfortable during the interviewing process.
When I know what I'm doing, such as . . ., I'm very relaxed.
When I know what I want, such as . . ., I'm assertive.
When I'm helping someone else, such as . . ., I'm brave.
When I'm doing something I really enjoy, such as . . ., I'm daring.

Empowering Belief: "I can always be comfortable and at ease, and be at my best in any situation."

FIGURE 9-2:
Neutralizing Limiting Beliefs (continued)

• • •

Limiting Belief: "I'm too serious."

Exceptions:

When I'm with my friends, such as . . ., I'm easygoing.
When I'm with customers, such as . . ., I'm in a lively mood.
When I'm with kids, I'm lighthearted.
When I'm at a party, I'm cheerful and upbeat.
When I'm on vacation, I'm joyful.
When I'm working on a project I truly enjoy, such as . . ., I'm cheerful and happy.
When I'm fixing things, such as . . ., I'm upbeat.

Empowering Belief: "I can always be at the right emotional level and mood, to be effective in every situation."

The procedure is to take each limiting belief, and write it out on a piece of paper. Leave several blank lines, and then write the opposite empowering belief to the limiting one. Next, on the lines in-between, list "counterexamples," "contradictions," and "exceptions" to the limiting belief. Make them as specific as possible. Don't just list it as a co-worker, a friend, or a neighbor, write out specific names. Remember, the idea is to be detailed enough, so that you create a picture of what you're dealing with, and make it real.

Counterexamples can be from your own experience or the experience of others. For instance, someone might feel that they are "too short" to be successful. Growing up they heard that short people were less able, and they were the object of countless jokes. A belief is created, "short is bad," that filters all other perceptions.

What are some counterexamples to "too short" to be successful? Look at all the well-known people that are short, from Mahatma Gandhi to Napoleon to Mother Teresa. There are many places to look for counterexamples such as books, magazines, newspapers, television, radio, in your own life, from friends, etc. Continue to add to your list to maintain your focus and increase your conviction. As you notice counterexamples to a limiting belief, the belief is no longer valid for you. *"What we concentrate on, we tend to create."*

"Too young" and "Too old" come up quite frequently. Yet there's an organization of multi-millionaires where you must be under forty to be a member, with many of the members achieving wealth in their twenties. And least we forget Col. Sanders, who began Kentucky Fried Chicken while in his sixties.

After coming up with exceptions to the limiting belief, then install and enhance the appropriate empowering belief, using the steps from the *Empowering Belief Management* chapter. What if presently, you don't locate any counterexamples, contradictions, and exceptions to your limiting beliefs? To handle this situation, keep building the opposite empowering beliefs and make them so strong that the limiting beliefs by contrast become unbelievable. Use enough proof and "BECAUSE'S" to make the empowering beliefs outweigh the limiting ones.

Just the mere act of being aware of and writing down any limiting beliefs weakens them. If you do nothing more than that, you're way ahead. Putting together the opposite empowering beliefs greatly furthers the removal of limiting beliefs. Then searching for counterexamples can free you of past presumed restrictions, opening up all kinds of positive possibilities. And convincingly proving and establishing the opposite empowering beliefs, completes the first phase of the process of neutralizing limiting beliefs. Due to the search, expectations change, changing the actions you will take and the way you take them, and the motivation to keep going is intensified.

Maintaining a limiting belief is a possible choice that might make sense if someone wishes to keep things the way they are. If you believe you are "too shy" to be a salesperson, you're probably right. And as long as you have this belief, you will most likely continue to be "too shy" to be as effective as you can be in this line of work. This is especially true if you believe that being shy would make someone unfit to do sales work. Therefore, if being outgoing, aggressive, thick-skinned, assertive, persuasive, and taking risks, is too uncomfortable and different from the self-concept someone wants to have, the belief change will have difficulty taking place. For a belief change to last, it must be in alignment with the whole system, including values, beliefs, skills, etc., as well as the self-concept.

Putting the Past Behind You

Now we move farther down the road in placing limiting beliefs, or restrictive often incorrect memories, in proper perspective. What were, and would have been, the consequences of accepting and maintaining a limiting belief? What effects did it have, and would it have had, on your family, career, health, finances, friendships, etc.? As in Figure 9-3, write out your answer using the structure in the examples, leaving plenty of space for your responses. Therefore, your answer would contain the following concepts and phrases:

"In the past, when I had thought (the limiting belief),
the gain was . . .,
and the loss was . . ."

The purpose of this procedure is to assist you in shifting your mental patterns, and to dissolve any limiting beliefs into disbelief. It's about recognizing the past, and putting it behind you. And remember, a second ago, is in the past.

When I present *Anatomy of Success* in a seminar, I have participants verbalize the above statements out loud. Saying and hearing the words builds greater involvement and expands the effectiveness of the technique. After you've written out your responses, say them aloud for maximum benefit. Send a message loud and clear, of what is now past and no longer acceptable to you.

Permit yourself to let your mind give you whatever comes up. The answers to these statements can be very revealing and illuminating. Often impressions and ideas that you never had a conscious awareness of, will surface. Be truthful with yourself and allow all of your deepest thoughts to be released by writing them down. Finishing this section can be extremely freeing as you open up your boundaries of what is possible and appropriate for you. And repositioning one limiting belief, can have a positive effect on repositioning many others.

Use this technique for each of your limiting beliefs. As always, keep adding to each part as you move closer to your goal. In many instances, what you learn in one segment will give you valuable insight into another.

FIGURE 9-3:
Repositioning Limiting Beliefs

• • •

Career: Getting a New Job

In the past, when I had thought (the limiting belief), the gain was: (possible answers)

o   I didn't risk the frustration of failing.
o   I would have less responsibility.
o   I would have less stress.
o   I could feel sorry for myself.
o   I could stay home and do personal tasks.
o   I could stay in an easy job and keep things the way they were.
o   I could be with my friends during the day.
o   I would know who I am.
o   I wouldn't have to commute to a job.
o   I would have an excuse for not getting a new job.
o   I wouldn't need to put out the effort to learn new things.
o   I could fit in with my friends.

and the *loss* was: (possible answers)

o   I would stay stuck in a lousy job.
o   I would not be able to get a job.
o   I would lose my self-esteem.
o   I would not have the money I wanted.
o   I would have conflict with my family.
o   I would have difficulty with my friends.
o   I would have health problems.
o   I would not live up to my potential.
o   I would disappoint my parents.
o   I would be bored and frustrated.
o   I would be envious of others.
o   I would feel restricted.

Figure 9-3:
Repositioning Limiting Beliefs (continued)

━━━━━━━━━━━━━━━━━━━━━   ● ● ●   ━━━━━━━━━━━━━━

EXAMPLES:

"In the past, when I had thought that I can't learn new skills required to get a job, the gain was I could keep things the same, I didn't need to change, and I avoided the frustration and effort of learning something new; and the *loss* was that I would be stuck in a job with no future, I would not live up to my potential, my self-esteem would suffer, and my relationships with my family and friends would be strained."

"In the past, when I had thought that I'm too old to get a job, the gain was I could feel sorry for myself, I could stay home and do things around the house, and I wouldn't risk being rejected; and the loss was that I would have no sense of purpose, I would wither up and vegetate, and people would lose respect for me."

Is it necessary to continually work on limiting beliefs? Possibly. There can be many negative influences in someone's life. Due to new experiences, more information, a change in values, etc., belief management could be an ongoing process. But at least now, you have the process, and you are in command.

Summarizing the steps to neutralizing limiting beliefs:

1. Write down the limiting belief.
2. Write out the opposite empowering belief.
3. Come up with counterexamples, contradictions, and exceptions to the limiting belief, from your own or others' experiences.
4. Install the empowering belief with the "Proof Menu" and "BECAUSE'S," from chapter 7. (Note: the counterexamples will frequently provide proof for the empowering belief)
5. List the consequences of the empowering belief, as demonstrated in chapter 7, Figure 7-3.
6. List the consequences of the limiting belief, using the specific phrasing described earlier in this chapter, and in Figure 9-3.

In some cases, you may find it useful to vary the sequence of these steps. Experiment with what works best in each situation. What's important is that the steps are completed at some point, and that everything is written down in detail.

In the next chapter we'll work with a method to uncover any negative consequences if you don't succeed.

Chapter 10

NEGATIVE CONSEQUENCES

● ● ●

NOT ACHIEVING YOUR GOAL

Negative consequences is another element of maximum motivation. In many situations, it is the most forceful one because "pain pushes." When we are uncomfortable, we take action. We regularly reach thresholds in life that cause us to respond. In *The Benefits* chapter, we talked about the positive things that could develop a threshold. In this chapter, we'll explore the opposite side, the negatives.

Whether it's hunger, thirst, tiredness, loneliness, fear (giving up smoking and fatty foods or die, finishing a project or lose a job), etc., we arrive at points, at levels of intensity, where we feel compelled to act. We feel a need to change an unpleasant state, and have a different feeling. It's moving away from the pain to neutral feelings, or possibly to pleasure.

Recognizing feelings that are very distasteful to you, is the first step in understanding how negative consequences affect you. Figure 10-1, lists feelings that could be very unpleasant. What are feelings that are so uncomfortable and distressing to you, that you will take massive action to avoid them? What are feelings that are so horrible to you, that you are driven to eliminate them, and have other ones in their place? What are feelings that push your hot buttons to move away from them as quickly as possible? Underline or circle each feeling on this list that you NEVER want to experience!

Negative consequences can play a main role in reaching your goals. The fear of loss can even be a more powerful motivator, than the possibility of gain. How does it feel to lose something? People commonly experience a very intense, sometimes overwhelming, emotional response to losing, or the thought of losing, something. This energy can be used as part of the motivating drive to achieve your ambitions.

FIGURE 10-1:
What are feelings you want to AVOID?

• • •

abandoned	hated	repulsive
abused	helpless	resentment
addicted	hopeless	restless
aimless	hostile	restricted
alone	humiliated	ridiculed
angry	ignorant	sad
anxious	ignored	scared
awkward	immoral	self-conscious
belittled	incompetent	self-pity
bored	indecisive	shame
burned out	indifferent	sickly
clumsy	inferior	sorrow
confined	insecure	stingy
confused	intimidated	stressed
controlled	irritated	stupid
crazy	isolated	submissive
criticized	jealous	tense
decaying	lazy	threatened
defeated	listless	timid
dependent	lost	trapped
depressed	manipulated	unappreciated
desperate	mean	unattractive
dirty	negative	unconnected
dishonest	nervous	unloved
disorganized	offensive	unlucky
dissatisfied	old	unsettled
doomed	ordinary	untrustful
doubted	outdated	unwanted
embarrassed	out of control	used
empty	overwhelmed	useless
exhausted	paranoid	vengeful
failure	passionless	victim
fearful	pathetic	vulnerable
foolish	persecuted	wasteful
forgotten	phony	weak
frigid	poor	weird
frustrated	powerless	worried
grief	regretful	worthless
guilty	rejected	wrong

Losing $10,000 can feel much more painful, than the pleasure of gaining $10,000. Accumulating $10,000 is real, it comes from doing something, from effort. You know what it took for you to get it. It may represent a lot of "blood, sweat, and tears." Therefore, there's a strong emotional element involved with losing. In some ways, it can be tied into our survival mechanism. For most people, there is a supreme instinct to survive. Losing goes against this instinct, and can produce a feeling of insecurity.

If someone feels they lose too often, they can feel hopeless. Why bother taking action if you never succeed? This kind of thinking feeds on itself and leads to a downward spiral. Giving up emotionally, can then lead to giving up physically, with illness and death the final outcome.

If your goal is not attained, are there any negative consequences? Are there any negative feelings you would experience? What could you possibly lose? What will be the effect on all aspects of your life? What would not achieving it prevent you from doing, having, and being? Would anyone else suffer? In *The Benefits* chapter, you listed the advantages of accomplishing a project, and then the benefit of each benefit until you arrived at a stopping point. The same method works here.

Setup a page as in Figure 10-2, which is an example of not getting a job. Write out all the negative consequences of not attaining a goal, at the top of the page. Then take each one separately and ask what is the consequence of each consequence until you get a feeling, or until no more ideas and links surface, and your thoughts stop. As with the benefits of the benefits, there are no right or wrong answers.

Ideas may often come up more than once. Some answers may not seem to make sense. Some may seem to have nothing to do with the prior thought. The key is to not evaluate, and to just let the ideas and impressions flow freely. Each time a word or concept repeats itself, it might be linked to different ideas. Be open with yourself, and allow whatever comes up to be recorded. Even death, as in one of the examples in Figure 10-2, might not be the end of the string. Remember, this is a process. Its purpose is to uncover what really matters to you. And the larger the list, the more powerfully motivating it will be for you.

FIGURE 10-2:
Consequences of the Negative Consequences

• • •

"Not getting a job as a . . ."

POSSIBLE NEGATIVE CONSEQUENCES: No money, low self-esteem, stress with mate, restricted, health suffer, stagnate, no future, lonely, no growth, boredom, feel unwanted, feel worthless, can't relocate, lose car, can't be with friends, can't help parents, shame, homeless, resentment, insecurity, depression, anger, can't take care of family, confusion.

"No money"—can't pay bills, restricted, no vacations, no entertainment, feel suffocated, stressed, poor health, no energy, sadness, friends avoid me, be alone, boredom, fear, stressed out, anxiety, confusion, can't get organized, waste time, feel useless, depression, giving up, hopelessness, no action, feel hopeless, death, family all alone, children have no love, children scared, kids get into trouble, their lives are ruined, they never reach their potential, lives are wasted.

"Low self-esteem"—feel worthless, feel sad, unhappy, no energy, never do anything, no fun, life a waste, feel depressed, people avoid me, being isolated, unconnected, isolated, no companionship, being alone, no one to count on, feel helpless, feel weak, no self-confidence, poor performance, no advancement, feel stuck, no joy, feel hopeless, frustration, tension, anger, can't connect with people, no one to share things with, stress, confusion, feel insecure, can't think clearly, can't make decisions, no action, vegetate, not really living, give up, never knowing what life has to offer, missing out, feel deprived, resentment, end up all alone, be lonely, misery.

"Stress with mate"—no love, tension, arguments, anger, no love, feel alone, feel worthless, shut down, no emotions, no feeling, no life, emptiness, anxiety, can't function, nothingness, feel dead, nothingness, ache deep inside, feel lost, confusion, feel overwhelmed, can't deal with things, can't fulfill responsibilities, feel worthless.

"Restricted"—feel closed in, feel cooped up, can't be spontaneous, feel limited, not self, feel phony, unsure who I am, can't relate to people, people won't like me, arguments, lose friends, no one to talk to, take up bad habits, gain weight, unable to engage in sports, watch television all the time, not be with people, boredom, become uninteresting, unable to connect with people, do everything by myself, no one to enjoy things with, no pleasure, dull life, wasted life, jealousy, envy others, feel less than, failure.

Negative consequences can be very influential. Depending on the goal, some deep fundamental issues of a person's subconscious can unfold. Again, the issue of survival can be at stake. When I work with unemployed people on career goals, using this process is often what it takes to help them break free, get unstuck, and be able to use their abilities. The fear of loss, can be the energizing force that starts the wheels of change rolling.

If you want to take the intensity of this process down to a lower level, one way is to do it with someone else. In my workshops, I often will demonstrate this technique by gathering negative consequences from several people. Then as a group, we go through possible negative consequences of each consequence. In this way, everyone learns how to use the tool, and yet not feel its full force.

ONLY do this exercise at a level that is comfortable and practical for you with each goal. Just writing out a few negative consequences may be enough for you to give you the understanding and motivating effect you want. Or in some special cases, leave out this process altogether, and stick solely with the benefits and all the wonderful positive feelings a goal will help you to achieve.

Threshold is what we're working towards. In other words, what future gain and loss will cause you to take positive, appropriate, and practical action now and on a consistent basis? What are those key points that move you to act in effective ways to have the quality of life that you desire? Go back over your benefits and negative consequences exercises, and pick out the main ideas and issues that are the most significant to you. Use them as important parts of the system to achieve and maintain MAXIMUM MOTIVATION.

In many instances, the negative consequences of not obtaining a goal could be minimal. You want to run the entire twenty-six miles in a marathon, but twenty is the most that you can do. You want to travel around the world, but you only get half way. You want to become the president of the company you work for, but the highest you go is to general manager. Depending on many factors in your life, especially your values and beliefs, the negative consequences may play a major or a minor role.

The next chapter deals with how to manage your time, and setting up an action plan.

Chapter 11

MANAGING
YOUR TIME

● ● ●

TAKING ACTION:
ONE SMALL STEP AT A TIME

One precious commodity it's difficult to get more of, is time. Every moment we are engaged in some use of it. Effective time management is based on constructing a thorough plan, and performing the plan efficiently. Taking the right actions, in the right way, and at the right time, will yield the best results.

> *"Even if you're on the right track,*
> *you'll get run over if you just sit there."*
> *—Will Rogers*

Motivation, as stated earlier, has seven elements to it. Setting up a clear, specific, detailed, prioritized, practical action plan is a major ingredient in the formula. Without this part, the rest of the system will be diminished. Establishing workable time frames leads to being productive, maximizing the use of one's time, and a successful feeling of accomplishment that inspires more action. Using this system, could save you well over an hour a day, as well as increasing your comfort and productivity.

Planning on paper, *POP*, helps you to anticipate what works, and to think things through in detail. It's like a dress rehearsal where you can safely iron out the bugs. Writing something down captures it, increasing involvement and understanding. "Trying" to remember things, can take a tremendous amount of time and energy. Repeating something over and over again in an attempt to memorize it, can cause pressure and stress, and still not yield the desired result. Have you ever looked up a phone number, and found that by the time you started dialing the phone, you couldn't remember the entire number? Save time and energy, and increase your efficiency by letting pen and paper do the work for you. From now on, set a goal to write everything down!

Andrew Carnegie, the steel tycoon, is reported in the late 1800s, to have paid a consultant $64,000 for two ideas. They are to write down what you must do today, and do the most important things first. We know this is sound advice, and yet so many people fail to use it.

Detailed planning will help you get a handle on things and give you a sense of control. Frequently when a client comes to me overwhelmed with life and anxious, it's because they haven't applied *POP*, or the concepts we'll discuss in this portion of the book. By utilizing the five-step formula that is explained in this chapter, an entire week can be planned out for someone, often in only twenty to thirty minutes.

Awareness is critical, therefore first let's find out where all your time is being used. We can't effectively change something, until we know what the current status is. To accomplish this, for a seven day period, actually log every moment, using Figure 11-1 as a guide. Record how your time is used during a "typical" week, keeping track of where every minute goes.

FIGURE 11-1:
Seven-Day Log

• • •

	Sunday	Monday	Tuesday	Wednesday	Thursday	Friday	Saturday
6:00AM							
6:30AM							
7:00AM							
7:30AM							
8:00AM							
8:30AM							
9:00AM							
9:30AM							
10:00AM							
10:30AM							
11:00AM							
11:30AM							
NOON							
12:30PM							
1:00PM							
1:30PM							
2:00PM							
2:30PM							
3:00PM							
3:30PM							
4:00PM							
4:30PM							
5:00PM							
5:30PM							
6:00PM							
6:30PM							
7:00PM							
7:30PM							
8:00PM							
8:30PM							
9:00PM							
9:30PM							
10:00PM							
10:30PM							
11:00PM							
11:30PM							
12:00AM							

Goal Categories

Taking the analysis further, we'll look at time usage in terms of categories. There are basically 1C categories that cover most human activities, as discussed in the *Building a Foundation* chapter. Again, they are:

Health	*Family*
Spiritual	*Friends*
Career	*Community*
Financial	*Recreation*
Home	*Personal*

This list is not in any order of importance, since for each person it would be different. And not everyone might have activity or goals in all 10 categories.

Before putting your time usage into groupings and percentages, the categories need some explanation. Figure 11-2, gives ideas on the breakdown of activities. Some may fall into more than one classification. Going to a dance class for two hours could be part health, part recreation, and part career. Dancing vigorously for 30 minutes is for health, leisurely playing around for an hour is recreation, and discussing business for half an hour with a potential client fits under career.

The following are not hard and fast definitions. They are general guidelines to give you insight into the current conditions, so that you can make productive and satisfying adjustments as to how you utilize your time in the future. Which category an activity fits under has to do with its purpose. Why you do something is the determining factor. If you take the kids to a ball game to stay close, it would come under family. If it's primarily because you want to see the game and you may as well take the kids along, it's more under recreation.

Health is anything you do to support being alive. This could include sleeping, exercising, shopping for food, preparing food, eating, cleaning up after eating, taking a cooking class, reading a health magazine, resting, and getting a massage. For some people, health could also involve doctor visits, therapy, taking medicines, and going to the pharmacy.

Family is anything to do with parents, spouse, children, siblings, relatives, and their families. It's the time you spend with them directly, in person, or on the phone, and the time you spend indirectly, such as doing things for them.

Community is somewhat of a broad category covering several areas. It could be involvement with neighbors, volunteer work, charitable work, political work, and the PTA. It's activities that are geared toward a participation or contribution to the world at large.

Friends is simply about people you choose to associate with because you value connecting and sharing with them. Ideally these are people who you care a great deal about and would do anything for, and vice versa. Casual socializing with people you may never see again, could come under this section. In other words, you're in a situation where you are enjoying interacting with someone, even though it's only temporary. You give each other some companionship, and satisfy the good feeling of joining and relating to another human being.

Career is what you do to make a living. It's what you do to be able to support yourself and others. It's what you do because you need to earn money. Anything related to getting a paycheck such as grooming, reading the paper, seminars, meals with customers, listening to tapes, doing research, or taking clothes to the cleaners, would be added to the total time.

There are many people who are financially independent, and work for reasons other than money. It could be for a sense of worth and self-esteem, which would be under health. It could be to help others, which would come under community. It could be to learn and grow, which would come under personal. And it could just be so much fun, that it could be under recreation. Money is just a way to keep score and to know if they can do it.

Spiritual for most people is dealing with activities of a religious nature. This could be whether someone belongs to an organized religion, or follows their beliefs in their own personal way. For some people being spiritual is communing with nature, meditating, helping others, or any activity of a nonmaterialistic nature. This is a concept of very personal definitions.

Financial is anything to do with money outside of career. Included would be paying bills, borrowing, handling insurance, making investments, retirement plans, reading financial information, college funds for the children, etc. This category can be taking up a surprising amount of time, for some people four to eight hours per week.

Recreation is about fun. How much time are you engaged in activities that are for the pure pleasure of it? It could be attending a sporting or musical event, going to a movie, playing checkers, reading, writing, attending a lecture, having a debate, dancing, taking a walk, going to the mall, taking care of a pet, playing golf, collecting stamps, watching television, vacations, or daydreaming.

Home deals with your living environment. If you live in an apartment, it could include cleaning, arranging, taking out the trash, or decorating. If you own a home, it's usually a never ending story of things that need to be fixed, replaced, or maintained. You may not do the work yourself, but making sure others do it, can still take a lot of time.

Personal is a general heading. It's for activities that don't easily fit into any of the other categories. Taking care of the car, doing laundry, and organizing personal files, could belong here. Learning for learning's sake, with the main benefit to acquire knowledge, to satisfy curiosity, could be here. Getting to know and understand yourself, as with many of the exercises in this book, perhaps would come under this section.

Romance and dating are special situations that can be in one of several groupings. If the purpose is for forming a union and marriage, then it's under family. If it's for companionship and caring without marriage, then it's under friendship. And if it's just for the fun of it, with no intention of beyond the moment, then it's under recreation.

Where Does The Time Go?

Next, based on the above definitions, or ones of your own, take a typical week and figure out where all your time goes in each category. Use Figure 11-2, to help plot out your time usage. Note, for this exercise, the amount of time involved in planning, organizing, procrastinating, waiting, and commuting, would be added to that activity. If you spend 20 minutes planning what to buy at the grocery store, 10 minutes organizing your money and checkbook, 5 minutes procrastinating whether or not to go, 10 minutes waiting for a friend to pick you up, and 60 minutes driving round trip, you would add 105 minutes to the time you are actually at the store.

FIGURE 11-2:
Where Is Your Time Being Spent?

• • •

In hours, jot down the total amount of time spent with each item in a typical 7 day week, and be sure to add items that aren't on this list.

Note: add planning, organizing, procrastinating, waiting, and commuting time to the activity.

HEALTH:
o Sleeping _____
o Exercising _____
o Buying food _____
o Preparing food _____
o Eating _____
o Cleaning kitchen _____
o Therapy
o Taking medicine _____
o Health, learning _____
o Resting _____

Family:
o Visiting with mate _____
o Visiting with children _____
  Visiting with family _____

Community:
o Political _____
o Volunteering _____

Friends:
o Visiting with friends _____
o Socializing _____

Career:
o Working _____
o Learning _____

Spiritual _____

Financial _____

Recreation:
o Sports _____
o Dancing _____
o Watching TV _____
o Listening to music _____
o Hobbies, games _____
o Pets _____
o Movies, plays, concerts _____
o Daydreaming _____

Home _____

Personal:
o Grooming _____
o Maintaining wardrobe _____
o Reading mail _____
o Maintaining car _____

After you record and know how your time is spent for one week, convert the hours into percentages. There are 168 hours in a week. To make the calculations easy, use the following approximations: *1* hour = ½%; *2* hours = 1½%; *3* hours = 2%; *4* hours = 2½%; *5* hours = 3%; *6* hours = 3½%; *7* hours = 4%; *8* hours = 4½%; *9* hours = 5½%; *10* hours = 6%; *11* hours = 6½%; *12* hours = 7%; *13* hours = 7½%; *14* hours = 8%, and so on. Remember, the percentages when totaled, should equal somewhere around 100%.

Once you've arrived at the percentages, lay them out next to each goal category as in Figure 11-3. Put the current percentage of time you spend in each category on the left, and your desired percentage of time to spend in each category on the right. Again, not everyone might have goals in all 10 categories.

Knowing what the percentages are, can be very illuminating. It will provide you with the reality of where your time is being spent, and why perhaps certain goals are not being met in your life. This awareness will also help in showing where adjustments in your time usage can and need to be made, so that you'll have enough time for the most important things.

Altering your time usage can be a major challenge. Sometimes there are so many goals that it becomes unmanageable, and something has to give. A familiar way of coping and to get more waking hours, is to get less sleep. This can work for a time, but long-term it can be less than suitable.

Explore different ways to achieve all your goals, and realize that some may need to be postponed until another time. There are some people that are so compulsive about doing things, that the quality of their accomplishments is less than rewarding. Balance, and stopping to smell the roses, can be essential to overall life satisfaction.

Another beneficial aspect of doing this exercise, is that it assists motivation. By creating a conscious knowing of the difference between where time is spent and desired time usage, a clarity is developed from where you are now to where you want to be. Plotting this information out, can be like a snapshot of your life, and why the quality might be less than it could be. This can help to inspire you to take action now.

When many people do this log, they are very surprised to learn where their time is actually going. So often, people underestimate how long something will take to finish. By establishing a time consciousness, time estimates can become much more accurate and efficient. If you never seem to have sufficient time for the most important things, this can help you to know where you need to make adjustments.

FIGURE 11-3:
Goal Categories

• • •

What percentage of your time and energy do you currently spend in each category? What percentage would you prefer and desire?

Hours	=	Current %		Hours	=	Desired %
77	=	46%	Health	70	=	41%
11	=	7%	Family	19	=	12%
1	=	1%	Community	5	=	3%
6	=	3%	Friends	11	=	7%
55	=	33%	Career	38	=	22%
4	=	2%	Spiritual	7	=	4%
4	=	2%	Financial	0	=	0%
3	=	2%	Recreational	12	=	7%
4	=	2%	Home	0	=	0%
3	=	2%	Personal	6	=	4%
168		**100%**		**168**		**100%**

How to Tame Time

Next are some general concepts and principles that will assist you in controlling and maximizing the use of your time.

- Have "A" and "B" lists for the various goals in your life. "A" list items, are things that you must do to attain an objective. "B" list items, are things that you want to do, when it's possible, but there are no negative consequences if you never do them. For instance, eating nutritious food, drinking pure water, and exercising regularly, are required for being healthy, and are "A" list elements. Whereas learning about gourmet cooking or the latest in exercise fashion, would be "B" list objects. Fun, but not necessary. "B" list items are important in that they are things we look forward to doing or having. They can give richness to today, by providing us with satisfying future possibilities. Unfortunately, I constantly see people do "B" list tasks when they need to do "A" list ones, and they get into time crunches. Using this program will help you to avoid this situation. Keep asking, "Is this action necessary, at this time, to achieve my goals?"

- Always establish specific time frames, when giving or getting a project. As mentioned in the *Wording Your Goals* chapter, if you are giving a task to someone, tell them when is the latest it can be completed by, and why. And if you are getting a project from someone else, be sure to learn the latest it can be finished by. Without doing this, a lot of time and energy can be wasted.

- To handle complex projects that have many steps, cut out 1½" to 2" squares of paper, and put each step on its own separate square. This makes it easier to organize, sequence, and rearrange each task. When I began writing this book, all the information I had accumulated over the years for it, presented a tremendous mass of data. By taking each idea and putting it on an individual piece of paper, I was able to organize a huge amount of material into categories, then chapters, and finally into paragraphs.

  When dealing with complicated pursuits, it can also be useful to warm-up before diving in. Before writing a lengthy contract, get up to speed by writing a brief note or editing a letter. Before making a very important phone call, make one or two brief calls where you are in control, and where you know they will be positive. Invest a few moments to be ready for the major events.

- If someone else is going to complete a step, write their name and phone number next to it on your work sheet. This will make it easy to remember who's responsible for what, and who to go to to stay on top of things. Let the paper do the remembering for you. Also, give your directions to them in writing to eliminate the possibility of error. And make sure that when you delegate to someone, that they have the skills, resources, time, and authority to do what you want them to do.

- Sometimes a venture can be difficult to get started. What steps need to be taken, in what order, in what way, what resources are needed, etc., could overload one's brain. At times people feel so overwhelmed, that they are unable to begin project, let alone keep it going and complete it. One usual solution to getting unstuck, is to get the input of someone who's already accomplished the type of undertaking you're working on.

  Another way to get moving, is to imagine you need to tell someone else how to manage and complete a task. With you in an objective role, explain to someone what they need to do, how they need to do it, and when they need to do it, to achieve the desired result. So often, we have the answers we seek, we just need to ask the right questions to become aware of them. "How would I tell a stranger to do this project?," is such a question.

- Alternate types of tasks, to keep yourself alert and energetic. Doing too much of the same thing, can lead to decreasing returns. Depending on the project, take a three to five minute change of pace break, somewhere between 30-90 minutes of sustained activity. During these few minutes, do something totally different. If you're doing a very mental function such as writing or taxes, do a physical or simple job such as moving some boxes or making a brief phone call to get some information. The idea is to switch the parts of your brain that you're using, to stay at peak performance.

- Prepare the night before everything that you'll need for the next day. Whether it's your clothes, food, materials for a meeting, your "to do" list, etc., put it all together the prior day when you have greater control over your time. Too often people leave things unfinished until the morning, and in a mad scramble "try" to get ready. This is a stress that with some planning, can be avoided.

- To have quality free time, it's useful to plan for it. In other words, schedule your unscheduled time. Leave certain periods of time unplanned and unscheduled so that you can be spontaneous, and at times just go with the flow. Or so that you can merely relax and be mindless, and able to recharge your mind, body, and spirit. Some people's lives are so full that this could seem impossible. But even five to ten minute time-outs, can help to clear the mind and rejuvenate the focus.

- To handle interruptions, use the technique of "because." Tell the person disturbing you, why you can't visit with them right now, and ask when would be a good time to get back to them. As an example, "Because a client is waiting for this report I'm working on right now, I'll need to get back to you later. When is a good time for you?"

- Create checklists for all your projects. Whether it's travelling, holding a meeting, or how to do a report, checklists will help to ensure that everything is accounted for, as well as save a tremendous amount of time. See Figure 11-4. I have a checklist of over 85 items for the materials I need to have for my various workshops. In subsequent chapters, there are checklists for career, management, and relationships to give you additional ideas.

- And the classic of, "Have a place for everything, and put everything in its place." Whether it's the car keys, clothes, or the monthly bills, have those specific places for each item so you automatically know where it is.

Clarity and knowing specifically what you want, the *UER*, is the first thing that needs to be determined to get organized. As discussed in the *Wording Your Goals* chapter, deciding on the results you want, serves as a beacon to guide your thoughts and actions, and to keep you on course. Once the *UER* is established, you can then know what to do, how to do it, and when to do it. Remember, to get the maximum assistance of others, you need to be able to explain to them what you want, so that they fully understand your wishes.

FIGURE 11-4:
Creating Checklists

● ● ●

TRAVEL

○ Cash	○ Undershirts	○ Extra wristwatch
○ Traveler's checks	○ Dress socks	○ Suntan lotion
○ Tickets	○ Sports socks	○ Sunglasses
○ Credit cards	○ Sweater	○ Hair dryer
○ Suits	○ Pajamas	○ Reading materials
○ Sports jacket	○ Raincoat	○ Business cards
○ Slacks	○ Gloves	○ Flashlight
○ Dress shirts	○ Shorts	○ Extra batteries
○ Neckties	○ Jacket	○ Camera
○ Casual shirts	○ Bathing suit	○ Film
○ Belts	○ Maps	○ Vitamins
○ Dress shoes	○ Address book	○ Medicine
○ Casual shoes	○ Umbrella	○ Iron
○ Sandals	○ Alarm clock	○ Exercise equipment
○ underpants	○ Stereo	○ Power cord
○ Running shoes	○ Tapes/CDs	○ Laundry bag
○ Sweats	○ First aid kit	○ Toiletries
○ Casual pants	○ Extra pens	○ Money pouch
○ Hats	○ Army knife	○ Set timers
○ Jeans	○ Snacks	○ Take out garbage
○ Mail picked-up	○ Big repellent	○ Water plants

MEETINGS

○ Determine purpose	○ Notify attendees	○ Equipment needed
○ Create agenda	○ Confirm attendees	○ Handouts
○ Who attend	○ Who lead	○ Beverages, food
○ Location	○ Determine style	○ Record session
○ When	○ Arrange seating	○ Distribute notes

When beginning to organize a plan, to help get your thoughts centered and your brain in gear, use some of the techniques from the *Effective Visualization* chapter. Imagine a time in the future after you have attained your goal, look back to now, and see how you did it. What were the steps you took? Were there any other people involved? How did you do what you did? Be sure to enjoy the feeling of success.

After you have the vision, tell someone (or a tape recorder) the story of how you did it. Relate it as if you're reliving it. As if someone were interviewing you about your achievement, tell them all the details, who, what, where, why, when, and how. Tell them everything you did, all the actions you took, and all the experiences you had, that gave you your success. Help them to fully understand what happened. Share with the interviewer how happy and grateful you are about this accomplishment. Make it as real as you can. This is the beginning of brainstorming the possibilities.

Five major questions will assist you in setting up your action plan and managing your time. The questions are:

- What steps or actions need to be taken?
- How long will each step take to complete?
- What are the smallest steps that each action can be divided into?
- When should each step be taken/completed?
- What priority or sequence should the steps be in?

The order that you ask these questions in depends on the project and circumstances. Often it's more productive to prioritize the steps before determining when to do each one. The idea is to be flexible, and that effective time management is a fluid process.

Format a sheet of paper as in Figure 11-5, which is an sample work sheet for getting a new job. Title each page with the goal that it's for, and use separate sheets for each project. First write out all the obvious steps that come to mind to accomplish a goal, as quickly as possible. Do this without regard for time, when, priority, or who will do it. Just get the ball rolling by getting something down on paper.

FIGURE 11-5:
Setting Up An Action Plan

• • •

Goal: *Having a new job as a . . .*

- What actions are needed, time required, priority, and when?
- List and prioritize actions into the smallest, specific attainable steps.

Priority	Steps	@	Hours	→	When
	redo resume	@	6	→	9/23
2	list past jobs	@	½	→	9/17
8	write out accomplishments of job A	@	½	→	9/18
9	write out accomplishments of job B	@	½	→	9/18
14	write out accomplishments of job C	@	¼	→	9/19
	get addresses and phone numbers of past jobs	@	1	→	9/19
6A	get new phone number of job A	@	¼	→	9/17
6B	make copy of school certificate	@	¼	→	9/18
15	get address and phone number of job C	@	½	→	9/19
	contact employment agencies	@	2	→	9/19
6	prepare list of employment agencies	@	½	→	9/17
7	contact employment agency A	@	¼	→	9/18
10	contact employment agency B	@	¼	→	9/19
13	contact employment agency C	@	1	→	9/19
4	prepare list of interview questions	@	2	→	9/17
5	practice answering salary questions	@	¼	→	9/17
5A	practice answering interviewing questions	@	1½	→	9/17
16	get address and phone number of job D	@	¼	→	9/19
20	list accomplishments of job D	@	½	→	9/20
12	get new briefcase	@	¾	→	9/19
17	have shoes repaired	@	½	→	9/19
22	get car washed	@	½	→	9/21
19	pick up suit from the cleaners	@	½	→	9/20
26	research industry trends	@	2	→	9/21
21	call library for hours of operation	@	¼	→	9/20
18	discuss relocating with the family	@	¾	→	9/19
11	meet with career counselor	@	2	→	9/19
1	set appointment with career counselor	@	¼	→	9/16
12A	prepare new stationery	@	1	→	9/19
3	get postage	@	¼	→	9/17
21A	contact employment agency C again	@	¼	→	9/20

FIGURE 11-5:
Setting Up an Action Plan (continued)

• • •

	compile lists of references	@	2 ½	$\rightarrow$	9/21
23	compile list of 3 personal references	@	1	$\rightarrow$	9/21
24	compile list of 3 business references	@	1 ½	$\rightarrow$	9/21
25	call personal reference A	@	½	$\rightarrow$	9/21
27	call business reference A	@	½	$\rightarrow$	9/22
28	send thank you note to XYZ company, V.P	@	¾	$\rightarrow$	9/22
29	send thank you note to XYZ company, receptionist	@	½	$\rightarrow$	9/22
10A	prepare copies of materials for career counselor	@	1	$\rightarrow$	9/19

Projects that are very complex will require many work sheets. When doing production work on films, the master sheet had hire cast, hire crew, secure locations, etc. Then each of these sub goals was given its own work sheet. Hiring each of the lead actors had so many steps, that each was a separate goal, and therefore each had its own work sheet. How many work sheets to use is determined by what will it take to keep everything organized and manageable.

Some useful questions to ask to generate the actions required are, "What do I need to do to achieve this goal? How can I effectively complete this task?" Keep asking "What else do I need to do?" This is a good time to involve your people resources. Get viewpoints from others, and the benefit of their experience to know what to do, and what not to do. Also, if someone else has done it, how did they do it? Would they do things differently from the way that you do them?

After you've listed as many steps as come to mind easily, then estimate how long each action will take, and jot it down. This is a vital element. Envisioning the time required to do something, creates a future orientation and a time consciousness. This helps to make the goal real and to make connections in the brain about what needs to be done, and how to do it. To figure out how long something should take to complete, you have to mentally experience it, and go through all steps to compute the time demands. Have you ever underestimated how long it would take to do a task, and suffered the consequences?

The more you figure out and write down time estimates, the more accurate your projections will become, and the more efficient your usage of time. Also estimating the time required, will help you to prepare for how much energy you'll need for each step. If you think something will take thirty minutes to do, and it takes forty-five, it can seem like drudgery. But if you think it will take an hour, and it only takes forty-five minutes, you'll still have energy left over. Expectation can have a major effect on us. Make a habit of writing out time projections and enjoy all the benefits.

Estimating that a step will take over 60-90 minutes to complete, usually means that a step is too big, and that there are smaller steps it can be broken down into. A reason people often get bogged down and procrastinate, is that they make their steps too large. For instance, redoing a resume is not one step, as so many of my students can confirm. There might be 20-50 or more steps to do, to put together an effective resume.

Investigate each step, and see if it can be broken down into smaller ones, as small as possible. This is a critical distinction. The key is to plan out actions that are the smallest steps possible, regardless of how obvious they may seem. This makes each one simpler to do, gives you a sense of accomplishment, and promotes taking more action. To illustrate this point, often when I teach time management, I have the group come up with the amount of steps it takes to get in a locked car and drive off. It's around 20 steps, depending on how careful a person is in their driving habits.

Keep asking if there are smaller steps to each step. Aim for a target of having steps that will take 15 minutes or less to complete. Each step is actually a separate goal. When something is unfinished, it can inhibit us from being at our best. Making your steps small enough to easily finish, makes it easier to devote one-hundred per cent to them, and to increase your efficiency.

Next, write down when each step will be taken and finalized. Be sure to make it a specific date by determining a particular day you will do an action. This is another way to monitor whether or not your steps are too big. If the start date and completion date of a step are not the same date, then that's telling you that you need to break the step into smaller ones. Specific dates help to motivate, create commitment, plan, and initiate action. There seems to be a human tendency that tasks take as long to complete as we allow for. With practical and tight time schedules, time is used productively.

Many projects, such as building a house, launching a new business, or producing a film, starting with the completion date and working backwards can be best. With the target date in mind, and an estimate of how long each step will take, you can get an idea of when you need to start. Be sure to build in enough extra time as a safeguard to allow for all the unseen variables that might show up.

Once the dates for each step are listed, then put the steps in priority. In what order should the steps be performed, for maximum efficiency? When specifically, at what time of the day, will each step be worked on? Depending on the nature of a project, it might be best to set the priorities before the dates. Experiment with different sequencing, and see which gives you the best results. Note how some steps in Figure 11-5, do not have priority numbers. This is because they are such large steps, that they have smaller steps in them, which have the priority numbers.

Prioritizing the steps are usually obvious, but it's critical that you stay flexible and are willing to change them as conditions change. Have you ever worked on something that could have been done later, and found that you didn't have enough time to do what was really needed? Most people seem to have a need for closure, meaning that once we begin a task, we want to finish it before moving on to another one.

Change is the only thing we can be certain of, and at an ever accelerating pace. So it's vital to be able to shift from one thing to another as is necessary. Choose to do what is the best use of your time to fulfill your goals, versus what are the easiest or closest things to do. Having everything written out, will help to keep you on target. And keep asking yourself, "Right now, what is the best use of my time to achieve my goals?"

When I was putting products in films, I usually had over seventy clients to represent, and typically had twenty-five to thirty films to service at any one time. Since films are so often dealing with crises (bad weather, equipment failure, incapacitated actors), things are in a constant state of change. There were days when almost every phone call meant that every priority in our company needed to be revised. This ability to adapt to ever changing circumstances, was one of the reasons we were so successful.

Another idea that's useful if you have to reset your priorities, is to use letters with the numbers. Say you're doing your resume and you remember two more things you need to do between steps 11 and 12. Rather than redo all the numbering, make the additional steps 11A and 11B. In some cases you may use up the entire alphabet and go to AA, BB, etc. By using letters you can simplify any rearranging that needs to be done.

Flexibility also deals with being open to the feedback that your actions are giving you. You need to constantly monitor and evaluate your results, and be willing to make adjustments if appropriate. If you do something in a certain way and you don't get the result you want, it's telling you that you need to make a shift to get a different outcome. If you want the color purple, you need to mix blue and red in certain proportions. But you continue to mix blue and yellow and can't understand why you keep getting green. No matter how stubbornly and energetically you combine blue and yellow, it still won't give you purple. Sound familiar? So if we want things to change, we must change what we do, when we do it, and how we do it.

Now that you have your steps laid out, estimated how long each will take, divided them into the smallest units of activity, when they'll be done, and in what priority, the next move is to transfer the steps to your daily calendar. A part of this transfer, is to have determined the specific time frames for each step, 9:00–9:45 A.M., 10:00–11:30 A.M., etc. Use a calendar that provides you with plenty of space to write out all your notes. Find one that suits the type of goals that you have. Give yourself a tool that allows you to easily organize your kind of projects. For many of the people in my classes, an appointment calendar that's broken down into 15-minute time slots works best.

Once you've completed a step, either check it off or put a line through it. Check it off if you may need the information at a later date, or if you're waiting, such as leaving a message for someone to call you back. Put a line through it, if it's a one-time event or if it's totally handled, such as returning someone's phone call or picking up your dry cleaning. Also, for many steps, it's usually a good idea to write down the date and time it was done. This is especially useful in communication, such as leaving a message, returning a call, faxing something, e-mail, ordering something, etc. Keeping this record will help you to know when to follow-up if necessary. For example, if you order something, jot down in your calendar on the day it's due to arrive, the day it was ordered, the phone number, who took your order, and any other required information.

The format in Figure 11-5, also works as your general "to do" list for daily activities. Therefore, one page may contain steps from many different goals. In this case, the "when" column would be used for listing the specific time of day a step would be performed.

People often ask about putting this method into a computer program. I find that it works best to use pen and paper. It's more mobile, flexible, immediate, and functional, to have a work sheet that can be used anywhere. Individual pages also allow for comparison and analysis of many projects simultaneously. Explore and find out what works best for you with your type of goals.

When is the best time to do your planning? In most situations, lay out your steps for tomorrow at the end of each day. This provides a sense of achievement, focus, and mastery. Then do it again at the beginning of each day to manage any changes and necessary adjustments. Of course, shifts will occur throughout the day as things develop, but without an initial blueprint, time is sure to be wasted.

Team situations also work well with this method. First, establish the *UER* for the project being worked on, with everyone's participation. Then get their input as to what actions they feel need to be done, time required for each action, when to be finished, and priority. After these items are decided upon, determine who will handle each task and write their name next to it. This creates involvement, commitment, and a sense of team, and helps all concerned to know who's responsible for what.

Figure 11-6 is an example of putting together an action plan for career development. The examples are from different people with different aspirations, and are designed to give you ideas to construct your own plans. They are models to help get you started on your path to fulfilling your wishes and dreams. Notice how some steps in Figure 11-6, have letters in the 'when' column. Simply use 'D' for something you want to do on daily basis, 'W' for weekly, 'M' for monthly, and 'O' for ongoing. These will act as constant reminders of things that you want to be put in your schedule.

The next chapter deals with how to keep yourself on track through the use of a daily log, and is the last segment of the primary *Anatomy of Success* system.

FIGURE 11-6:
Setting Up an Action Plan

• • •

Goal: *Developing my career.*

- What actions are needed, time required, priority, and when?
- List and prioritize actions into the smallest, specific attainable steps.

Priority	Steps	@	Hours	→	When
	learn new computer software	@	10	→	8/20
2A	get phone number of computer school	@	¼	→	7/15
4	register for computer school	@	¼	→	7/17
5	get book on public speaking	@	½	→	7/18
4A	call bookstore for public speaking book	@	¼	→	7/17
6	arrange sitter for kids	@	½	→	7/18
	write an article for a trade magazine	@	4	→	8/1
16A	join local Chamber of Commerce	@	1	→	7/24
12	get Lynn to be a mentor	@	1	→	7/21
	start attending all company events	@	50	→	O
3	get a list of company functions	@	1	→	7/15
	request more responsibility	@	3	→	7/20
2	make appointment to meet with supervisor	@	¼	→	7/15
1	decide where I can handle more responsibility	@	1	→	7/15
11	meet with supervisor on more responsibility	@	¾	→	7/20
7	setup accomplishments book	@	1	→	7/19
8	start recording accomplishments daily	@	¼	→	D
	give speeches to industry groups	@	6	→	M
13	sign up for public speaking class	@	¼	→	7/21
17A	meet with staff on increasing productivity	@	1	→	7/25
14	develop agenda for meeting with staff	@	1	→	W
9	notify staff of meeting on productivity	@	½	→	7/20
	research what the competition is doing	@	3	→	7/29
10	find out if library has trade magazine	@	¼	→	7/20
15	compile list of articles on the competition	@	1	→	7/23
16	look up information about the competition	@	1 ½	→	7/23
18	prepare report about the competition	@	2	→	7/25
17	organize notes about the competition	@	1	→	7/25

Chapter 12

DAILY LOG

● ● ●

RECORDING YOUR PROGRESS

At this point, by doing all of the preceding steps, you know what you want, why you want it, and what you need to be doing to reach your objectives. There's one more piece of the process that will assist you in being connected to your target and staying on track, and that's utilizing a daily log.

Each day write down what steps you took to achieve each of your goals. By documenting your daily activities, you get a sense of progress, and you have something on paper that shows you are moving closer toward your destinations. This keeps you in the success cycle, for it encourages taking more action. Therefore the motivation to succeed is maintained and reinforced. The act of recording what you're actually doing, keeps your goals as part of your ongoing consciousness. It also provides you with continuous feedback as to how things are measuring up to your plan. This in turn helps to keep you directed and advancing forward.

To get you started on keeping an account of your actions, setup a sheet of lined three-hole notebook paper for each of your main goals, as in Figure 12-1. Full-sized college ruled paper works well, for it allows you to log around one month per side, if you log several days in the blank space above the lines. In the upper left-hand corner write the year, then your name, and lastly a goal. Enter these headings on both sides of the sheet as a constant reminder of what you want and to establish ownership of each project. In addition, put together a three ring binder with an separate section for each of your goals to keep it all organized.

FIGURE 12-1:
Daily Log

• • •

(year) (name)_____ —(goal) "I always want to be totally healthy."

(month/day)
1/1   exercised, relaxed with friends.
1/2   walked 2 miles, took up a new hobby, sailing.
1/3   read article on healthy cooking.
1/4   —
1/5   —
1/6   helped friend solve a problem, exercised.
1/7   did volunteer work.
1/8   bought new cooking device.
1/9   installed water filter, exercised.
1/10 got massage, watched sunset.
1/11 —
1/12 bought new walking shoes, did visualization.
1/13 went to party and danced, walked up 6 flights of stairs.
1/14 watched television show on health.
1/15 went grocery shopping.
1/16 —
1/17 made appointment for physical exam.
1/18 checked out new sporting goods store.
1/19 helped neighbor move furniture.
1/20 organized closets and gave clothes to charity.
1/21 hiked in the forest.
1/22 —
1/23 set goals for exercise program.

Keep in mind, as mentioned in the prior chapter, that some activities might apply to more than one goal. For instance, if you go to a party it can relate to satisfying business, family, and health outcomes. At the event you might network and make professional contacts, spend time with family members, and dance so much that you have an aerobic workout. Therefore this one function would have entries under three different projects.

The best time to note what you do each day toward fulfilling your dreams, is at night before you go to sleep. In the left-hand column write the date and then jot down everything you did that day in the pursuit of each ambition. Use abbreviations whenever you can so that you can get a lot of information condensed in a small space. Since it usually averages only twenty to forty seconds to list the actions for each goal, the time involved is minimal. As well as your specific actions, list any positive results that you attain each day. All this information contributes to a feeling of accomplishment, and it tells your brain what to work on as you sleep.

What if there's a day that you do nothing toward a goal, what should you do? Still set down the date and simply mark a dash on the line to show that no activity occurred that day. This helps you to have a graphic representation of your current priorities, an issue we'll discuss shortly.

Another issue comes up, and that is what if you miss making entries for a day or two. This can happen quite frequently especially when you do a lot of traveling. If you miss logging for a period of time, just fill-in the data as soon as you can to the best of your recollections. Whatever you come up with no matter how incomplete, will still help you to stay on target.

An additional suggestion is to take your Benefits page for each goal, and place them opposite the daily log sheets. This will require punching holes on the right-hand side for when you write on the front side of the log sheet. By having holes on both sides, you can always have the Benefits page facing the log sheet. In this way the Benefits page acts as a constant reinforcement, strengthening your motivation and desire. Sometimes why we want something, why it's important to us, can get lost in the shuffle. Glancing at the benefits of each goal each day as you write out the actions you took, helps to maintain your focus and perspective.

After several weeks of putting what you've done on paper, you'll begin to see an accurate picture of your current commitment to a project. Many times people talk so much about wanting something, that they feel they're doing a lot to have it. Then when they look at their daily log and notice very few entries and numerous blank lines, the truth becomes obvious. Besides understanding yourself, there's another benefit to this awareness.

Have you ever felt that you had to obtain a certain result, and that not having it generated too much frustration and stress? Here's an occasion where your daily log is very useful in increasing your comfort level. When you look at your log and observe little or no activity, you know that the goal right now isn't critically important to you, and that there are other more significant needs in your life. Or that in some way, you are not properly prepared in terms of clarity, skills, knowledge, beliefs, etc. You may require more experience, more information, more empowering beliefs, to neutralize some limiting beliefs, etc.

Looking at your log can help you to be okay with your existing situation, and keep stress at an appropriate level. Too much stress and you might be too frustrated, feel hopeless, and quit. Too little stress, and you can lose your motivation. Having balance, based on the truth, should yield the best results.

When we absolutely positively must have something, we take steps to acquire it. The proof is in the doing. Often we hear someone complain about not having something and yet they do nothing to change their condition. By using a daily log you face the reality that you must take the initiative if you want to receive the results. So if one of your log sheets is basically bare, accept the fact that it's okay to not have this outcome at the present time because you're not doing enough to make it happen.

Does this mean to give up? No! It just means to be realistic with what can be accomplished at any one time, and to allow yourself to resolve any internal conflicts. Sometimes one goal must be secured before another one can be fully pursued. Acknowledge that right now obtaining a particular outcome may require more output than is currently practical, and that you will continue to do what you can under the present circumstances toward its fulfillment. You can now be comfortable with waiting because you know you have made a choice. You can replace frustration and stress with understanding.

What if one of your log sheets shows that you're taking massive action on a project and yet you still have no real results? A lot of activity doesn't necessarily equal victory. Remember it's not just what you do, but also how and when you do it. Sometimes job seekers that I work with tell me that they contact many companies each day, and they get discouraged due to the poor replies that they get. We then dig into how they approach these companies, what attitude they put out. Too often the attitude is negative, defensive, fearful, needy, hostile, lifeless, indecisive, impolite, confused, etc. Too often they do not research a company, and are not communicating how they could be of value to a prospective employer. Taking action is crucial to success, but it must be the right kind of action, presented in the right way, at the right time, suitable to each situation.

Your daily log gives you valuable feedback, it helps to provide you with a reality check. After pursuing a goal for a period of time, you might realize that its attainment is impractical at the moment. Again, you may need more skills, more knowledge, more people, more time, more planning, more money, to realign your values, to change beliefs, etc. You can reach a point where you decide to regroup or to postpone a particular destination to follow other paths. There are times when we have to get more than our feet wet to know that the water is too cold. We can choose to put on a wet suit, or to swim another day. Keep in mind that regardless of the effects you produce, you can always benefit and grow from them, by asking "What can I learn from this?"

When a positive result occurs, indicate it in your log in some special way. Many people use different colored stars like the ones used in elementary school. Each color is assigned a meaning. Green could be for executing a beginning type of action, like setting an appointment or ordering a loan application. Silver could be for actually having a meeting. Red for concluding a major step, and gold for completing a project. The concept is to reward yourself in some way for the triumphs you achieve and to continually support your motivation.

When you accomplish a goal, confirm your success by signing and dating your log sheet. This gives you a sense of closure. The end has been reached and now it's time for another venture. Add each achievement to your success list, so that they also become resources for other objectives. Certain goals, such as being healthy, will probably remain forever, and therefore will always be ongoing.

This concludes the *Anatomy of Success* system. The next chapter is an overview of the system, with ideas on how to use and adapt the steps in your daily life. After that, there are special chapters with checklists for career, management, and relationships.

Chapter 13

OVERVIEW

● ● ●

Applying The System

Anatomy of Success consists of many steps, processes, and techniques, as listed in Figure 13-1 at the end of this chapter. Do you have to do all of them for every goal? For optimum results, in one way or another, yes. Certain goals, such as which television to buy or where to get your hair done, won't require a complete session, as many of the answers to the system are already in place. But for major goals, such as health, relationships, and career it's recommended to do every section completely. And the more you use the system, the faster and more automatic it becomes. We'll use an illustration of buying a new car, to see how using the various components of the system would work.

Using *Positive Language Patterns* will be helpful in all situations. They affect your thinking and your behavior, and therefore your results. The self-awareness techniques from the *Building a Foundation* chapter, are ongoing processes that are involved in almost every aspect of your life.

Is wording a clear concise specific positive goal statement useful? Absolutely. Your goal statement, establishing the *UER*, is creating the instructions for your mind. Only when this is completed do you know what to pay attention to, and what choices to make. Have you ever made a purchase or decision without knowing specifically what you want, and later been unhappy with the result? In choosing a car, some of the things you might consider are:

- the style
- the color
- the size

- cost of insurance
- theft rate
- theft deterrent system

- the price
- financing options
- cost of operating
- ease of entry & exit
- trunk capacity
- comfort of the seating
- interior
- the handling
- length of warranty
- resale value

- mechanical quality
- ease of getting service
- maintenance schedule
- status and prestige
- noise level
- type of audio system
- rear visibility
- the engine power
- type of accessories
- safety record

Moving to other steps, you would want to determine when you want to own the car so that you can arrange for the financing and the sale of your old car. How long you intend to keep the car might indicate whether to lease or buy, and if an extended warranty makes sense. Where to buy could be meaningful in terms of a dealer's reputation, and the ease of having the maintenance done.

Do you need to spend a lot of time on the benefits? It depends. If everyone concerned agrees that it's time to buy a new car, then the benefits are already handled. If you need to convince someone that it's a good idea, or if owning it will require a great deal of effort on your part, then doing the whole benefits of the benefit until the underlying feelings surface, would be advantageous. Projecting into the future how buying this new car would impact your life six months, one year, and five years later is beneficial to be sure you'll be satisfied with this choice later.

Visualizing you having and enjoying the car would be useful. Imagining all the different ways you would be using the vehicle, could assist you in determining which is the best selection. Visualization gives you an efficient method for doing a type of test drive, from the comfort of your home.

Planning what resources you need would make sense. What skills would be helpful in buying a car? Researching, analyzing, organizing, budgeting, interviewing, communicating, deciding, persuading, and negotiating could come into play when making almost any purchase. Information besides the criteria items above, such as lists of dealers, dealer's reputation, dealer's cost, manufacturer rebates, inventory levels, any recalls, test reports, and the market value of your old car, are things you would want to know. Determining specifically how much money you can and are willing to spend, is certainly important. People that could contribute could be owners of the same model, mechanics, insurance agent, banker, and a friend to assist with the negotiating. Location to work in won't probably be an issue, but certain equipment might be required. From books, magazines, and a computer for research, to a calculator for all the figuring, to taking a test drive, could all assist you in making the best choice and deal that you can.

Some beliefs to establish in others could be, that your old car is worth a certain price, and that you will only pay a specific amount for the new car. You may need to establish the belief in whomever you borrow the money from, that you can and will pay back your loan. And you may need to install the belief in your spouse to put money into a new car instead of something else.

What are some self beliefs that would serve you in buying a car? That you will choose the best car with the right equipment. That now is the best time for you to buy. That you will get the best deal possible. That you deserve to have a new car. That you can afford a new car. That it's worthwhile to buy a new car. And checking out the potential loss and the gain of these beliefs, will help you to know if these beliefs are beneficial to you or could cause you difficulties.

Looking at what could cause you not to achieve your goal, will help you to be aware of what you need to do. Analyzing how your relationships with others might be affected, can help you to prepare to deal with it. Will your spouse be supportive of the purchase? Will others, such as friends or co-workers, be jealous? Are there benefits of not buying the car, such as less debt and lower insurance premiums? Understanding what could be lost after you buy a new car, can help you in removing things that could hold you back.

Are there limiting beliefs, such as you'll never sell your old car, that you don't deserve it, that you can't get the financing, that it's not worth it, that you'll buy the wrong car at the wrong dealer, etc.? It would definitely be desirable to neutralize these beliefs and replace them with opposite empowering ones. Or learn that you're not prepared to buy a new car at this time.

Recognizing the negative consequences of not getting a new car, is valuable in discovering whether you really need to make the purchase now. What's the downside if you don't do it?

Setting up an action plan would be important. You'd certainly want to figure out what actions to take, how long each would take, what order to do them in, and when. An organized game plan will help you to maximize the use of your time and energy. And logging what you do each day to achieve getting a new car, will assist you in keeping on track and focused.

Many times people ask me if it's necessary to do the steps in the exact order as listed here. The answer is not necessarily, except for the wording and the constructing of your goal statements. It's usually best to thoroughly complete this part first so that you have clarity, and know where you want to end up. Then do the rest of the steps in the order that is most suitable for each of your goals. Quite often someone's sense of who they are, values, beliefs, self-concept, skills, abilities, etc., needs to be dealt with before they can move forward with full enthusiasm. This can be necessary before someone is able to use their capacity and potential.

As you can see, these questions, processes, and techniques work for you in the pursuit of any goal. Just asking all the questions from *Anatomy of Success* even if you don't do all the steps or write everything down, will be beneficial. Just asking all the questions causes connections in your brain, helping you to achieve better results.

Each night write out your goals for the next day. In today's ever changing world, be sure to allow for flexibility. As conditions change you need to be able to change with them. Along with this, start each day with reading your major goals out loud. This activates more of your senses and increases your commitment to having what you want. Make this verbalization more potent by being in an appropriate physical pattern, and using a voice tone that is believable.

Another idea is to create a detailed audiotape of what your goals are, and play it as you go to sleep at night. This will assist your brain in knowing what to work on as you sleep and contribute to insights as you awaken. Also, do brief visualizations of you succeeding, as often as is practical. The mind is always active. Continue to fill it with what you want, or someone else may do it for you. Summarize each of your goals, with the main benefits and feelings, on small cards that you can carry with you. They act as constant reminders keeping your *UER*, your *Ultimate End Results*, in sight.

The next chapter is a checklist to help you determine what you want in a job or career. It will assist you in creating a clear picture of what works best for you.

FIGURE 13-1:
"Anatomy of Success"

• • •

Outline

POSITIVE LANGUAGE PATTERNS—Chapter 1:
- Always use Positive Language Patterns. Work for the most effective wording to use in each situation to achieve your *UER*.
- Replace Mischievous Metaphors, Sorrowful Similes, and Adverse Analogies with the positive of what you do want.

BUILDING A FOUNDATION—Chapter 2:
- Maintain self-awareness through knowing and monitoring your values, beliefs, self-concept, skills, successes, life purpose, and goals.
- Keep developing your success self-concept, and make choices that are consistent with who you wish to be.

WORDING YOUR GOALS—Chapter 3:
- Word your goals very specifically, with enough detail to form an image of the *UER*.
  a) Determine how you will know you have achieved each objective, what is your criteria?
  b) When is each goal desired, where, and for how long?

THE BENEFITS—Chapter 4:
- Why have a goal? What will it allow you to do, have, and be? Write out the benefits of the benefits, until the underlying feelings are known.
- After attaining a goal, what is different in your life (do, have, and be) 6 months, 1 year, and 5 years later?

FIGURE 13-1:
"Anatomy of Success" (continued)

———————————————   • • •   ———————————————

EFFECTIVE VISUALIZATION—Chapter 5:
- Use "Full Spectrum" and "Reflection Realization" visualization techniques to imagine yourself having and enjoying your goals, in vivid detail.
- Adjust all the elements until your visions are the most appealing to you.

READYING YOUR RESOURCES—Chapter 6:
- Use SIMPLE to determine what resources are needed.

EMPOWERING BELIEF MANAGEMENT—Chapter 7:
- What beliefs do you need to establish to achieve a goal?
  a) What beliefs do you need to establish in others so that they willingly help you?
  b) What beliefs do you need to install in yourself to empower you?
  c) Use the "Proof Menu" and "BECAUSE'S" to install the beliefs.
  d) What are the consequences, loss and gain, of your empowering beliefs?

WHY NOT—Chapter 8:
- Could anything cause you not to achieve a goal?
  a) Will relationships with others change?
  b) Are there any benefits of not achieving a goal?
  c) Could anything be lost after a goal is achieved?

NEUTRALIZING LIMITING BELIEFS—Chapter 9:
- Are there any limiting beliefs that could hold you back, and that need to be neutralized or replaced?
  a) What are past limiting beliefs that have changed to positive ones?
  b) Write down any limiting beliefs.
  c) What are the opposite empowering beliefs?
  d) What are counterexamples and exceptions to the limiting beliefs?

FIGURE 13-1:
"Anatomy of Success" (continued)

• • •

e) Install the empowering beliefs with the "Proof Menu" and "BECAUSE'S."
f) What are the consequences, loss and gain, of each empowering belief?
g) What were, and would have been, the consequences of each limiting belief?

NEGATIVE CONSEQUENCES—Chapter 10:
- What are negative feelings that you always want to avoid?
- If a goal is not achieved, are there any negative consequences?
  a) What would you lose, what would you be prevented from doing, having, and being if you don't succeed?
  b) Write out the consequences of each negative consequence until no more ideas surface, and your thoughts stop.
- Threshold—what future gain and loss will cause you to take action, now?

MANAGING YOUR TIME—Chapter 11:
- Write out an action plan for each goal, and for each day, of what steps are needed, time required to do each step, when each step is to be completed, and prioritize the steps into an efficient sequence.
- Constantly break your steps down into the smallest steps possible.

DAILY LOG—Chapter 12:
- Each day record the steps you've taken toward the achievement of each goal.
- Keep adding to your list of successes.

Chapter 14

CAREER CHECKLIST

● ● ●

GAINING CLARITY FOR YOUR VOCATION

In the *Wording Your Goals* chapter, we dealt with being focused and developing a list of the elements you want a goal to have. Getting specific enables you to make better choices and achieve desirable results. Not being specific can limit your motivation, for lack of a definite destination inhibits taking action. Also, writing everything down gives you a sense of control and helps to handle all the ideas that can be flying around inside one's brain at tremendous speed.

This chapter is a guide to help you prepare a detailed list for what you want in a job or career. It covers general things to consider in determining whether a position or career is suitable for you. In some cases it will assist you in knowing if you are suitable for the position. Clearly knowing what you want, will empower you to get it. You will present yourself with confidence and inspire others to have confidence in you. And for best results, both you and the employer must be satisfying the high points of each other's wish lists.

From the points on Figure 14-1, use the items that are important to you, and then add others that are of special interest to you. As with other examples, these came from several different people. Setup a piece of paper writing out each item from the list, and then write out what you want. Put each of your answers on a separate line, so that you can rate it, as discussed in the next paragraph. Complete your ideas for each entry before moving to the next item. We often have so many options that it can be difficult to make a decision. Assembling the data of what you want will make it easier for you to know where to look and what to do.

After you jot down your replies, then determine their importance or VALUE. On a scale of 1-10, 1 being of little importance and 10 being absolutely necessary, assign a number to each of your responses. Say you would like to work for an old established company, but it's only a preference and a newer company is acceptable. Therefore the rating might only be a 3 or 4. In the case of overnight travel, because of family responsibilities, none is crucial to you, so this would be a 10.

In addition, analyze how closely what you've been getting comes to your desired level. Rate the NOW status of your current position, or if you're between jobs, evaluate the last one. For instance, if it's very significant to you for your manager to give you praise on a regular basis, if its value is a 10, and you rarely receive praise, the NOW rating might be a 2. And it's possible that what you are or have received is better than what you require. You may be okay with commuting two hours per day, rating it a 6 or 7, and you may only be commuting one hour per day, so the NOW rating would be a 9 or 10.

What's the likelihood of a job or career fulfilling all your requirements? There are too many variables to answer this question. But since we rarely get more than we ask for, creating your checklist will help you to get more of what you want. It will help you to make decisions that work for you.

The sequence of items in Figure 14-1 is not in any special order. Each person's requirements are unique. Some of the parts, such as location, might be more straightforward than others, such as type of supervisor. If you have difficulty getting a clear answer as to what you want for an item, just write out whatever comes to mind. Leave some blank lines and come back to it later. By completing the whole list, you may find that the answer to one issue will generate an answer for another. Also, with many of the ideas, such as salary and commuting time, a range could be appropriate.

In some cases, doing this checklist from two other viewpoints, besides the one in this chapter, would be useful. One would be for your ultimate ideal job or career situation. Dream the big dream, which might include being the president of your own company, earning over $1,000,000 per year, commuting 10 minutes a day, etc. Another outlook could be for what you absolutely positively don't want and find totally unacceptable regardless of the money. This might include commuting over four hours per day, relocating, doing overnight travel 70% of the time, unfriendly co-workers, or having a boss who's a screamer. After filling out all this information, you should have a clear idea of what path to pursue.

FIGURE 14-1:
Job and Career Checklist

• • •

	VALUE - NOW

JOB DUTIES: responsible for the product being
produced; hands-on working with staff and customers.   9 - 8

SKILLS USED: managing, hiring, organizing, planning,
purchasing.   8 - 6

SALARY: $70,000.   7 - 8

BENEFITS AND PERKS: medical, dental, profit sharing.   9 - 7

LOCATION: downtown business district.   8 - 10

COMMUTING TIME: two hours per day.   7 - 10

TYPE OF CO-WORKERS: friendly, hardworking, upbeat,
honest.   10 - 7

TYPE OF SUPERVISOR: fair, organized, decisive, smart.   7 - 7

TYPE OF PRODUCT OR SERVICE: real estate.   9 - 9

TYPE OF CUSTOMERS: corporate, middle management.   7 - 6

SIZE OF COMPANY: medium, 100-300 people.   6 - 8

AGE OF COMPANY: 10-12 years old.   8 - 5

TURNOVER: very low.   5 - 7

WORK STRUCTURE: mostly work as part of a team.   8 - 8

COMPANY IMAGE: excellent reputation for quality.   10 - 6

FUTURE POTENTIAL: not an issue, I'm doing what I want.   1 - 10

ENVIRONMENT: a lot of light, lots of windows, clean.   9 - 8

WORK HOURS: start 8:30 A.M., end 5:30 P.M., maximum
60 hours per week.   10 - 10

PRESTIGE: want a supervisory title, and be highly visible.   7 - 10

OVERNIGHT TRAVEL: 3 nights per month.   10 - 9

JOB SECURITY: want security and where I can stay
for at least 5 years.   9 - 7

PACE: somewhat hectic with a lot of activity.   8 - 9

STRUCTURED OR UNSTRUCTURED: prefer doing
basically similar work each day.   8 - 10

PUBLIC OR PRIVATE: public where I can buy stock.   6 - 0

FIGURE 14-1:
Job and Career Checklist (continued)

• • •

TRAINING: like ongoing skill development.	7 -	6
VACATIONS: 2 weeks paid, and 1 week unpaid.	3 -	10
DRESS CODE: casual based on personal preferences.	5 -	2
EMOTIONS: satisfied, productive, involved.	10 -	6
EXPERIENCES CAUSING EMOTIONS: see happy customers, work well with co-workers, get clear goals from supervisor.	9 -	7

It's been said do what you love and the money will follow. How often is this true? Most of the financially successful people that I know and have interviewed, do love what they do. But I also know many people, especially in the arts, who are doing what they love, and yet can barely survive. There are many actors, writers, dancers, singers, musicians, designers, photographers, directors, comedians, poets, and artists who live for their work and who are just getting by. Having functional flexibility may be a wise choice. Being flexible might be working at an art gallery, a theater, a school, a production company, or a publisher to be close to one's passion, and following the dream during personal time.

As we discussed earlier, we do everything to have a certain feeling. Sometimes when we understand the feelings behind an occupational goal that doesn't seem to work for us, then perhaps we can find another more practical career that provides the same feelings. I'm not suggesting to give up on a dream, however, if it's not working after a realistic amount of time, or if the price you have to pay is too great, a change in direction may be in order. How does the pursuit of your career balance with the rest of your life?

The following are brief descriptions of the items in Figure 14-1:

• Job duties: what do you specifically want to do, what types of tasks? What kinds of projects do you want to be working on? What would you do on a typical workday? What do you want to be responsible for accomplishing? Do you want to manage, sell, manufacture, design, train, research, build, drive, audit, cook, farm, keep books, handle customers, negotiate, hire, write, etc.? Do you want to work with people, machines, or ideas? Do you like to work face-to-face, or through technology?

- Skills: which ones do you want to be using? Do you want to be communicating, analyzing, creating, organizing, coordinating, persuading, advising, demonstrating, coaching, budgeting, inspecting, measuring, forecasting, assembling, memorizing, computing, and so on?

- Salary: what's a realistic amount of compensation based on your abilities, skills, experience, education, the responsibilities of the job, the industry, and current conditions? What's the minimum you'll work for? How often do you want a salary review? What do you want raises to be based on? Do you want to be able to earn bonuses?

- Benefits and perks: what extras do you want, such as medical, dental, eye care, pension plan, profit sharing, stock, stock options, day care, education reimbursement, car, expense account, severance package, title, office, staff, vacations, personal time, sick leave, health club, clothing allowance, signing bonus, life insurance, disability insurance, and a credit union?

- Location: do you want to work in a certain area, such as a central business district or out in the suburbs? Does it need to be near public transportation? Do you want to work only in a particular part of the country, or are you willing to relocate? Do you want to be at the home office or a regional office?

- Commuting time: how much time do you want to spend going to work? What's the maximum amount of time or distance that you are comfortable travelling each day?

- Type of co-workers: what kind of people do you want to work with? People who are honest, friendly, quiet, fun, clean, outgoing, hardworking, dependable, liberal, conservative, trustworthy, male, female, young, old, intelligent, optimistic, respectful, considerate, calm, cooperative, competent, happy, interesting, etc.?

- Type of supervisor: what sort of manager do you want? Someone that works very closely with you or one that leaves you alone? Do you want constant praise, occasional praise, or do you know yourself when you've done a good job? Do you want a supervisor who tells you how everything is to be done, or who tells you the outcome and leaves it up to you how to accomplish it? What level of independence do you want? What qualities do you want them to have, such as fair, organized, nurturing, creative, loyal, accepting, cheerful, honest, logical, ambitious, sympathetic, thorough, patient, stable, sincere, and polite?

- Type of product or service: what kind of company or field do you want to work in? Do you want to work in retail, manufacturing, automotive, real estate, banking, insurance, education, entertainment, government, travel, legal, financial, medical, technology, transportation, food services, leisure, publishing, etc.?
- Type of customers: do you want work with corporations, the government, or the public? Do you want to work with male, female, young, old, managers, salespeople, etc., or do you like to work every kind and type of customer?
- Size of company: do you want to be a part of a small local organization, a huge international conglomerate, or something in between? What number of employees is desirable to you? Is there a level of sales volume that you prefer?
- Age of company: do you want a company with a long history and proven track record, or a new start-up where you would be part of its birth and growth?
- Turnover: do you want a place where people stay forever or where people move around a lot? Must turnover be from promotions and growth, or are you okay with it being from people being unhappy with the company and leaving?
- Work structure: do you want to work alone or as part of a team? What percentage of the time do you want to be in either situation? Is having a flexible work schedule desirable?
- Company image: what kind of reputation is important to you? If a job was perfect for you but the company had a negative image, would it matter to you? Do you want to be involved with the recognized leader in a field?
- Future potential: do you want to be in an organization where you can advance, or is it acceptable to you to remain in the same position, and perhaps move to another organization to advance?
- Environment: what physical surroundings are important for your effectiveness? How do you feel about size of work area, desk placement, furniture, noise level, air quality, lighting, temperature, aromas, windows, music, and decor?
- Work hours: how many hours a week are you willing to work? What hours during the day do you want to work, start times and stop times? How do you feel about working nights and weekends?
- Prestige: how important is the rank or status of a job? Is an impressive title meaningful to you?

- Overnight travel: what amount of overnight travel is desirable? Is it zero, one day a month, one day a week, or leave Sunday and come back Friday?
- Job security: do you want something that is very secure, or are you okay in a position with challenge and uncertainty?
- Pace: do you want a job that's very active and busy or slow and easy? How much stress and pressure are you comfortable with? Do you like to work on one thing at a time until it's completed, or handle several projects at the same time?
- Work pattern: do you want a structured situation where you basically do the same tasks each day, or an unstructured position where each day is different?
- Public or private: do you want to work for a public company where you can buy its stock, or one that is privately owned?
- Training: do you want a job where they provide ongoing training and skill development, or are you okay with gaining new skills on your own?
- Vacations: how much time off is necessary, even if unpaid? Do you want to be able to accumulate vacation days?
- Dress code: is a strict code of appearance acceptable or do you want an open casual code? Are you willing to wear a uniform?
- Emotions: what feelings do you want to have at the end of the workday? Do you want to feel satisfied, relaxed, appreciated, productive, important, energetic, competent, involved, thankful, happy, etc.? What are feelings you need to have to make a job worthwhile to you?
- Experiences causing emotions: what would you actually do, or experience, during the day that would provide you with the feelings that you want? Would you produce a quality product, be efficient and organized, have cooperative co-workers, receive praise from staff, help people, see happy customers, get compliments from suppliers, etc.?

Once you finish with these questions, be sure to add your own special items of importance.

Clarity is what these questions will help you to have, so that you know what works and doesn't work for you in a job or career. Can someone be too specific? Yes. In some cases people are so particular that nothing will ever satisfy them. Doing this exercise helps many people to get realistic. When they see that too many of their answers have ratings of eight, nine, or ten, they begin to realize that they might need to be more flexible. Or it may become very obvious that a job is not suitable and it is time to make a change.

This checklist is a tool for you to gather information to improve your present position and improve how you feel about it. It will also help you to decide on your next position with greater understanding.

In the next chapter, we'll explore a checklist that deals with managing an organization.

---------*Chapter 15*---------

ORGANIZATION CHECKLIST

● ● ●

COVERING ALL THE BASES

Success of an organization, whether it be business, nonprofit, or governmental, can be enhanced by constantly monitoring activities against a standard. This is especially true when it comes to employees. Constantly improving employees quality of performance and satisfaction, is as necessary to having success, as is having a quality product.

Focusing energies and keeping activities on target, is what the questions in this checklist are about. Not every question will apply to every situation. Simply mark off those that are appropriate to your situation, and add others that are useful to you.

Rating of the various items on this checklist is on a scale of 0-10. A "10" status means that you are satisfied with the level of achievement you have concerning a given question. A "0" status means that you feel a question addresses something that you feel is worthwhile, but have not yet implemented. Anything in between would be an indication of how close you are to the desired level. For instance, you may feel that certain employees should visit and learn your customer's operations. This is happening but not to the extent that your staff knows everything they need to know about your customers. Therefore the rating might be a 6 or 7. The activity is taking place, but more still needs to be done.

How often would it be useful to use the checklist and measure what's being accomplished? It depends on many variables; the organization, the department, the project, etc. As a general guideline, when you first start to use it, do it every three to four weeks. As things progress, you'll get an idea of the best time intervals to use to measure the status of your operations.

Most of the questions on this list are self-explanatory. Others I'll give more detail on as we go along. As with other checklists, the sequence of the questions is not necessarily in terms of importance. This is an individual matter depending on the organization.

Evaluating Operations

STATUS

[   ] Are short, medium, and long term goals being set
for the organization, and for each department?   _____

[   ] Are customers needs being fulfilled?   _____
(Everyone has customers. Some are internal and
some are external. In other words, a customer is
anyone we are accountable to for the completion of
a task. A customer is someone who is counting on
us to provide goods or services, or both. So
whether you answer the phone, file papers, assemble the product, load the trucks, send out the bills,
etc., you have customers. It could be the driver of
the truck, the next person on the assembly line, the
supervisor, the ultimate buyer, or the stockholders.
And the customers must be satisfied for the organization to prosper.)

[   ] Are customers asked, on an ongoing basis, what's
important to them, and how you could improve the
relationship? Are they being asked what they like
and dislike about your product and service?   _____

[   ] Are employees visiting and learning the customers'
operations?   _____

[   ] Are the customers' customers known and understood?   _____

[   ] Are customers contacted on a regular basis, and
with helpful information?   _____

[   ] Is customer service effective; are problems resolved
quickly?   _____

[   ] If a customer leaves, are they contacted to find
out why?   _____

[   ] Is everyone always looking for ways to improve
their work, and is change accepted as desirable?   _____

[   ] Do employees write ongoing reports evaluating
their own work and how they could improve it?   _____

[   ] Are employees encouraged to make suggestions
to improve the organization?   _____

[   ] Are employee suggestions being responded to in
a timely fashion?   _____

[   ] Do employees know how what they do contributes
to meeting the overall goals of the organization; do
they feel involved?   _____

[   ] Do employees have the authority to meet their
responsibilities?   _____

[   ] Is the most efficient system used to fulfill each
function?   _____

[   ] Is there too much emphasis on quotas at the
expense of quality?   _____

[   ] Are the hiring practices effective, with suitable
job profiles?   _____

[   ] Is an effective orientation given to new employees;
are they helped to fit in and understand how the
organization works?   _____

[   ] Is there an effective amount of teamwork?   _____

[   ] Is there good communication between departments,
and is everyone being kept informed?   _____

[   ] Is there sufficient delegation, with employees
knowing "why" something needs to be done in a
certain way, and by a certain time?   _____

[   ] Are employees being helped to set their own
realistic goals; do they know what's expected of
them and have a clear yardstick for success: tasks,
output, quality, attitude, time, etc.?   _____
(Studies have indicated that many employees aren't
totally sure of what they are supposed to do and
how their performance is measured. This confusion
causes stress and lowers productivity.)

[   ] Do employees get enough regular feedback on how
they're doing?   _____

[   ] Do employees receive enough praise, recognition,
and respect?   _____

[   ] Is there sufficient ongoing training?   _____

[   ] Do employees and the organization have compatible
values?   _____

[   ] Are the right people assigned to appropriate projects?   _____

[   ] Are employees finding self-fulfillment in the
attainment of the organization's goals; is the work
satisfying for the employees?   _____
[   ] Do employees receive equal treatment?   _____
[   ] Are the leaders leading by example?   _____
[   ] Is the work environment productive: lighting,
noise, space, layout, colors, furniture, air quality, etc.?   _____
[   ] Are employees being paid appropriately for their work?   _____
[   ] Are the benefits and perks adequate (medical, dental,
profit sharing, time off, expense accounts, day care,
personal time, tuition reimbursement, etc.)?   _____
[   ] Do employees have an optimal workload, not too
much and not too little?   _____
[   ] Is the best form of motivation being used for each
employee?   _____
[   ] Are there functions such as purchasing, accounting,
advertising, hiring, legal, warehousing, etc., that
can be combined?   _____
[   ] Is there enough equipment for everyone to do their job?   _____
[   ] Is the best equipment being used for the task?   _____
[   ] Is there enough working capital?   _____
[   ] Are the best locations being used for each area,
such as manufacturing, warehousing,
administrative, etc.?   _____
[   ] Is appropriate insurance being used, and at the
best price?   _____
[   ] Is there an understanding of governmental
regulations, federal, state, and local, and are
they being met?   _____
[   ] Are the best production methods being used?   _____
[   ] Are the most effective suppliers being used:
quality, price, quantity, delivery, service,
payment terms, warranty, etc.?   _____
[   ] Is the quality of the product at the right level to
meet and fulfill the customers' expectations?   _____
[   ] Does the product have a good design, is it easy to use?   _____
[   ] Is the product packaging appealing and appropriate?   _____
[   ] Are instruction manuals easy to understand and use?   _____
[   ] Is the best packaging being used for shipping
and storage?   _____

[　] Is there too much or too little inventory? _____

[　] Does the product have an adequate warranty? _____

[　] Is it easy for customers to get warranty service? _____

[　] Is repair turnaround time satisfactory? _____

[　] Is the delivery of the product being done in a
timely manner? _____

[　] Is the product priced at an optimal level? _____

[　] Is there an effective amount of product choices? _____

[　] Is the competition known and understood;
their strengths and weaknesses? _____

[　] Is an advantage over the competition being
maintained? _____

[　] Is the right image of the organization promoted
at all levels? _____
(This includes advertising, salespeople, customer
service, quality of the product, product packaging,
building signs, office decor, stationery, dress code,
logos, trucks, etc.)

[　] Are the right markets being approached? _____

[　] Are all potential product uses being considered? _____

[　] Are new customers being considered for existing
products? _____

[　] Are new products being considered for existing
customers? _____

[　] Are new products being considered to reach
new customers? _____

[　] Is the market research effective, the right
sampling with the right questions? _____

[　] Is there enough market research? _____

[　] Is an optimal number of salespeople being used? _____

[　] Are salespeople effectively trained and equipped? _____

[　] Are salespeople being given enough support? _____

[　] Are the best sales distribution channels being used:
retail, direct mail, sales reps, trade shows,
coupon packs, Internet, infomercials, card
decks, wholesalers, franchisees, referrals,
telemarketing, etc.? _____

[　] Is there enough advertising, frequency and saturation? _____

[　] Is the right message being used in the advertising? _____

[   ] Is the best choice of advertising medium being used:
radio, newspapers, magazines, billboards, mailers,
buses, yellow pages, television, Internet,
sponsoring events, etc.?   _____

[   ] Is the quality of the advertising sufficient; is it
consistent with the quality of the product?   _____

[   ] Are decisions viewed from several points of view,
such as customers, customers' customers,
employees, suppliers, lenders, the government,
the competition, stockholders, etc.?   _____

[   ] Are the wants and needs the organization
satisfies, its purpose for being, clearly defined?
Is there a specific mission statement that's
being communicated?   _____

One key question is: "Do all activities move towards the achievement of the organization's goals?" It's also a very good idea to have all of the employees answer and rate these same questions. Their feedback will yield information that is very valuable. In addition, asking for their input helps to establish their involvement in the organization, especially if their input is acted upon. Too often employees are asked for their opinions but nothing is ever done with what they say. This only tends to widen the gap between management and worker.

Doing this rating of your organization on a regular basis will provide many benefits. Paying attention to the nature of things and measuring the status with the purpose to constantly improve, will create positive change.

"What we concentrate on, we tend to create."

The next chapter provides a checklist for enhancing relationships, particularly romantic ones.

Chapter 16

ENHANCING RELATIONSHIPS

● ● ●

101 QUESTIONS TO ASK BEFORE YOU BEGIN OR END A RELATIONSHIP

Quality romantic relationships can be a major part of the quality of our lives. Understanding what we, and our mate, want and don't want, can lead to acceptance and mutually gratifying connections. It can be difficult to be comfortable with something that we don't understand.

This chapter provides you with questions and a checklist to establish the awareness and knowledge necessary for successful relationships. These tools are to enhance a current relationship, pave the way for a new one, or aid in the letting go of a past one. Often, regardless of how long people are together, they really don't know each other. This chapter assists you in the process of knowing. How can you take the proper action unless you have the proper information?

"If I would have known you felt that way, I . . ."

Equally important to knowing what you want, is to clearly know what the other person wants. How much needless stress and confusion occurs because people don't effectively communicate? It's not just are they right for you, but also are you right for them! Unfortunately due to certain limiting beliefs, some people only choose partners that are wrong for them, thereby living out a limiting script of what they feel is possible for them.

247

Chemistry?

Checklists in relationships to some people, are felt to be too restricting and dehumanizing. They say that it all comes down to whether or not there's chemistry. We all generate an energy and create an impression by the manner in which we present ourselves. This is based upon our script, our values and beliefs. The way we walk, talk, breathe, move, our facial expression, muscular tension, look in our eyes, etc., are a representation of what we are thinking and feeling.

All of verbal and nonverbal information we put out, and receive from someone else, is quickly interpreted. Then we get a sense of whether or not there is chemistry. This feeling is founded on something real, on conscious and unconscious input that creates mental and physical responses. This checklist will help you to discover what it is for you.

Everyone has a checklist. When we like or dislike someone, it's because what we see, hear, and feel from them is associated to something pleasant or unpleasant from our past experiences. Research has shown that a certain unconscious smell is also experienced during the initial attraction phase.

The idea of this checklist is to give you control by bringing to the conscious level what does and doesn't work for you, as well as the other person. The checklist is designed to give you clarity so that you can be realistic and truthful with yourself. It will show you if your standards are so rigid, that no one will ever be good enough or acceptable to you. It's also a safe effective way for two people to know and gain an understanding of each other.

Before people form a relationship, get married, or breakup a relationship, going through this checklist could make all the difference in the world. In many instances, it would be obvious that a mistake was being made in trying to form a partnership. In other situations, people may realize that they really do care about each other, and that staying together and working things out is the best path to follow. The better the information we have, the better choices we can make, for ourselves and for others. For optimum coupling, everyone must be satisfied. If you get what you want, but the other person is miserable, your joy will tend to be short-lived.

The checklist in this chapter has been assembled over a period of many years, and the examples are from many different people, male and female. Of course not every item will be important to everyone. You'll most likely have things that you'll want to add and things you'll want to delete. But each idea is significant to someone, and that's how it got on the list. Remember, everyone is special and unique, and that everyone has their own individual reality.

How much compatibility is necessary for two people to have a mutually rewarding relationship? It depends on the couple's *values* and *beliefs*. If they are in sync, then most likely other considerations can be worked out. If the *values* and *beliefs* are in conflict, then they have different goals and they will be moving in different directions. The basis for a mutually supportive relationship just isn't there. This checklist is an aid in opening up communication and removing the barriers that might be keeping you apart.

It can take several hours to answer all the questions in this chapter. Sometimes it's best to work on it in pieces, committing 30 to 40 minutes at a time. This small investment in time and energy will provide you with lifelong benefits.

Should you do this checklist with your mate? Some couples answer all the questions themselves and then they share them. Other couples do it together by interviewing each other, and recording each other's responses. Regardless of the method, the key is to openly accept each other's viewpoints without judgment. Listen and learn. This is not suggesting to agree with everything, but to understand each other.

Many of the questions address subjects that strongly impact our lives, and yet we rarely discuss them. So often people don't really know each other, or for that matter themselves. They can spend a lifetime together feeling dissatisfied, never opening up and experiencing the joy of mutual knowing and understanding.

Values and Beliefs

In the *Building a Foundation* chapter, we explored your life values and beliefs to know yourself and if a goal was in alignment with them. At this point we'll narrow the focus to your relationship values and beliefs, and if they will be supportive of you having the type of relationship that you want. And it's very important to discover if your partner's values and beliefs about relationships are in harmony with yours. If they are too different from yours, or what you want yours to be, you both will potentially be in for a lot of stress and friction.

There seem to be people who are happy in their misery, who constantly get into the same kind of wrong relationships. Again this is a function of living out their script, their values and beliefs. Some people constantly sabotage relationships when they are going along smoothly, and they find people who are right for them, boring.

Values and beliefs determine what happens in a relationship. If someone believes that there must be arguments, fights, and conflicts, they will create them if there is too much harmony. We see this happen time and time again. Listen to a person's script to understand what they will do. Listen to how they talk about others, and what they pay attention to. By listening, we can know what their attitude is, and what scenario they are playing out. If someone feels that they are a victim, they might create scenes where they are a victim.

Values

"Exchange values before exchanging vows!"

Since our values are what is truly important to us, and what we will spend time and energy and resources to have, it is critical that both parties values are in agreement. Our whole lifestyle and life situation is influenced by our values. Two people need to be moving, or want to move, in the same direction, or appreciate the direction of the other person, or conflict will occur. Regardless of how strong the "chemistry" is, compatible values are necessary for sustained mutually beneficial and satisfying relationships. Therefore, first compare life values as illustrated in chapter 2, Figure 2-1.

As with your life values, to uncover what your relationship values are, ask yourself, "What's really important to me about a romantic relationship?" First write them down, and then put them in order of importance, as in Figure 16-1. If in a relationship, also rate on a scale of 1-10, 10 being ideal, how close each value is experienced compared to your desired level. For example, say respect is one of your values and a mate often criticizes your ideas, you might rate the current or experienced level at a 4 or 5. If the value of respect is experienced at your desired level, you would rate it a 10.

FIGURE 16-1:
Romantic Relationships

• • •

Values

List and Prioritize		Prioritized		Current Level
(3)	consideration	(1)	respect	(7)
(1)	respect	(2)	trust	(6)
(8)	fun	(3)	consideration	(6)
(11)	acceptance	(4)	passion	(10)
(6)	compatibility	(5)	friendship	(6)
(10)	sharing	(6)	compatibility	(8)
(7)	freedom	(7)	freedom	(6)
(4)	passion	(8)	fun	(4)
(2)	trust	(9)	loyalty	(9)
(9)	loyalty	(10)	sharing	(5)
(5)	friendship	(11)	acceptance	(7)

Figure 16-2 takes the process one step further. To gain additional clarity about what is true for you, ask yourself how you know each of your values is being fulfilled, and how you know when it isn't being fulfilled. What actually needs to happen? What experience, what feedback will you receive that tells you whether or not a specific value is being met?

FIGURE 16-2:
Romantic Relationships

———————— • • • ————————

Values

How do you know you have each value being fulfilled? How do you know when you don't have it?

(1) *Respect*—my opinion is valued, I'm listened to, my feelings are considered valid, I'm treated well in public.
Don't have: My needs and feelings aren't being considered, someone tries to force their opinions on me, being treated like a child with my judgment being challenged.

(2) *Trust*—they believe in me, each partner upholds and keeps their commitments.
Don't have: They're suspicious and I'm accused of things, my opinions are not valued, my partner is overly protective and critical.

(3) *Consideration*—when both of us are focusing on each other's wants and needs.
Don't have: Being neglected, not wanting to be together, not being concerned about them.

(4) *Passion:*—being held, cuddled, touched, and massaged tenderly whenever appropriate. Kissing and making love.
Don't have: Not touching, either partner tenses up when the other comes near, and a barrier is sensed between us.

(5) *Friendship*—we share everything, talk about everything, like to do things together, feel comfortable to be totally open with each other, caring about their well being, fun, feel comfortable to be totally myself.
Don't have: Expected to play a role, lack of trust, other person sees me as less than they are, no caring, they try to take advantage of me.

(6) *Compatibility*—like to do the same things, like to do things together, like the same type of people, having similar lifestyle, and being comfortable living together.
Don't have: Having opposite lifestyles and patterns, different values, different goals.

FIGURE 16-2:
Romantic Relationships—Values (continued)

• • •

(7) *Freedom*—do whatever you want to do, feel accepted as is.
Don't have: Being restricted by monopolizing my time, complaining about where I go and what I do, complaining about my friends, criticizing my ideas.

Beliefs

As we said before, beliefs are the most foundational element of what we do, how we do it, when we do it, and how we feel about it afterward. Without the appropriate beliefs about a goal, it's like building a house on quicksand. At first it's solid, but at some point it will definitely collapse and fall. To have a warm, loving, caring, mutually beneficial and satisfying relationship, certain beliefs need to be present. This goes for both people. Make a list of your beliefs about relationships. Then separate your list into two parts, one your empowering beliefs, Figure 16-3, and the other any beliefs that could be limiting, Figure 16-4.

What beliefs do you need to have, to have the type of relationship that you want? In addition to the examples in Figure 16-3, we can go back to the "Fundamental Four," the beliefs that: I *can* have, that it's *worth* having, that I *will* have, and that I *deserve* to have my ideal relationship. If you and your significant other do not have these and the other beliefs you feel you need to have this goal, then go back to the belief change steps and keep working on it until you have them installed. And along with implanting the positive beliefs, be sure to neutralize and replace any negative limiting beliefs. *"Either we control our beliefs, or they control us."*

Beliefs about the sexes can be an interesting exercise. In some of my workshops, I write at the top of a board, "Men are . . .," and I ask the women to fill-in the blanks. Too often 99.99% of the comments are negative. Things such as selfish, dishonest, cold, egotistical, self-centered, sloppy, cheap, clumsy, insensitive, poor listeners, impatient, rude, competitive, unreliable, boring, weak, critical, demanding, controlling, immature, emotionally unavailable, inconsiderate, unappreciative, rude, domineering, jealous, and petty, are common responses.

FIGURE 16-3:
Romantic Relationships

• • •

Possible Empowering Beliefs

"Relationships continue to grow and get better over time."
"Giving helps to bring out the best in each other, with each nourishing the other."
"Relationships need to have mutual respect."
"People need to have a genuine liking for each other and consider their mate their best friend."
"There needs to be honesty, integrity, and total trust in the relationship."
"When you love, you feel so caring that you place the other person's needs above your own."
"Differences need to be resolved as soon as they come up."
"Your mate is a completion of you."
"Each person is fulfilled and balanced by the relationship."
"There is no questioning in a true relationship, it has full acceptance for both parties, as is."
"You love them because of their faults, not in spite of them."
"Each person needs to be an open and receptive listener."
"A committed relationship is actually freeing instead of restricting."
"You need to essentially have the qualities in yourself that you want your mate to have."
"Open honest communication is crucial to success."
"Because I'm a worthy person, I know I can work things out."
"There is always an ideal mate for everyone."
"People in love can overcome any obstacles that come their way."
"The greatest joy in life is spending quiet intimate moments cuddling with your mate."
"There is a truth and beauty when people are truly in love."
"Both partners need to willingly put their full energies into the relationship."
"The relationship needs to be the most important one in each partner's life."
"Everything in life is better when shared with someone you love."

FIGURE 16-4:
Romantic Relationships

• • •

Possible Limiting Beliefs

"If I have a committed relationship it will hurt my family, I won't have time for them."

"It verges on being impossible to find my ideal mate, all the good ones are already taken."

"A committed relationship will interfere with my career, and my friendships."

"If I find the right mate, they won't want me."

"I can't get someone that I want, so I'll have to settle for someone less than I want, like most people do."

"Because I came from a dysfunctional family, I only attract people who are dysfunctional."

"Men only care about how a woman looks, and would rather be with a woman who is young and beautiful, rather than a woman who is intelligent."

"Women only want a man who's wealthy."

"I won't know what to do with someone who fulfills my criteria, and I'll screw it up."

"If I get into a committed relationship, eventually they'll abandon me and I'll be all alone, and worse off than before."

"A committed relationship will mean that I'll be overeating all the time and become overweight."

"There are always power struggles and conflict between the sexes."

"Men can't understand the problems of women."

"There's always another one around the corner, but they're also going to be the wrong one."

"I only see myself having short-term relationships."

"Familiarity breeds contempt."

"Men are not that trustworthy."

"Romance always disappears soon after the honeymoon."

"Marriage is a series of painful compromises."

"If you don't sleep with them fairly soon, they'll drop you."

"Fighting and arguing are normal parts of a relationship."

FIGURE 16-4:
Romantic Relationships—Possible Limiting Beliefs (continued)

• • •

"No relationship ever turns out to be the way you think it will be, and you
end up being disappointed."
"Relationships involve a lot of 'masks,' with people hiding who they really
are."
"There are too many expectations on both sides, and therefore both parties
become disappointed and frustrated."
"Good communication between the sexes is impossible, we're too different."
"Long-term loving relationships only happen in the movies."

"Women are . . .," is then put on the board, and the men have their
say. Again it's usually negative, with comments such as insecure, nosey,
gossipy, selfish, materialistic, compulsive, too sensitive, slow, too talkative, whiny, weak, fearful, self-centered, complainers, nagging, critical,
petty, manipulative, demanding, controlling, too emotional, and possessive, are regular answers. Is it any wonder that relationships can be so
challenging?

Building on a concept stated earlier, I commonly see people who
believe that fighting and arguing are normal parts of a relationship, that
will cause fights with each other. When everything is going along
smoothly and harmoniously, people with this belief start to get nervous.
Since they believe that arguing is normal, they feel that it's only a matter
of time before it happens. If too much time passes without a fight, tension
builds due to the anticipation of the assumed conflict. They then create a
problem to get it over with, and fulfill their expectations.

If you have all the appropriate beliefs but your partner doesn't, they
might sabotage what could be wonderful for both of you. Can your beliefs
be so strong that they can balance out and counteract the limitations of the
other person? Yes. However, at what price? Will you pay the price without
resentment? Will you do it with total understanding, love, and acceptance?
Are you willing to always be in the role of nurturer, or do you need to set a
time limit on it?

How Do You Know . . . Love?

Before we get into the detailed checklist, there are two broad questions that can help to setup a base to build upon. All of these inquiries are designed to give you a clear specific criteria of what does and doesn't work for you and your partner. Everyone has their own code, formula, and recipe for what love is. And over time, this coding can change. To be able to, "Do unto others as they want done unto them," we need to understand what their particular combination is.

"How do you know when you're receiving love?" is the first question to guide each other through. What makes your partner believe that someone is giving them love? What do they experience that says to them that someone loves them? Find out what they see, hear, feel, smell, and taste, as in Figure 16-5. After you learn their code, let them know what yours is. What are your answers to these questions? What literally happens that convinces you someone loves you? Do the easiest ones first.

"How do you know when you're giving love, what do you do?" is the second question to work on. What is their behavior when they really care? What actual specific things do they say and do when they love someone? Figure 16-6 provides some samples. Then share your answers.

There are many benefits to writing out your replies to these questions. Often people don't understand the meaning of their partners behavior. Many times people really love each other but their expression of that love takes totally different forms. Once people know what works for each other, they can effectively communicate and enhance the relationship. For instance, a man may open the car door for his mate to show he cares. However, she may feel that it's demeaning and treating her like child. Or a woman may ask a man how his day was to show she cares, and he might feel like he's being interrogated.

We all have our own unique strategies for love. Become aware of what yours and your mate's are, and you both can benefit. Instead of feeling that what you do isn't appreciated, understand that your actions may not fit the code of your mate. How often do you hear someone say that if their mate really cared, that they would know what to do? People are not mind readers. Everyone sees and experiences the world differently.

FIGURE 16-5:
Love Strategies—Receiving

————————————— • • • —————————————

How do you know when you're receiving love? What does someone do and say? What do you see, hear, feel, smell, and taste?

See: Doing things together; us sitting close together; they look happy to be with me; they look at me with a special look in their eyes; they give me gifts; they send me little cards and notes; they take me to places I enjoy; they get along with my family and friends; they wear clothes that I like; they voluntarily do things for me.

Hear: They call me a lot; they express concern for me; they take an interest in my interests; they want me to take an interest in their interests; they give me a lot of compliments; they tell me that they love me; they read poetry to me; they sing to me; they share their hopes and dreams with me; they want my opinion on things; they laugh at my jokes; they say nice things about me to other people; they patiently explain things to me; they call me by a "pet" name; they use a loving tone when speaking to me.

Feel: They touch me a lot; we hold hands a lot; they like to put their arms around me; they caress my face; they're very sensual with me; we cuddle each night; we sit next to each other in restaurants; they gives me massages. I feel accepted, and free to be myself.

Smell and Taste: They wear a cologne that I love; the aromas of the dinner they cook for me; the flowers they give to me; a sweet taste when they kiss me.

FIGURE 16-6:
Love Strategies—Giving

• • •

How do you know when you're giving love, what do you say and do?

I give them a lot of compliments.
I compliment them in front of other people.
I express appreciation for being together.
I spend a lot of time with them.
I show that I care about their interests and that I want to be involved in
    them.
I'm supportive of their goals.
I get to know their family and friends.
I call them during the day to see how they're doing.
I buy them flowers.
I buy them little gifts.
I send them cards expressing my love.
I let them choose where we go and what we do on the weekend.
I share in the housework.
I help with the children.
I make sure to look my best for them and that I'm attractive to them.
I keep learning so that I am interesting to them.
I take care of them and cater to them.
I'm respectful and patient, even when they make obvious mistakes.
I give them space when they need it.
I ask for their opinion on important issues.
I make love to them a lot.
I'm open about my feelings.
I call them by a "pet" name.
I tell them how much I care, and how special I think they are.
I'm very affectionate with them.
I'm accepting of them and their ideas.

It's up to each of us to let our partner know how we feel, and to understand that our requests may not be comfortable for the other person to fulfill regardless of how much they care. We must let the other person know us, and create an environment where they feel safe to let us know them. Then with this knowledge, and with mutual acceptance, each partner can work to make the relationship mutually satisfying.

Getting Specific

The questions in the checklist in Figure 16-7, are not in a particular order since each one's importance will vary from person to person. Answer those questions that you feel are worthwhile, with what you would like, and then rate it on a scale of 1-10.

General guidelines for rating your answers basically have four levels. A rating of 1–3 would mean that it would be nice but it's unimportant. A rating of 4–6 means that it's somewhat important, a strong preference, but it's not essential. A rating of 7–9 means that something is very important and you probably won't be happy without it. Rating something a 10, means that it's nonnegotiable, that it's crucial, that it "must" be present in the relationship or you won't be satisfied. A zero rating comes into play when rating what you receive from another person, and indicates that you are getting something totally unacceptable.

After you answer each question and give it a rating, evaluate them. How many 8s, 9s, and 10s do you have? Do you have too many? Many of my clients rate over half their list at this level, and as they look at it, they realize it's unrealistic. What's the likelihood of one person being able to satisfy your entire criteria? Do you need to adjust downward some of your ratings? Do you have limiting beliefs that cause you to have such strict ratings as a way to keep you from having a worthwhile relationship?

If you are in a relationship, also rate how closely each item comes to your desired level. This can assist you in clearly defining what's working for you, and areas that need some attention. What can both of you do to bring the current level of satisfaction up to the desired level?

In some instances what you get may be more than necessary, as shown in some of the examples. Someone's looks or monetary status could actually be much greater than what you require. You want someone who is between 5'11" to 6'2" tall, rating it an 8, and your partner is 6'2", so in the now column you would give it a 10. You may feel that perfect teeth is a 7, and the person may have a 9 for this item. You may want someone who earns a certain amount of money which is at an 8 in importance, and they earn twice that much, so you would give it a 10.

When there are many strong differences in key areas, it's very unlikely that the relationship will be a satisfactory one. Again key areas for one person may be totally different from another. Having different sleep habits may seem trivial, but if you never get a good nights sleep, wake up everyday exhausted, and therefore have no energy, it can then become very meaningful.

FIGURE 16-7:
Relationship Checklist

● ● ●

The following is a general list of points that could be important to someone in a relationship. Choose the ones important to you, and write out what you want next to each item. Then assign a *Value* to each, on a scale of 1-10, with 1 meaning of very little importance, and 10 extremely important, a "must." If a relationship exists now, or to let go of a past one, also assign a rating under *Now*, of how close what you received comes to your desired level. For relationships other than romantic, such as friends, family, or career, create separate lists of your key elements. (Note: on several items, especially appearance, the person rated higher than was necessary.)

	Value	- Now
Age, range: 38 to 50	6	- 10
Height, range: 5'11" to 6'2"	8	- 10
Weight, range: 170 to 210	8	- 10
Hair color: dark	1	- 10
Hair style: short and groomed, no bald spots	5	- 9
Body type (large, small): medium build	5	- 10
Eye color: blue	3	- 10
Teeth: straight and white	7	- 9
Skin, complexion: olive and smooth	5	- 10
Hairiness, facial: no facial hair	8	- 10
Hairiness, body: some on chest and none on back	7	- 10
Posture: straight and upright	10	- 10
Walking style (determined, casual): fast and straight	4	- 2
Facial expressions (serious, relaxed): bright, cheerful	7	- 7
Gestures: a lot, very animated	3	- 6
Energy level: a lot, very lively	8	- 8
Voice—pace, volume, tone: fast pace, medium volume, a lot of inflection and animation	7	- 7
Clothes style (conservative, casual): conservative but with lively colors	7	- 8
Affection: a lot but not all the time	10	- 2
Sensuality: lovemaking daily, with a lot cuddling afterward	10	- 10

FIGURE 16-7:
Relationship Checklist (continued)

• • •

	Value	- Now
Feelings desired: free, calm, accepted, secure, respected, desired, admired, excitement, fun, gentleness, nurtured, romantic, mentally stimulated	10	- 3
Money (conservative, loose): generous within their means, without going into debt	7	- 9
Money, living expenses: we split according to income	10	- 10
Structure (planned, spontaneous): spontaneous	7	- 3
Change (frequent, infrequent): infrequent	7	- 5
Status conscious: it's important	8	- 10
Temper: easygoing and mild tempered	10	-- 2
Emotionality: somewhat, medium amount	6	- 2
Expressiveness (open, closed): open and very communicative	10	- 3
Children: have one child together and that they never had any children	10	- 0
Family, parents, siblings: friendly close-knit family	5	- 0
Family, time: socialize with at least twice a month	9	- 2
Childhood: stable and good relationship with family	6	- 2
Health: excellent, very healthy	10	- 8
Food, types: healthy simple foods, with a lot of variety	9	- 7
Eating habits: eat quickly but with etiquette and manners	8	- 3
Sleep habits (position, temperature, bed type): each person on their own side of the bed, slightly cool, very firm king-size mattress, totally darkened room, and no snoring.	10	- 0
Sports, types: baseball, golf, and fast walking	6	- 2
Exercise: someone who exercises daily	10	- 10
Temperature, home, car: 70° for both	8	- 8
Work type; attitude: attorney, psychologist, or business owner; someone who loves their work	9	- 10
Income: over $100,000 per year	6	- 10
Work hours: 8:00 A.M. to 7:00 P.M., maximum 55 hours per week	10	- 3
Work travel, overnight: average one day per month	8	- 8

FIGURE 16-7:
Relationship Checklist (continued)

• • •

	Value	- Now
Religion: have the same religion	7	- 0
Religious practices: be interested in and observant on a daily basis	9	- 2
Humor: a lot, able to laugh at self and life	9	- 7
Friendliness: open and accepting of people	8	- 3
Independent or group: a balance of both	8	- 6
Poise: very poised and self-confident	10	- 10
Conversations, topics: current events, philosophy, law, self-growth, religion, health	10	- 2
Politics, time: liberal, averaging 6 hours per month	5	- 0
Ideal day—who, what, where: exercise first thing in the morning, a two-hour hike, have brunch at a beautiful restaurant overlooking the water, read the NY Times together, go to see a matinee performance of a musical, pick up food at a gourmet food shop, cook dinner together, after dinner share a bubble bath, wash each other, dry each other, make love for hours, cuddle and talk quietly until we fall asleep in each other's arms	8	- 3
Role models: people who have made a positive difference in world, socially conscious people	7	- 2
Goals—life: being successful, strives for good health, helping other people, improving our educational system	10	- 2
Goals—relationship: having a strong family unit; having a supportive, nurturing, growing, loving, committed relationship; to have a child; to constantly improve the communication and depth of our relationship	10	- 2
Beliefs about self: they think they're a good person, that they can accomplish their goals, sees a bright and active future ahead, can handle any challenges, that they would make a good parent and mate	9	- 7

FIGURE 16-7:
Relationship Checklist (continued)

——————————————— • • • ———————————————

	Value	- Now
Beliefs about relationships: there are solutions to problems, that stability is important, sharing activities is important, that there is enough time to have a career and a relationship, lovemaking and romance is important, friendship with one's spouse is essential, that a relationship can always be kept vibrant and alive	10	- 10
Music, type, volume: easy listening, low volume	6	- 2
Dancing, type, how often: disco, swing; once a month	4	- 4
Attitude, conservative or liberal: very liberal	8	- 3
Charity, time, money: four hours per month; 5% of net	7	- 8
Colors (bright, subdued): subdued and conservative	6	- 6
Friends, types: bright, friendly, talkative, active	8	- 5
Gambling, time, money: once a year with a small $ amount	8	- 3
Liquor: nondrinker or light social drinker	10	- 0
Drugs: no drugs	10	- 10
Smoking: nonsmoker	10	- 8
Neatness: basically neat but not fanatical	10	- 9
Cleanliness: very clean	10	- 10
Day or night: day, up early and to sleep by midnight	9	- 7
Risk level, investments, sports, business: some but basically a low risk approach	9	- 6
Each other's best friend: very important, crucial	10	- 2
Integrity—business: a lot, someone who is fair	10	- 8
Integrity—personal: totally honest and trustworthy	10	- 2
Education: at least some college	6	- 0
Intelligence: above average, high I.Q.	9	- 7
Vocabulary: proper grammar and little swearing	10	- 8
Car, type: large expensive four-door sedan	7	- 10
Driving style: confident, competent, and polite	8	- 7
Cooking: share the activity	10	- 9
Shopping: share the activity	9	- 9
Restaurants: Italian, E. Indian, seafood; eat out no more than twice a week	7	- 7

FIGURE 16-7:
Relationship Checklist (continued)

• • •

	Value	- Now
Hobbies: anything as long as it doesn't detract from our relationship	9	- 1
Indoor or outdoor: balance of both	9	- 9
Pets: a small dog that they are not too attached to	4	- 4
Reading material: daily newspaper, non-fiction, some novels, a weekly news magazine	9	- 1
Television: 7 - 10 hours/week, mostly news and movies	10	- 3
Movies: once per week, all types except horror	5	- 0
Art: French Impressionists, art deco, modern	6	- 6
Vacations—type, how long: different types, sightseeing, adventure, skiing, sailing; two weeks at a time maximum	8	- 8
Vacation travel mode (car, plane, boat): flying	6	- 6
Home, type, size, grounds: one-story modern, 2,800 square feet, on one acre, hot tub, with a lot of trees and flowers	8	- 7
Home location: in a suburb of a large city	8	- 8
Furnishings: French Provincial, yet simple and uncluttered	7	- 5
Plants: a lot and many different types	6	- 6
Household tasks: everything shared down the middle	9	- 9
OTHER: someone who is okay with me doing things without them	10	- 4

Remember we're working for understanding and acceptance. The goal is to know enough about each other so that things can be worked out. However, if you want someone who is affectionate, nurturing, even-tempered, and an open communicator, and you pair with someone who is not, you're probably only kidding yourself or fulfilling a limiting belief. We can ask someone to change in certain ways, and if they don't, we can either lovingly accept them the way they are, or argue and fight, or move out of the relationship.

Another possibility is for us to be a certain way that encourages our mate to be the way that we want. If we want affection and warmth, are we affectionate and warm enough? If we want nurturing and acceptance, do we nurture and accept enough? If we want open communication, do we openly communicate enough? Are conditions being created where your mate is comfortable enough, to freely and willingly contribute to the way you want things to be?

Someone was once asked why they felt they were so successful with the opposite sex. Their reply was that they didn't *compete* with them. A concept that may be useful to many people. Competition isn't always obvious. It can be the little challenges we throw out, the little "humorous putdowns," the little one-upmanships, that individually may seem harmless, but that collectively can be very destructive. Do you find yourself criticizing or complimenting? Neglecting or nourishing? Putting down or praising? Humiliating or honoring? Suppressing or supporting? Embarrassing or encouraging?

Let's clarify some of the questions from Figure 16-7. *Feelings desired* refers to how you want to feel when you are with your mate. The feelings in the example seem to come up quite frequently. If the feelings you desire are not experienced when you're with someone, will the relationship be good for you? Could you be in the relationship for the wrong reasons, such as fulfilling negative beliefs?

Structure deals with how planned or how spontaneously you like to live. Some people need to have months at a time totally booked up, and others like to live from moment to moment. Do you have a strong preference at either of these extremes, or is it somewhere in between?

Change is concerned with the issue of the frequency of altering things. Some people thrive on change, other people are stressed out by it. Have you ever noticed how some people are always changing things such as hairstyles, clothing styles, vacation spots, home furnishings, and cars, and some people are so habitual that they never change anything unless they must? What's your approach, and will you adjust it if it makes your mate uncomfortable?

Independent or group refers to whether or not you like to do things with just the two of you, or with groups of people. As you perhaps have seen, some people dislike being alone, and thrive in crowded situations such as clubs and team activities. Their home can be a continual open house for everyone. Other people tend to be very private and prefer solitude, socializing in groups on an infrequent basis. Which do you prefer, and how strong is your preference?

Conversations is concerned with what you like to talk about. It can be a reflection of whether you have the same interests, as well as the comfort level in the discussion of those interests. As you may have experienced, with some people the exchange of words just flows naturally, and with others it's very uncomfortable and awkward. In the sample, the importance of good dialogue was a 10, and the status was a 2. Unless this couple was busy doing something, one of them was very frustrated and felt isolated. What do you like to talk about, and how important is it to discuss ideas with your mate?

Ideal day deserves some special attention. In the example there is a very wide difference between what one person wanted, and what they received. What would your *ideal day* be like? Put all your dreams and desires down on paper. Are these shared by your mate, or do they feel your ideas are silly, stupid, or boring? This can be very revealing as to what you have in common, and how compatible you are.

Goals is a topic that's in two sections. What are your life *goals*, and what are your relationship *goals*? How closely aligned are your *goals* with the *goals* of your mate? Another issue comes up, and that is how supportive is the relationship of each partner achieving their *goals*? Without alignment and support from each other for each other, there can be great turmoil. As you can see by the differences in the ratings in the example, these two people would have a lot of conflict in their relationship.

Beliefs about self and relationships, are asking what you want your mate to believe. How close does your partner come to having the type of *beliefs* that you feel are important? In the example with a rating of 10, these types of *beliefs* were viewed as essential by this person. Their partner came pretty close in fulfilling some *beliefs*, but was way off on some of the others.

Colors is looking at the issue of the types of *colors* preferred in decorating the home, personal items, car, etc. Some people like big, bold, bright *colors* that are very stimulating. They like things that stand out, like having a bright red car. Other people prefer soft quiet *colors* that blend into the surroundings. This could seem like a minor point, but *colors* do affect us, and living in an environment that is irritating or that stifles one's energy, could be very uncomfortable.

Day or night is addressing the issue of internal time clocks. There can be primarily *day* people or *night* people. Some people love to get up early every morning and go to sleep by 10:00 P.M. Others get up at noon and get to bed around three or four in morning. These differences can put a definite strain on the amount and quality of shared time. In some cases it can make continuing a relationship all but impossible. But as with so many things, this can be worked out.

I know a couple where one spouse gets up at five in the morning and is asleep by 10:00 P.M. The other spouse gets up between 10:00 and

11:00 A.M. and goes to sleep around 2:00 A.M. Since they understand that they have different biological clocks, they work things out. Neither is offended because their mate falls asleep or awakens at a time different from their own. They make sure they speak during the day, have dinner together, and are together as the first one falls asleep. The night owl then does paperwork until it's time for sleep. Through understanding they have mutual acceptance and respect, and a quality relationship.

Friendship is a critical item! Do you consider each other each other's best *friend*? Surveys have shown that the most common thing in successful long-term relationships is *friendship*. That each person considers their mate their best *friend*, and vice versa. It makes sense. If we are not best *friends* with the person we share the most important things with, the person we have chosen to spend the rest of our lives with, then most likely we will never feel free and content.

What does *friendship* mean? Some of the ideas that come up often are things such as compatibility, trust, caring, acceptance, support, sharing, understanding, respect, feeling understood, comfort, consideration, etc. Another way to say some of these concepts, is that one feels "free" to be oneself. What's feeling "free" worth? How valuable is it? If you don't feel "free" to be yourself in your primary relationship, what's the quality of it going to be? Also, are you providing conditions where your partner feels "free" to be themselves? If you are already in a relationship, constantly look for ways to be a true *friend*. If you are considering beginning a new relationship, ask yourself if the two of you can be each other's best *friend*. If the answer is no, then either put a halt to the proceedings, or accept it for what it reasonably will be, a temporary fling or a relationship filled with conflict and stress. Over time, physical passion usually declines, but real *friendship* can last a lifetime.

Being best *friends* with someone doesn't guarantee that this is someone you can have a lifelong romantic relationship with. *Friends* may be all that you can be to each other. But NOT being *friends* almost guarantees that the relationship will not be a successful and joyful one.

Hobbies and interests if not shared can be a significant area of disharmony. Relationships are enhanced and bonded through shared experiences. If one partner has many *hobbies* and activities that are not shared by the other, and which require a lot of time apart, distancing can occur. If the *hobbies* take priority over being together, then something fundamental is probably out of balance. At the first sign of discomfort, communication needs to occur so that each partner can understand the position of the other. Understanding paves the way for resolving differences.

Indoor or outdoor first refers to how some people prefer to be home most of the time, and some people like to be out and about as much as possible. The other part is that some people love *outdoor* activities such as walking, hiking, camping, skiing, biking, golf, etc. Are you at one end of the spectrum or somewhere in between, and how important is it to you?

Other

No checklist will be complete for everyone. At this point add *other* things that are of importance to you. Some items that have come up are being a pack rat, being divorced, having a police record, and having phobias. Are there any additional things that must or must not be present in the other person, and the relationship, for it to work for you? Remember many pet peeves and irritations are merely smoke screens for more fundamental issues, which again, are based on values and beliefs.

Quirks and Joys

Quirks and *joys* are two concepts that can act as feedback devices to help you know to what extent you really care about someone. They are not that meaningful in and of themselves, but as indications of true feelings. Examples in Figure 16-8.

Quirks are unique habits, behaviors, or mannerisms that a person has. They are those particular ways that someone has of thinking and of doing things. *Quirks* are the distinctive styles of functioning a human being has. They are the rituals and routines that a person exhibits. From the way they eat, brush their teeth, how they laugh, what they laugh about, how they get up in the morning, to how they prepare for sleep at night, people have their uniqueness.

The question is, how do you feel about their *quirks*? Do they annoy you or do you enjoy them? This can give you valuable insight. If you find yourself annoyed by their *quirks*, it's telling you that something much more important is involved. It's telling you that there are incompatibilities, unresolved issues, or other things that need to be attended to in order for the relationship to prosper. On the other hand, if you find that you enjoy their quirks, it's telling you that there is something very special in how you feel about this person.

FIGURE 16-8:
Quirks (their unique habits), Dislike Or Like?

——————————————————   • • •   ——————————————————

DISLIKE: Turns on the TV as soon as they come home, gambles regularly, is always late, leaves clothes on furniture, picks teeth with fingernail, eats like there's no tomorrow, leaves hair in the sink, has a 30 minute routine before coming to bed.

LIKE: Totally gets into whatever they do, helpful to people in need, sings in the shower, sees beauty everywhere, makes conversation with people wherever we are, very curious about everything, has a cute little laugh when they get confused, gets a special look on their face when they're learning, always has to organize everything, can't decide what they want to eat for dinner.

Do you ENJOY their JOYS?

Golf, boating, stamp collecting, cooking, decorating, working on car, planning parties, talking with friends, playing games, fishing, shopping, discussions (sports, relationships, politics, etc.), travelling, dancing, volunteering, pets, movies, grooming, learning, photography, music, reading, gardening, knitting, concerts, sporting events, antiques, soap operas, baseball, painting, football, etc.

Enjoying their joys is another indicator of what your true feelings are. How do you find yourself reacting to what they enjoy, to what gives them pleasure? If a man loves to watch football games or work on his car, do you respond positively or negatively? If a woman loves to go shopping or read romance novels, what kind of feelings come up? If your mate has a hobby or activity that they get great *joy* out of, how do you find yourself reacting? If you do not enjoy the *joy* that they are experiencing, again this is an indication that something deeper is out of alignment.

If you find yourself *enjoying their joys*, even if you feel their *joys* are silly, useless, or boring, then it's most likely a good sign that you have something real. We can use the example of children. A child can get hours of *joy* out of playing with a piece of string. We watch this, and talk about how cute it is. We give gifts to children so that we can *enjoy their joy* as we see them light up with excitement over their new possessions. Become aware of how you are affected by *quirks* and *joys*, and use this information to enhance your relationship.

Traits

Traits, qualities, and characteristics is the next area to consider. What are the most important ones you want your mate to have? Figure 16-9 will give you some suggestions. After you make your choices, rate their importance and place the rating in front of each item. It's also a good idea, to write out how you know someone has each of the desired traits, qualities, and characteristics. What is the evidence and proof that someone has these attributes? What do they say and do that convinces you, they are the type of person that you would have mutual happiness with?

What About You?

So far we've been looking at what you want, which also gives you clarity about who you are. Another thing that needs to be addressed is *what do you have to be* to have the type of relationship that you want? Do you have the traits, qualities, and characteristics necessary to attract and to have the type of relationship that you desire?

Using Figure 16-9 as a guide, pick all things that you believe you need to be to have a satisfying relationship. Then after each item, rate yourself on how closely you possess each quality at a level you feel is sufficient to have the result you desire. Rate something a 10 if you feel you're at the right level, and on down the scale indicating how much you need to work on a trait.

For instance, you feel you need be patient, dependable, and accepting. As you interact with your mate, you notice that you are very impatient, that you are sometimes late, and that sometimes you are too critical. Therefore you might rate yourself a 3 on patience, an 8 on dependability, and a 7 on acceptance. By doing this you can easily gauge your own behavior, and know ways that you can improve the relationship for both of you.

FIGURE 16-9:
Traits, Qualities, and Characteristics

• • •

Choose those desired in Mate, Rate Importance 1-10, Define, & at end, Rate how close you come to the desired level, 1-10:

[9]   Accepting—they're okay with the way I am now (6)
[10] Affectionate—constantly touching and cuddling (7)
[6]   Appreciative—their thankful for what I do for them (8)
[7]   Available—they make time for me (7)
[7]   Cheerful—happy about life, smiles a lot (8)
[8]   Clean—keeps things neat and dirt free (9)
[7]   Confident—they're sure of themselves, poised, calm (9)
[8]   Considerate—think about the needs of others (9)
[6]   Decisive—they clearly know what they want and they act on it (8)
[10] Dependable—they keep their word, do what they say they'll do (10)
[8]   Down-to-earth—nonmaterialistic, likes the outdoors and simple things (8)
[7]   Energetic—lively and active, sparkle in the eye, ready to have fun (7)
[9]   Fair—does what's right in dealing with people (9)
[8]   Flexible—okay with change and being spontaneous (6)
[7]   Friendly—open and outgoing with people, likes people (6)
[8]   Fun—good sense of humor, likes to play, willing to try new things (9)
[7]   Giving—likes to share and to help others (5)
[10] Healthy—mentally and physically in harmony and balance (8)
[10] Honesty—is truthful and tells the facts because it feels right (10)
[7]   Kind—gentle in handling people (7)
[9]   Loving—warm, soft, and caring (7)
[10] Loyal—stands by people no matter what (10)
[6]   Neat—keeps things organized and orderly (7)
[7]   Nurturing—likes to help people feel good about themselves (8)
[7]   Open-minded—receptive to new ideas and points of view (6)
[7]   Optimistic—sees a bright future, and looks at what's going right (6)
[8]   Patient—okay with waiting for results, takes things in stride (7)
[9]   Practical—make realistic and useful choices, only calculated risks (7)

FIGURE 16-9:
Traits, Qualities, and Characteristics (continued)

● ● ●

[9] Respectful—takes other people's feelings into account (8)
[6] Romantic—express that they care in many little ways (6)
[9] Sensual—very physical and make love with a lot of affection (7)
[10] Sincere—straightforward, steady, and reliable (9)
[6] Supportive—helps and encourages others in achieving their goals (7)
[9] Understanding—sympathetic and grasps what I'm feeling (8)

Can you be too good, too perfect, too kind, too giving, etc.? Yes and no. If the relationship is genuine, is based on truth and honesty, then the more you give the more you get. If the relationship is filled with lies, with falsehoods, with people that have limiting beliefs such as that they don't deserve to have happiness, then you can have a situation where the more you give the more they take.

Some people have such low self-esteem, that they lose respect for anyone who respects them. At the subconscious level, since they believe they are unworthy, they might feel that anyone who likes them is trying to use them, is being phony, or is unworthy themselves. Dealing with these people becomes a self-fulfilling prophesy of conflict. Keep in mind, that a person's beliefs set the course, and that they just go along for the ride. We can rarely change others, especially without their consent, but we can change ourselves.

Do you need to have all of the qualities that you want in the other person? Probably not all of them. If it's issues such as honesty, loyalty, and kindness, most likely you would have to have them. But things such as creativity, humor, and athletic ability are not necessarily required by both parties. You could enjoy reading their poems, laugh at their jokes, and cheer them on in their favorite sport.

Putting the Past Behind You

Besides dealing with future or current situations, this chapter can help you to let go of some past relationships. After answering each question, and giving it a value of importance, you then rate how close your prior partner came to your desired level. For instance, you want someone who is a nonsmoker, it's extremely important to you, so you give it a maximum value of 10. The person you were trying to be with was a chain smoker, so you would rate this item's level of fulfillment a zero.

When you see all your answers laid out in front of you on paper, you can consciously realize why a relationship was the way it was. Realize that each of you were fulfilling your scripts, and that now you can let go of it. Realize that there were too many differences, and it would never have been a satisfying long-term union. You can put things in perspective, and accept that each of you was doing the best you could with the resources and script that each of you had at the time. Often there are no villains, no right or wrong, just differences.

Other Uses

Relationships other than romantic, is another area where this chapter can be useful. Many of the questions can be helpful in identifying ways for you to enhance relationships with friends, family members, co-workers, and customers. The checklist assists you in knowing what's working for both parties, and what could be improved. It promotes people seeing things from each other's point of view. The more we recognize that each person's behavior is logical from their perspective, the more we can understand each other, the better the world will be. Again, the fact that someone does something, means that from their viewpoint it makes sense. Otherwise they wouldn't do it!

Asking a friend their friendship values with, "What's really important to you in a friendship?" can be very illuminating. Then following up with, "How do you know when you're giving friendship?" and "How do you know when you're receiving friendship?" can give you an insight you may never have otherwise. This knowledge and understanding can assist both of you in bonding at very rewarding levels.

Hiring new employees is another way this checklist can be valuable. Depending on the position, 30 to 50 of the items on the list could apply in assisting you in determining what you're looking for in a staff member. What is the profile of the ideal candidate? At times, too little thought is given to what qualities are required for a particular job, the wrong person is hired, they don't work out, and the whole process needs to be done all over again. What is the cost in time, money, and frustration? And not only do we need to know if an applicant is right for us, but that we are right for them.

Summarizing some of the key ideas for a successful romantic relationship, can help to keep you focused and on track, and to achieve the quality of experience that you're looking for.

"Are we, or can we be, each other's best friend?"

"Do we enjoy, respect, encourage, and accept each other as is?"

"Do we have similar values and compatible goals?"

"Do we constantly want to give to each other?"

"Do we consider our relationship more important than any other relationship?"

"Do we resolve our differences as soon as possible, and always go to sleep in harmony with each other?"

"Do we openly communicate so that we truly know each other?"

"Do we regularly do things together so that we have shared experiences?"

"Do we daily express caring and appreciation for each other?"

"Are we both committed to make the relationship work for both of us?"

Use these type of questions to enhance your relationships for a lifetime of mutual learning, understanding, and satisfaction.

Mother Teresa said two things that have stuck with me, that would seem to improve any relationship. Use them and experience the riches they can provide. They are:

"Do small things with great love."

"It's not how much we give, but how much love we put in the giving."

Epilogue
• • •

Each Day Is A New Beginning

Life is about setting and achieving goals. Each day is a new beginning. Plotting a course on a daily basis, puts you in control. What we do today, forms our tomorrow's.

Keep setting new objectives so that as you attain one goal, you can begin on another one. A major part of a full rich life, is made up of having things to look forward to experiencing. Imagine you are 125 years old and you're looking back at now. What would you say? What would you want your biography to state? How would you feel about it? Learn from the past, enjoy the present, and focus on the wonderful possibilities of the future.

Thank you for the privilege of sharing *Anatomy of Success* with you. Wishing you the success and fulfillment you desire, and remember:

"What we concentrate on, we tend to create!"

Glossary

• • •

Beliefs—What we accept as true, regardless if it is actually true. Beliefs tend to only allow us to be aware of what is consistent with them, and change when there is sufficient experience to establish new beliefs.

BOSS—Belief Operating System Structure; an accumulation of beliefs that forms the programs run by the brain.

Full Spectrum Visualization—Imagining having a desired result by seeing it from every angle and viewpoint, and by adjusting all the possible elements to make it as satisfying and fulfilling as possible.

Fundamental Four—Four core empowering beliefs, can, worth, will, and deserve, that assist someone in using their potential.

Goal—a result that someone desires to have, toward which they expend mental and/or physical energy.

New Three Rs—Doing the Right Thing, in the Right Way, and at the Right Time, to achieve a goal.

Physical Pattern—Using a certain posture, facial expression, breathing pattern, muscular tension, voice pattern, movement, etc., that creates a certain emotional state.

POP—Planning on Paper; writing everything down to have clarity, control, and commitment.

Positive Language Patterns—Ways of communicating in an effective, productive, and empowering manner.

Proof Menu—A list of possible ways to support your ideas and generate certain beliefs in yourself and others.

Reflection Realization Visualization—Imagining having a desired result as if seeing it as it would be reflected in a mirror.

Return, Revise, and Resolve—A visualization exercise to remedy and heal past situations.

Self-Concept—The beliefs a person has about themselves in terms of traits, qualities, and characteristics, and therefore influences behavior.

Skill—An ability or capacity to do something, that has been developed into a level of competency and expertise.

Success—Achieving and fulfilling certain desired results and feelings.

Threshold—Arriving at a point, a level of positive or negative intensity where someone feels compelled to do, or not do, something.

UER—Ultimate End Result; the absolute bottom line outcome that's desired. It's so specific and detailed, that anyone reading it would understand what it is.

Values—What we feel that are very important and worthwhile, and that ultimately come down to feelings.

Visualization—Forming mental images or pictures of a desired outcome and result.

WIN—Whatever Is Necessary; the willingness to do what's required to reach an objective.

Index

• • •

A
addictions, 23
addicts, 75
affirmations, 101–103
analogies, 46, 150–151
    examples of, 48–49, 150
Anatomy of Success, outline, 229–231
anger. *See* language patterns, physical
    pattern
asking, 165
attitude, defined, 65

B
Belief Operating System Structure, 64, 75
    and limiting beliefs, 175
    and self-concept, 81
    defined, 59–60
beliefs, 59–64
    analyzing, 63
    anatomy of, 64–65
    consequences, 160–161
    defined, 59
    emotions, 20
    examples of, 61–62
    installing, 154
    installing in others, 145–146, 148–
        152
    installing in self, 153–154
    life, 60
    recognizing, 63
    versus facts, 63, 177
    See also empowering beliefs, limiting
        beliefs
benefits
    determining, 116, 118
    examples of, 120–121
    failing, 168
    motivation, 115, 122
    time frames, 122, 124
    uncovering, 116
    See also motivation
BOSS *See* Belief Operating System
    Structure
brain, xv, 2, 3, 5, 9, 15, 54

C
car, buying, 225
career checklist, 233–240
career, questions, 139
change, 22, 23, 81
    and others, 166
    and success, 168
charisma, 60
checklists, creating, 209
chemistry, romantic, 248
communicating, 9, 136
complaining, 40
compliments, receiving, 46

D
daily log, 219–223
    example of, 220
delegating, 13, 96, 206, 243

E
Edison, Thomas Alva, 33
emotions, negative, 2
empowering beliefs, 75–78
    assembling, 76
    examples of, 77, 178–186
    Fundamental Four, 75–76, 153–154
    job interview, 155
    job, getting, 155–159

F
feelings
    motivation, 115
    motivation, examples of, 117
    negative, 191
    negative, examples of, 192
friends, 7, 274
Full Spectrum Visualization. *See under*
    visualization

G
goals
    business owner, 100
    career examples, 104–105
    categories of, 200–202
    criteria for, 103

About the Author

Ronald A. Kaufman is an acknowledged expert in communication skills and has become known as the "guru" of goal setting. After careers as a stockbroker and in film production and promotion, working on films such as "E.T.," "Ghostbusters," and "Rocky III" with Fortune 500

companies, he became a seminar leader and executive coach. In his workshops, he has successfully trained thousands of people on how to fulfill their potential and achieve their desired results. Noted for his upbeat enthusiastic style, he gives individuals proven real world tools, techniques, and strategies that they can use immediately to enhance their lives.

In addition to conducting workshops, giving speeches, and working with clients one-on-one, Ronald is frequently involved with the media. He has appeared on numerous television shows such as "Vicki," "Love Stories," and "Home and Family," and has co-hosted "JTN Magazine" and "Spotlight on Jobs."

Ronald A. Kaufman & Associates

Ronald A. Kaufman & Associates provide one- to three-day workshops for companies and organizations on the topics listed below. All of our programs are customized and tailored to your specific group. The classes are fast paced, filled with exercises, and your satisfaction is 100% guaranteed. For information about our services and how we can assist you in achieving your goals, please contact us at:

(310) 226-6972
or
e-mail: anatomyofsuccess@yahoo.com

Workshops:

- *"THE SUCCESS STRATEGY"* – goal setting to produce maximum results
- *"EFFECTIVE PRESENTATION SKILLS"* – public speaking, whether your audience is 1 or 1,000
- *"ART OF NEGOTIATING"* – creating win/win agreements
- *"STRESS MANAGEMENT"* – recognizing and resolving the issues that cause the condition
- *"TEAM BUILDING"* – methods for achieving clarity, commitment, and harmony
- *"SELLING SKILLS"* – achieving the mindset of selling and techniques for completing the transaction
- *"MEDIA SKILLS"* – how to give effective interviews on television and radio, and deal with the press
- *"ENHANCING RELATIONSHIPS"* – '101' questions to ask before you begin or end a relationship
- *"THIS JOB'S FOR YOU"* – job interviewing skills and career transition
- *"TIME MANAGEMENT NOW"* – techniques to maximize efficiency and motivation

CPSIA information can be obtained at www.ICGtesting.com
Printed in the USA
LVOW070336191111

255720LV00002B/4/A